Early Thoughts on Performance Practice

Books by David Whitwell

The Sousa Oral History Project
The Art of Musical Conducting
The Longy Club: 1900–1917
La Téléphonie and the Universal Musical Language
Extraordinary Women
A Concise History of the Wind Band
Essays on the Modern Wind Band
Essays on Performance Practice
A New History of Wind Music
The College and University Band
The Early Symphonies of Mozart
Music of the French Revolution
Stories from the Podium

On Composers
Wagner on Bands
Berlioz on Bands
Chopin: A Self-Portrait
Liszt: A Self-Portrait
Schumann: A Self-Portrait in His Own Words
Mendelssohn: A Self-Portrait in His Own Words

On Education
Philosophic Foundations of Education
Foundations of Music Education
Music Education of the Future

Aesthetics of Music
Aesthetics of Music in Ancient Civilizations
Aesthetics of Music in the Middle Ages
Aesthetics of Music in the Early Renaissance
Aesthetics of Music in Sixteenth-Century Italy, France and Spain
Aesthetics of Music in Sixteenth-Century Germany, the Low Countries and England
Aesthetics of Baroque Music in Italy, Spain, the German-Speaking Countries and the Low Countries
Aesthetics of Baroque Music in France
Aesthetics of Baroque Music in England

The History and Literature of the Wind Band and Wind Ensemble Series
Volume 1 The Wind Band and Wind Ensemble Before 1500
Volume 2 The Renaissance Wind Band and Wind Ensemble
Volume 3 The Baroque Wind Band and Wind Ensemble
Volume 4 The Wind Band and Wind Ensemble of the Classical Period (1750–1800)
Volume 5 The Nineteenth-Century Wind Band and Wind Ensemble
Volume 6 A Catalog of Multi-Part Repertoire for Wind Instruments or for Undesignated Instrumentation before 1600
Volume 7 Baroque Wind Band and Wind Ensemble Repertoire
Volume 8 Classical Period Wind Band and Wind Ensemble Repertoire
Volume 9 Nineteenth-Century Wind Band and Wind Ensemble Repertoire
Volume 10 A Supplementary Catalog of Wind Band and Wind Ensemble Repertoire
Volume 11 A Catalog of Wind Repertoire before the Twentieth Century for One to Five Players
Volume 12 A Second Supplementary Catalog of Early Wind Band and Wind Ensemble Repertoire
Volume 13 Name Index, Volumes 1–12, The History and Literature of the Wind Band and Wind Ensemble

Ancient Voices
Ancient Views on Music and Religion
Ancient Views on the Natural World
Ancient Views on What Is Music
Contemporary Descriptions of Early Musicians
Early Views of Music and Ethics
Early Thoughts on Performance Practice
Music Performance in Ancient Societies

Renaissance Voices
Essays on Renaissance Philosophies of Music
Renaissance Men on Music

www.whitwellbooks.com

David Whitwell

Ancient Voices
Views on Music by Ancient and
Medieval Writers

Early Thoughts on Performance Practice

Edited by Craig Dabelstein

WHITWELL PUBLISHING • AUSTIN, TEXAS, USA

Ancient Voices: Views on music by ancient and medieval writers
Early Thoughts on Performance Practice
Dr. David Whitwell

WHITWELL PUBLISHING
AUSTIN, TX 78701
WWW.WHITWELLPUBLISHING.COM

Based on essays originally written between 2000 and 2005.
© 2013 by David Whitwell
All rights reserved.

Composed in Bembo Book.
Published in the United States of America.

ISBN-13: 9781936512768
Cover design by Daniel Ferla.

Contents

	Acknowledgements	vii
PART 1	MUSIC IN ANCIENT GREECE	
1	What Was Ancient Greek Music Like?	3
2	On the Ancient Greek Modes	17
3	On the Social Standing of Music in Ancient Societies	31
PART 2	VIEWS FROM THE CATHEDRAL	
4	Music Viewed by Early Church Philosophers	55
5	Boethius	71
6	Cassiodorus	79
7	Late Medieval Music Treatises	87
PART 3	EARLY DISCUSSIONS ON PERFORMANCE PRACTICE	
8	Early Reflections on Repertoire	105
9	Early Reflections on Acoustics and the Perception of Music	117
10	Early Experience with the 'Pyramid Principle'	137
11	Early Reflections on Tempi	145
12	Early Reflections on Instruments and Ensembles	155
13	Early Views on Percussion	167
14	Early Views on Memorization	175
	Bibliography	181
	About The Author	191
	About the Editor	193

Acknowledgments

I am indebted to my friend and colleague, Craig Dabelstein, for his help in preparing this book for publication.

David Whitwell
Austin, Texas

PART I
MUSIC IN ANCIENT GREECE

What Was Ancient Greek Music Like?

> *It is impossible for us now to recover the meaning of this dead music of ancient Greece.*[1]
>
> Henry S. Macran, 1974

WHEN MODERN MUSICOLOGY WAS FOUNDED in the nineteenth century a decision was made that you can only study music if you have the actual music in front of you. It is for this reason that most books on Renaissance music, for example, are almost entirely limited to discussion of Roman Church music and the secular madrigal types. The fact is that relatively few men living in the Renaissance would have ever heard any of that music. Ironically, there are abundant contemporary sources which discuss in detail what Renaissance music practice was *really* like.

This is the problem with ancient Greek music. From the Golden Age of Greece, the period of the lyric poets, Socrates, the great playwrights and Aristotle, no music survives. What has survived is a small body of melodies and fragments notated in a primitive alphabetic notation from only the most recent period of ancient Greece, the so-called 'Roman Period of Ancient Greece,' (146 BC–529 AD) a period identified by all writers as one of cultural decline and a period far removed from the earlier centuries of high Greek culture. Therefore, music historians have generally thrown up their hands and declared that nothing can be known of Greek music. The quotation above is representative of that viewpoint.

But a careful reading of Greek literature actually reveals much about ancient Greek music. First, there must have been similarities between the musical practice of the earlier civilizations of Egypt and ancient Greece. The relations between Egypt and Greece can be documented to very remote times, as, for example, in the case of Danaus, a probable brother to Amunoph III, who left Egypt and founded Argos, where he died in 1,425 BC. With the reign of Psammetichus I, Egypt, which had been a rather closed society, was opened to Greek travelers and settlers and from this date many notable Greek philosophers, from Thales and Solon to Plato spent time there. It is no surprise, therefore, that the earliest Greek musical traditions we know of seem quite similar to the accounts of the older Egyptian culture. When we read the writings of the early Greeks and look at the icons of the Egyptians we sense a common ground. Indeed, when Herodotus visited Egypt, he was astonished when he heard a song there which he had believed was a famous song of Greek origin.

---

[1] Aristoxenus, *The Elements of Harmony*, 16, trans. Henry S. Macran (Hildesheim: Georg Olms Verlag, 1974), 3.

We might briefly digress and note that, as we can infer from the Old Testament, many of the ancient Hebrew traditions also came from Egypt. Voltaire, a participant in the discussion during the Baroque Period of the relative merits of ancient and modern aesthetics in the arts, mentions this in his essay, 'Revolutions in the Tragic Art,' when he discusses the functional role of music in religion in ancient times.

> These public diversions were, among the Greeks, connected with their religious ceremonies. It is well known that among the Egyptians, songs, dances and representations made an essential part of the ceremonies reputed sacred. The Jews borrowed these customs from the Egyptians, as every ignorant and barbarous nation endeavors to imitate its learned and polite neighbors; hence those Jewish festivals, those dances of priests before the ark, those trumpets, those hymns, and so many other ceremonies entirely Egyptian.[2]

The association between the cultures of ancient Egypt and Greece may help explain why no music survives from the great centuries of ancient Greece. We know the Egyptians had no notated form of music and it is likely the Greeks followed suit. We do know the ancient Greeks did not even have names for the individual notes. But knowledge and notation are two different things. For example, while ancient Egypt had no notation, they nevertheless had conductors, music schools and music education. Again, we are not speaking of the alphabet notation of the most recent, and last, period.

But just because there was no notation, it would be a very great mistake to assume the music was therefore simple. We must remember that music functioned quite well for many centuries before the advent of notation.[3] People before notation, for example, still had the overtone series, with all its consequent implications—as is witnessed by more than one extant bone flutes dating ca. 8,000 to 12,000 years BC, or more, which have holes bored to produce a diatonic scale. It might be more fair to these ancient musicians and listeners to say that they remind us that music is, after all, for the ear and not the eye.

What *was* ancient Greek music like? As we have said, a great deal can be learned from the contemporary literature and a good, and important, place to begin is with harmony. Modern writers generally assume, based on the unaccompanied melodic fragments of the Roman Period, the last period of ancient Greece, that ancient Greek music consisted of single line melodies with no understanding of harmony.

But in some of the most ancient of Greek literature, the works of the great lyric poets, we read descriptions of harmony. In Pindar's (522–443 BC) *Ode for Aristocleides of Aegina,* Winner of the Pankration, we find the expression, 'strike chords.'

> Of song grant, of my skill, full measure. Strike,
> O daughter of the lord of cloud-capped heaven,
> Chords to his honor.[4]

---

[2] 'Revolutions in the Tragic Art,' in *The Works of Voltaire* (New York: St. Hubert Guild, 1901), XXXIX, 152.

[3] We are among those who wonder if perhaps we lost more than we gained when we began to put music on paper.

[4] Geoffrey S. Conway, *The Odes of Pindar* (London: Dent, 1972), 204.

The writer of comedies, Pherecrates (fifth century BC), introduces a character called Music, all bruised and battered and dressed in woman's clothes, representing a perceived decay in the practice of music. Justice asks what is wrong and in Music's reply we find the following lines which seem to indicate harmony,

> Wringing and racking all my veins,
> Ruined me quite, while nine small wires
> With harmonies twice six he tires.

A later reference to the 'twice six' makes clear this is a reference to a twelve string instrument:

> With his twelve cat-guts strongly bound,
> He leaves me helpless on the ground.[5]

But it is an earlier passage in Plato's (427–347 BC) *Symposium* which seems to be a clear documentation of harmony.

> Anyone who pays the least attention to the subject will also perceive that in music there is the same reconciliation of opposites; and I suppose that this must have been the meaning of Heracleitus, although his words are not accurate; for he says the One is united by disunion, like the harmony[6] of the bow and the lyre. Now it is the height of absurdity to say that harmony is discord or it is composed of elements which are still in a state of discord. But what he probably meant was, that harmony is attained through the art of music by the reconciliation of differing notes of higher and lower pitch which once disagreed; for if the higher and lower notes still disagreed, there could be no harmony,— clearly not. For harmony is a symphony, and symphony is a kind of agreement; but an agreement of disagreements while they disagree there cannot be; you cannot, I repeat, harmonize that which disagrees. In like manner rhythm is compounded of elements short and long, once differing and now in accord; which accordance, as in the former instance medicine, so in all these other cases music implants, making love and concord to grow up among them; and thus music, too, is a science of the phenomena of love in their application to harmony and rhythm. Again, in the constitution of a harmony as of a rhythm there is no difficulty in discerning love, and as yet there is no sign of its duality. But when you want to use them in actual life, either in the kind of composition to which the term 'lyrical' is applied or in the correct employment of melodies and meters already composed, which latter is called education, then indeed the difficulty begins, and the good artist is needed. Then the old tale has to be repeated of fair and heavenly love—the love that comes from Urania the fair and heavenly muse—and of the duty of gratifying the temperate,[7] and those who are as yet intemperate only that they may become temperate, and of preserving their love; and again, of the common love that comes from Polyhymnia, that must be used with circumspection in order that the pleasure be enjoyed, but may not generate licentiousness.[8]

---

5   Quoted by Plutarch, in 'Concerning Music.'

6   The Greeks sometimes used the word 'harmony' in a larger sense, the whole rather than one of the parts; indeed, it is often used as we might use today the word 'music' itself. The term 'symphony' was sometimes used to express what we mean by 'harmony.'

7   By temperance Plato means something like self-discipline.

8   *Symposium*, 187b.

Aristotle (384–322 BC) also seems to refer to harmony when he writes,

> we delight in concord because it is the mingling of contraries which stand in proportion to one another.[9]

Athenaeus says Stratonicus (fourth century BC) was 'the first to introduce multiplicity of notes in simple harp playing; he was also the first to receive pupils in harmony, and to compile a table of musical intervals.'[10]

It is with the generation after Aristotle that we come to the one person who should have answered all our questions about Greek music of the fourth and fifth centuries BC. His name is Aristoxenus (b. ca. 379 BC) and he was a student of Aristotle's and he wrote a number of books on music. Unfortunately, nearly all of his books are lost, among them a book called *Elements of Harmony*, of which only three chapters are extant. Nevertheless, the title alone seems to confirm harmony in the fourth century BC.

Tibullus (55–19 BC) also mentions harmony in a discussion of the Apollo myth. Here Apollo himself speaks:

> It is not told in mockery that I
> served as Admetus' shepherd, long ago,
> and lost the will to play the lyre, or try
> new harmonies for voice and strings to share—
> but used an unstopped pipe, in my despair.[11]

Ovid (43 BC–17 AD) describes a professional singer who begins his song with an appeal to Jove for inspiration. Before this, however, he gives us a rare reference to the musician tuning up, with an indisputable description of harmony.

> And when he had tried the chords by touching them with his thumb, and his ears told him that the notes were in harmony although they were of different pitch, he raised his voice in this song: 'From Jove, O Muse, my mother—for all things yield to the sway of Jove—inspire my song!'[12]

And finally, what about the reference by Athenaeus (ca. 200 AD) to players of the five-string *magadis*, 'Each man ringing out a different tone from the other …'?[13]

We may not have extant written examples of harmony from ancient Greece, but as the reader can see from the above contemporary commentary it is clear that some form of harmony is implied and that this music did not consist of melody alone.[14] Based on surviving

---

[9] *Problemata*, XIX, 38.
[10] Athenaeus, *Deipnosophistae*, VIII, 352.
[11] Tibullus, *Poems*, III, iv.
[12] Ovid, *Metamorphoses*, X, 143.
[13] Athenaeus, *Deipnosophistae*, XIV, 637.
[14] We have not mentioned the fact that there is iconography which shows the double-pipe aulos with the player's fingers clearly appearing with different finger positions on each pipe.

ancient instruments it seems likely that their harmony, like ours, was based on the overtone series. This series was something they understood by ear, even if they lacked knowledge of physics to notate it.

Rhythm also seems to have been well understood even if there were no apparent form of notation. Aside from the implied evidence of the well-known poetic rhythmic structures, there can be little doubt that peoples long before the ancient Greeks were familiar with the relationship of movement and music. This is certainly documented in some of the very oldest extant Greek literature, such as the following passage from about 800 BC which implies a group of people simultaneously beating time and singing.

> They set out to go, and the lord Apollo, son of Zeus, led the way,
> his step high and stately, and with the lyre in his hands
> played a lovely tune. The Cretans followed him
> to Pytho, beating time and singing the Iepaieon
> in the fashion of Cretans singing a paean when the divine
> Muse has put mellifluous song in their hearts.[15]

There is a very interesting discussion of rhythm by Aristides (d. 468 BC). He associates the beginning of rhythm with the rise and fall of marching feet: those rhythms associated with the *arsis* are restless and those associated with the *thesis* are more peaceful. But it is particularly interesting that he associates some emotional qualities with rhythm. Rhythms composed of short syllables, he says for example, are faster and 'more passionate' and those composed only of long syllables are slower and calm and mixtures have the qualities of both. Compound rhythms are more emotional and 'the impression they give is tempestuous, because the number from which they are constructed does not keep the same order of its parts in each position.' Running rhythms inspire us to action, other are supine and flabby.

Aristides finds rhythm closely associated with character and therefore he contends that it is possible to judge a person by his manner of walking.

> We find that people whose steps are of good length and equal, in the manner of the spondee, are stable and manly in character: those whose steps are long but unequal, in the manner of trochees or paions, are excessively passionate: those whose steps are equal but too short, in the manner of the pyrrhic, are spineless and lack nobility: while those whose steps are short and unequal, and approach rhythmical irrationality, are utterly dissipated. As to those who employ all the gaits in no particular order, you will realize that their minds are unstable and erratic.[16]

---

[15] 'To Apollon,' 514–519, trans. Apostolos N. Athanassakis, *The Homeric Hymns* (Baltimore: Johns Hopkins University Press, 1976).

[16] Quoted in Andrew Barker, *Greek Musical Writings* (Cambridge: Cambridge University Press, 1989), II.

This last style of walking, in uneven gaits, coincides with first-hand descriptions of the style of walk by both Mozart and Mahler.

Plutarch, in describing the fleet carrying the ashes of Demetrius (337–283 BC) as part of his funeral obsequies, clearly speaks of a rhythmic structure sophisticated enough to be coordinated with the melody by uneducated slaves.

> The most famous aulos player of the time, Xenophantus, was sitting close to it playing a solemn melody, to which the rowers kept time in rhythm. The beat of their oars, like funeral mourning, answered the strains of the aulos.[17]

And then there is Aristoxenus (b. ca. 379 BC), the student of Aristotle whom we have mentioned above, who wrote a book called, *Elements of Rhythm*, of which only a single chapter has survived. His discussion certainly lacks the step-by-step thoroughness of his teacher, Aristotle. One sometimes is not sure if Aristoxenus is describing elements of music not yet standardized, or whether the gaps in his own understanding does not permit him to provide the detail we need. The following, from his surviving chapter on Rhythm, will suffice.

> It hardly needs argument to convince us that not every arrangement of time-lengths is rhythmical. But we must pay attention to the analogies and try to understand what they reveal, until proof is provided by actual observation and experience.
>
> We are familiar with what happens in combinations of letters of the alphabet and combinations of musical intervals. We know that we cannot combine letters at random in speech or musical intervals in singing. There are only a few combinations that we actually use, and numerous ones that the voice cannot reproduce in pronunciation and our sense of hearing refuses to accept and rejects.[18]

It is important to point out that the phrase in the second paragraph here, 'combinations of letters of the alphabet and combinations of musical intervals,' is not a reference to the simple alphabetic notation found in the more recent Roman Period of ancient Greece. Instead he is referring to an interest the Greek philosophers apparently had in associating the intervals in the normal melodic tessitura of ordinary speech with meaning. The higher the pitch representing degrees of accent. For instance one finds still in the thirteenth century this comment by Roger Bacon:

> For accent is a kind of singing; whence it is called accent from *accino, accinis* [I sing, thou singest], because every syllable has its own proper sound either raised, lowered, or composite, and all syllables of one word are adapted or sung to one syllable on which rests the principal sound.[19]

---

[17] Plutarch, *Lives*, 'Demetrius,' 53.

[18] Aristoxenus, *Elementa Rhythmica* (Oxford: Clarendon Press, 1990), 8.

[19] *The Opus Majus of Robert Bacon*, trans. Robert Burke (New York: Russell & Russell, 1962), I, 259. Even today the pitch rises when we become excited, a carry-over from prehistoric man.

It is interesting that in discussing the division of Time, in two places he seems to suggest the existence of something like the modern conductor, once saying 'signals' are necessary to make the division and in another place, 'Rhythm cannot exist without … someone to divide the time.'[20]

In summary, then, we can see that the music of ancient Greece had rhythm characterized by pulse which could be coordinated with melody and consisted of subdivisions of the beat into long and short elements, which could also be mixed, and the knowledge generally well enough known to make possible ensemble performance with a conductor.

The aspect of ancient Greek music which early philosophers most emphasized was the Greek modes and the character they represented. We will devote the following essay to this aspect of ancient Greek music. The only theoretical information we have comes from the end of the period in the writings of Aristoxenus. By this time the emphasis seems to have been not so much on character but on emerging quasi-scale structures and the means of notating them. But we need more information. One can, of course, read what has survived from Aristoxenus and understand it on an objective level but there is too much missing here to be comfortable in making judgments on the actual use of these scale-like mode structures. It was in reference to this subject, specifically, that Henry Macran made the statement which stands at the head of this essay.

An example of the gaps in information in the extant material by Aristoxenus is his following observation, for which one can only wish he had left more discussion.

> [Just because] a man notes down the Phrygian scale it does not follow that he must know the *essence* of the Phrygian scale. Plainly then notation is not the ultimate limit of our science.[21]

Because some professors today place much importance on Arixtoxenus for understanding Greek music we feel inclined to wave a flag of caution. While we do know the titles of at least six lost books by Aristoxenus dealing with music, he apparently wrote more than four hundred other books, including works on philosophy and ethics. Music books, therefore, represent a very small part of his output and we have no way of knowing the basis of his authority on the subject of music or whether any of his contemporaries would have agreed with what he wrote. There is one passage during his 'scale' discussion, for example, which seems to reflect a clear lack of confidence on his part, if not an apology for writing about something he really does not quite understand.

---

[20] Michael Psellus, *Introduction to the Study of Rhythm*, quoted in Aristoxenus, *Elementa Rhythmica* (Oxford: Clarendon Press, 1990), 23, 25. Psellus is a later author who seems to have copied his material from portions of the Aristoxenus' books which are now lost.

[21] Ibid., 39.

> Here we would ask our hearers to receive these definitions in the right spirit, not with the jealous scrutiny of the degree of their exactness. We would ask him to aid us with his intelligent sympathy, and to consider our definition sufficiently instructive when it puts him in the way of understanding the thing defined. To supply a definition which affords an unexceptionable and exhaustive analysis is a difficult task.[22]

There is some surviving discussion of form in ancient Greek music. Plato, quoting Socrates, gives a brief review of even earlier forms and his comment about not allowing changes gives this a particular Egyptian character.

> AN ATHENIAN STRANGER. Let us speak of the laws about music,—that is to say, such music as then existed,—in order that we may trace the growth of the excess of freedom from the beginning. Now music was early divided among us into certain kinds and manners. One sort consisted of prayers to the Gods, which were called hymns; and there was another and opposite sort called lamentations, and another termed paeans, and another, celebrating (I believe) the birth of Dionysus, called 'dithyrambs.' And they used the actual word 'laws' for another kind of song; and to this they added the term 'citharoedic.' All these and others were duly distinguished, nor were the performers allowed to confuse one style of music with another.[23]

In another place Socrates mentions instrumental forms.

> AN ATHENIAN STRANGER. Because all discourses and vocal exercises have preludes and overtures, which are a sort of artistic beginnings intended to help the music which is to be performed; lyric measures and music of every other kind have preludes framed with wonderful care.[24]

The expression Socrates uses here, 'wonderful care,' probably included precision, as implied in his famous definition: 'Musically,' is the very 'name for correctness in the art of music.'[25]

A perceived aesthetic decline in music was mentioned by many early philosophers. Plutarch, who dated this decline early in the fourth century BC, apparently associated a 'mixing' of traditional forms with this decline. He quotes a passage from a lost work by Aristophanes which complains of the poet Philoxenus introducing lyric verses in the middle of the choruses.[26]

But to speak of harmony, rhythm and form do not really tell us much about what Greek music was really like, for these subjects are, after all, only the grammar of music. It is these early philosophers' discussion of aesthetics and values which give us a better feel for what the music must have been like.[27]

---

22 Aristoxenus, *The Elements of Harmony*, 16, trans. Henry S. Macran (Hildesheim: Georg Olms Verlag, 1974).

23 *Laws*, 700ff.

24 *Laws*, 722d.

25 *Alcibiades I*, 108d. A passage in *Laws*, 769b, speaks of the 'wonderful care' by painters.

26 'Concerning Music.'

27 Modes, which we treat in a separate essay, are very much instructive in this regard.

It is Plato who gives us a careful definition of the values of the highest, most aesthetic, kind of music. Taken altogether, his discussion gives us a portrait of a very high level of music and implies that these values were known and discussed. Here are the values Plato includes in his definition of the highest music, or what we might call today, art music.

The music must be inspired

In *Ion*, Plato writes,

> All good poets, epic as well as lyric, compose their beautiful poems not by art, but because they are inspired and possessed.[28]

In the *Apology*, he makes the point again.

> I learnt that not by wisdom do poets write poetry, but by a sort of genius and inspiration.[29]

Students in wind ensembles and bands in all levels of American educational institutions today almost never perform genuine, inspired music. They are given a diet of constructed, educational music whose origin lies in commercial interests.

The music must have Beauty

Plato asks,

> For what should be the end of music if not the love of beauty?[30]

This was very important to Plato's vision of his utopia. Not only did he wish for the blessings of Beauty for its own sake, but for its positive influence on the public.

> We would not have our guardians grow up amid images of moral deformity, as in some noxious pasture, and there browse and feed upon many a baneful herb and flower day by day, little by little, until they silently gather a festering mass of corruption in their own soul. Let us rather search for artists who are gifted to discern the true nature of the beautiful and graceful; then will our youth dwell in a land of health, amid fair sights and sounds, and receive the good in everything; and beauty, the effluence of fair works, shall flow into the eye and ear, like a health-giving breeze from a purer region, and insensibly draw the soul from the earliest years into likeness and sympathy with the beauty of reason.[31]

---

[28] *Ion*, 534.

[29] *Apology*, 22c.

[30] *Republic*, III, 403c.

[31] Ibid, 401b.

There must be a contemplative listener, not one seeking mere entertainment

Plato goes to some care to establish the point that the contemplation of the beautiful is not the same thing as experiencing mere 'pleasure' in music.

> AN ATHENIAN STRANGER. When anyone says that music is to be judged by pleasure, his doctrine cannot be admitted; and if there be any music of which pleasure is the criterion, such music is not to be sought out or deemed to have any real excellence, but only that other kind of music which is an imitation of the good, and bears a resemblance to its original.
> CLEINIAS. Very true.

When Plato writes of 'musical instruments used to charm the souls of men,'[32] we assume he is referring to attentive listeners.

The highest music has Truth

Plato continues,

> AN ATHENIAN STRANGER. And those who seek for the best kind of song and music ought not to seek for that which is pleasant, but for that which is True.[33]

There is a striking similarity between this passage and a statement given in Los Angeles by the famous conductor, Sergiu Celibadache.

> Anyone who still hasn't got past the stage of the beauty of music still knows nothing about music. Music is not beautiful. It has beauty as well, but the beauty is only the bait. Music is True.[34]

What do they mean by this? What does to be *true* mean in music? Plato's definition is based on the relationship of music to the soul. The most important music is that in which the emotions and meaning of the music corresponds to the highest virtue of the soul. For Plato, the question is not just a distinction between artistic truth and pleasure, but between good and evil. He makes here the strongest condemnation of entertainment music, or popular music, which he declares does nothing more than flatter the audience.

> SOCRATES. I would have you consider ... whether there are not other similar activities which have to do with the soul—some of them activities of art, making a provision for the soul's highest interest; others despising the interest, and as in the parallel case considering only the pleasure, of the soul, and how this may be acquired, but not considering what pleasures are good or bad, and having no other aim but to afford gratification, whether good or bad. In my opinion, Callicles, there are such activities, and this is the sort of thing which I term flattery, whether concerned with the body or the soul or anything else on which it is employed with a view to pleasure and without any consideration of good and evil. And now I wish that you would tell me whether you agree with us in this notion, or whether you differ.

---

32 *Symposium*, 215c.

33 *Laws*, 668b.

34 Quoted in *Los Angeles Philharmonic Notes*, April, 1989.

CALLICLES. I do not differ ...
SOCRATES. And is the notion true of one soul, or two or more?
CALLICLES. Equally true of two or more.
SOCRATES. Then a man may delight a whole assembly, and yet have no regard for their highest interests?
CALLICLES. Yes.[35]

Aristotle also discusses Truth as a synonym for the 'soul.' He would say that in speaking or in music the performer must express what is in his soul; the performance then has Truth.

> Voice is a kind of sound characteristic of what has soul in it; nothing that is without soul utters voice, it being only by a metaphor that we speak of the voice of the aulos or the lyre or generally of what (being without soul) possesses the power of producing a succession of notes which differ in length and pitch and timbre. The metaphor is based on the fact that all these differences are found also in voice.[36]

The voice is also one representation of the emotions of the soul, something which Aristotle finds universal in character.

> Words spoken are symbols or signs of emotions or impressions of the soul; written words are the symbols of words spoken. As writing, so also is speech not the same for all races of men. But the emotions themselves, of which these words are primarily signs, are the same for the whole of mankind.[37]

This is one of the most important of all of Aristotle's observations dealing with the arts. First, he points out correctly that the emotions are universal. This is the basis for the phrase, 'Music is the international language.'

Second, he reminds us that great music itself has no value in and of itself. Its value is that it represents and makes possible for the listener to understand the performer's emotions. This internal emotional foundation of music is the 'Truth' in music. And we must add that someday it will finally be understood that here is where the focus and purpose of music education should lie.

Taking these two together, Aristotle sets music (and grammar) apart from other kinds of knowing. Because the communication of feeling is the purpose of music, and because of the universality of emotions, all men receive a direct communication from the musician without need for intervening or additional knowledge.

> Knowledge, the genus, we define by a reference to something beyond it, for knowledge is knowledge *of* something. Particular branches, however, of knowledge are not thus explained. For example, we do not define by a reference to something external a knowledge of grammar or music. For these, if in

---

[35] *Gorgias*, 501b.

[36] *De Anima*, 420b.5.

[37] *On Interpretation*, I, trans. Harold P. Cook (Cambridge: Harvard University Press, 1962).

some sense relations, can only be taken for such in respect of their genus or knowledge. That is to say, we call grammar the knowledge, *not* grammar, of something, and music we call, in like manner, the knowledge, *not* music, of something.[38]

Music must have Virtue

By Virtue, Plato means that the good artist has a duty not to merely amuse his listeners, but to present them with the good.

> SOCRATES. Listen to me, then, while I recapitulate the argument: Is the pleasant the same as the good? Not the same. Callicles and I are agreed about that. And is the pleasant to be pursued for the sake of the good, or the good for the sake of the pleasant? The pleasant is to be pursued for the sake of the good. And that is pleasant at the presence of which we are pleased, and that is good by the presence of which we are good? To be sure. And we are good, and all good things whatever are good, when some virtue is present in us or them? That, Callicles, is my conviction. But the virtue of each thing, whether body or soul, instrument or creature, when given to them in the best way comes to them not by chance but as the result of the order and truth and art which are imparted to them: am I not right? I maintain that I am. And is not the virtue of each thing dependent on order or arrangement? Yes I say. And that which makes a thing good is its appropriate order inhering in each thing? Such is my view.[39]

Aristotle also stressed this definition of the highest music.

> We must see that every science and art has an end, and that too a good one; for no science or art exists for the sake of evil. Since then in all the arts the end is good, it is plain that the end of the best art will be the best good.[40]

Aristotle gives us an illustration of this with respect to music, and at the same time a definition of 'a musical man.'

> A good man is one that delights in virtuous actions and is vexed at vicious ones, as a musical man enjoys beautiful melodies but is pained at bad ones.[41]

In another place Aristotle addresses the good, or the virtuous, in art.

> Every art and every inquiry, and similarly every action and pursuit, is thought to aim at some good; and for this reason the good has rightly been declared to be that at which all things aim.[42]

Plutarch says the quality of Virtue was the reason the Greeks 'were so careful to teach their children music,'

---

38   *Categories*, VIII.
39   Ibid., 506d.
40   *Magna Moralia*, 1182a.33.
41   *Ethica Nicomachea*, 1170a.9.
42   Ibid., 1094a.

for they deemed it requisite by the assistance of music to form and compose the minds of youth to what was decent, sober, and virtuous; believing the use of music beneficially efficacious to incite to all serious actions.[43]

Strabo gives a similar explanation for the use of music in education to form character. The ancient Greeks, he said,

> assumed that every form of music is the work of the gods ... And by the same course of reasoning they also attribute to music the upbuilding of morals, believing that everything which tends to correct the mind is close to the gods.[44]

Aristotle adds some additional observations and definitions which reflect the highest music. First, he seemed to respect the human qualities reflected in the highest music. He made the observation, for example, that we get the most pleasure in hearing music which is 'expressive of meaning.'[45] It was also his judgment that 'a woeful and quiet character and type of music' is 'more human.'[46]

Athenaeus adds the quality of nobility in the highest music of the ancient Greeks.

> In olden times the feeling for nobility was always maintained in the art of music, and all its elements skillfully retained the orderly beauty appropriate to them.[47]

To this Plutarch summarizes, 'That music was ever accounted among them the best, which was most grave, simple, and natural.'[48]

'Noble, grave, simple and natural,' it is these words which so inflame our curiosity about the lost music of the ancient Greeks. How we wish we could hear once again the music which corresponded to Plutarch's fascinating discussion of the Spartans.[49]

> They spent a great part of their studies in poetry and music, which raised their minds above the ordinary level, and by a kind of [natural] enthusiasm inspired them with generous hearts and resolutions for action. Their compositions, consisting only of very grave and moral subjects, were easy and natural, in a plain dress, and without any paint or ornament, containing nothing else but the just commendations of those great personages whose singular wisdom and virtue had made their lives famous and exemplary, and whose courage in defense of their country had made their deaths honorable and happy.

---

43 *Concerning Music.*

44 *The Geography of Strabo*, trans. Horace L. Jones (Cambridge: Harvard University Press, 1960), X.3.10.

45 *Problemata*, 918a.33.

46 Ibid., 922b.20.

47 Athenaeus, *Deipnosophistae*, XIV 631.

48 'Concerning Music.'

49 'Customs of the Lacedaemonians.'

On the Ancient Greek Modes

As we have mentioned in the previous essay, the only fragments of ancient Greek music which have survived are from the last, and most recent period to us, the 'Roman Period.' There is no extant music from the great centuries of ancient Greece, the eighth through the fourth century BC. Similarly, there is no notation of, or discussion of the theory of the modes, before Aristoxenus, a pupil of Aristotle.

On the other hand, the most frequently mentioned aspect of ancient Greek music by ancient philosophers was these modes. Unlike the later Church modes of Western Europe which share the same names, such as 'Dorian,' and are characterized by, and taught as, varying accumulations of half- and whole-step intervals together with cadential centers, the ancient Greek mode names were names of societies of people. A label such as 'Dorian' was used to reflect the style of a specific society of people's music much as today we might speak of 'German' or 'French' music. Eventually they apparently became systems for tuning the lyre, at a time when the Greeks had no names for the actual notes of music. Later, Aristoxenus coined the term *tonos*, suggesting that perhaps they had become somewhat more like modern scales. But none of this tells us anything about the music itself.[1]

As we have said, the character of the music seemed to be widely understood as reflecting the character of the people. What did they mean by that? Athenaeus begins by agreeing with an argument, in a now lost book by Heracleides of Pontus, that really one should only speak of three Greek modes, the Dorian, Aeolian, and Ionian, as these represent the three main tribes of the Greeks. Phrygian and Lydian, he says originated with the 'barbarians' [meaning those who do not speak Greek well] and were learned by the Greeks from them. He then attempts to portray the character of these three tribes, with the obvious suggestion that the music of these modes represent somehow the same character.

> Now the Dorian mode exhibits the quality of manly vigor, of magnificent bearing, not relaxed or merry, but sober and intense, neither varied nor complicated. But the Aeolian character contains the elements of ostentation and turgidity, and even conceit; these qualities are in keeping with their horse-breeding and their way of meeting strangers; yet this does not mean malice, but is, rather, lofty and confident. Hence also their fondness for drinking is something appropriate to them, also their love affairs, and the entirely relaxed nature of their daily life.
>
> Next in order let us examine the Milesians' character, which the Ionians illustrate. Because of their excellent physical condition they bear themselves haughtily, they are full of irate spirit, hard to placate, fond of contention, never condescending to kindliness nor cheerfulness, displaying a lack of affection and a hardness in their character. Hence also the kind of music known as the Ionian mode

---

[1] Neither does the description in words by Athenaeus tell us anything about the taste of the 'Phrygian figs,' or the 'Lydian figs,' or the smell of the 'Phrygian odor' [*Deipnosophistae*, III, 75, 76 and XIV, 626].

is neither bright nor cheerful, but austere and hard, having a seriousness which is not ignoble; and so their mode is well-adapted to tragedy. But the character of the Ionians today is more voluptuous, and the character of their mode is much altered.[2]

The belief in these kinds of associations continued for centuries. Heinrich Glarean, for example, in his *Dodecachordon* of 1547, writes in a similar vein.

If I am allowed to make a rough judgment concerning this and the preceding modes, I shall say it in a few words: Each mode seems to me to reflect beautifully the customs of the people from which the names are taken. The Athenians were truly Ionians, the Spartans were Dorians; the former, although lovers of pleasant things and students of eloquence, were still always considered capricious. Yet the Spartans, renowned in war and bound by military discipline and the severe laws of Lycurgus, have preserved longer the harsh customs handed down from their ancestors. These modes have the same characteristics. The Ionian, devoted entirely to dancing, contains much sweetness and pleasantness, almost no severity. On the contrary, the Dorian presents a certain majesty and dignity which it is easier to admire than to explain. It is very suitable for [epic] poetry, as I have myself experienced at one time as a youth in Köln in the presence of the celebrated Kaiser Maximilian and many princes, not without the reward of the merited laurel branch (which is said without boasting).[3]

The great Baroque writer, Johann Mattheson, in his review of tonality[4] still refers to the association of the Greek modes with the peoples for whom they were named.

It is probable that the Dorians had a coarser, more manly, and deeper speaking voice than the Phrygians; and that on the other hand the Lydians sang finer and more effeminately than the others. For the Dorians were a modest, virtuous and peaceful people; the Phrygians however used more noise than foresight; whereas the Lydians, forefathers of the Tuscans, were everywhere described as sensual people.

Henry Agrippa, in his three volume *De occulta philosophia* (1509–1510), written in the old mold of Catholic Scholasticism, claims to have found ancient sources which tie the above associations with the ancient philosophers' theories on basic elements. He then adds to the mix the Renaissance ideas of the 'Humors' and the 'music of the spheres.'

Moreover, they that followed the number of the elements, did affirm, that the four kinds of music do agree to them, and also to the four humors, and did think the Dorian music to be consonant to the Water and phlegm, the Phrygian to choler and Fire, the Lydian to blood and Air, the mixed-Lydian to melancholy and Earth: others respecting the number and virtue of the heavens, have attributed the Dorian to the Sun, the Phrygian to Mars, the Lydian to Jupiter, the mixed-Lydian to Saturn, the hypo-Phrygian to Mercury, the hypo-Lydian to Venus, the hypo-Dorian to the Moon, the hypo-mixed-Lydian to the fixed star…[5]

---

2   Athenaeus. *Deipnosophistae*, XIV, 624–626.

3   Heinrich Glarean, *Dodecachordon*, trans. Clement Miller (American Institute of Musicology, 1965), I, 155ff.

4   Johann Mattheson, *Der vollkommene Capellmeister* [1739], trans. Ernest Harriss (Ann Arbor: UMI Research Press, 1981), I, ix.

5   Henry Cornelius Agrippa, *De occulta Philosophia*, II, xxvi. The best modern edition, which is highly recommended, is Donald Tyson, *Three Books of Occult Philosophy* (St. Paul: Llewellyn Publications, 1993).

In any event, the ancients believed in the relationship between music and character much more than anyone today. Even Aristotle, who wrote with little enthusiasm about music in general, took this relationship seriously.

> We accept the division of melodies … into ethical melodies, melodies of action, and passionate or inspiring melodies, each having, as they say, a mode corresponding to it …
>
> In education the most ethical modes are to be preferred, but in listening to the performances of others we may admit the modes of action and passions also. For feelings such as pity and fear, or, again, enthusiasm, exist very strongly in some souls, and have more or less influence over all. Some persons fall into a religious frenzy, whom we see as a result of the sacred melodies—when they have used the melodies that excite the soul to mystic frenzy—restored as through they had found healing and purgation. Those who are influenced by pity and fear, and every emotional nature, must have a like experience, and others in so far as each is susceptible to such emotions, and all are in a manner purged and their souls lightened and delighted. The purgative melodies likewise give an innocent pleasure to mankind.[6]

Let us, then, consider a representative sampling of these relationships as held by earlier philosophers.

Dorian

> Music of a moderate and settled temper … grave and manly.[7]
>   ……
>
> All men agree that Dorian music is the gravest and manliest.[8]
>   Aristotle (384–322 BC)
>
> Majestic.
>   Aristoxenus (b. ca. 179 BC)
>
> Exhibits the quality of manly vigor, of magnificent bearing, not relaxed or merry, but sober and instense, neither varied nor complicated.[9]
>   Athenaeus (ca. 200 AD)
>
> Warlike.[10]
>   Apuleius (123–180 AD)

---

6   *Politica*, 1342a.
7   *Probemata*, XIX, 48; *Politica*, VIII, 5, 7.
8   *Politica*, 1342a.27 and 1342b.14.
9   Athenaeus, *Deipnosophistae*, XIV, 624–626.
10 Erasmus quoting Apuleius in 'Adages,' in *The Collected Works of Erasmus* (Toronto: University of Toronto Press, 1992), XXXIII, 283ff.

Bestows wisdom to and causes chastity in the listener.[11]
    Ornithoparchus (1517)

Phrygian

Exciting and orgiastic and inspires enthusiasm.
    Aristotle

Causes wars and inflames fury.
    Ornithoparchus

More suitable to severe, religious music, as elegies, laments and funeral music.[12]
    Glarean (1547)

Here never does one sing in Phrygian modes,
Since nowhere is there argument and din.[13]
    Antonio Abbatini (1667)

The Phrygian mode lies at the center of one of the most frequently told tales regarding the character of these modes, an incident involving Alexander the Great. As Plutarch retells this moment,

> Even Alexander himself, when Antigenides played before him in the [Phrygian] mode, was so transported and warmed for battle by the charms of lofty melodies, that leaping from his seat all in his clattering armor he began to lay about him and attack those who stood next him, thereby verifying to the Spartans what was commonly sung among themselves,
>
> > The masculine touches of the well-tuned lyre
> > Unsheathe the sword and warlike rage inspire.[14]

Lydian

Relaxed.[15]
    Plato (427–347)

Sharpens the wit of the dull and moves the mind from earthly to heavenly desires.
    Ornithopaarchus

---

[11] *Ornithoparchus, Musicae active mirologus and Dowland, Introduction: Containing the Art of Singing* (New York: Dover, 1973), 156.

[12] Glarean, *Dodecachordon*, trans. Clement Miller (American Institute of Musicology, 1965), I, 130.

[13] Quoted in Lorenzo Bianconi, *Music in the Seventeenth Century*, trans. David Bryant (Cambridge: Cambridge University Press, 1989), 288.

[14] 'The Second Oration Concerning the Fortune or Virtue of Alexander the Great.'

[15] *Republic*, III, 398e.

Harsh.
　　Glarean

Aeolian

The Aeolian character contains the elements of ostentation and turgidity, and even conceit; these qualities are in keeping with their horse-breeding and their way of meeting strangers; yet this does not mean malice, but is, rather, lofty and confident. Hence also their fondness for drinking is something appropriate to them, also their love affairs, and the entirely relaxed nature of their daily life.
　　Athenaeus

Calms the tempest of the mind and, after having done so, lulls it to sleep.
　　Ornithoparchus

Ionian

Relaxed.
　　Plato

Associated with dancing. Because some men attribute a frivolous wantonness to this mode, it was rarely used in older Church music.
　　Glarean

Hypodorian

Magnificent and steadfast.
　　Aristotle

The lowest of all ... These tones ... have been shown to possess such great usefulness that they calm excited minds and cause even wild animals and serpents and birds and dolphins to approach and listen to their harmony.
　　Cassiodorus (480–573 AD)

Hypolydian [is good] for lamentations because of its doleful sound.[16]
　　John, *On Music* [ca. 1100 AD]

---

[16] Hucbald, 'Melodic Instruction' in *Hucbald, Guido, and John on Music*, trans. Warren Babb (New Haven: Yale University Press, 1978).

Hypophrygian

> Has the character of action.[17]
> Aristotle

Hypoionian

> Great charm in morning songs and love songs, especially in the Celtic tongue which the Swiss use.
> Glarean

Mixolydian

> Mixolydian makes men sad and grave ... woeful and quiet.
> Aristotle

> Pathetic.
> Aristoxenus

> The ancients heard Mixolydian as melancholic.[18]
> Plutarch (46–127 AD)

> A certain tranquil dignity which both moves and dominates the people.
> Glarean

Aside from these early descriptions of the character of the Greek modes, there are a few additional observations which seem to carry important information but lack sufficient detail to be helpful to the modern reader. First, a comment by Aristoxenus (b. ca. 379 BC), who wrote at a time when theorists were attempting to formulate a written form of the modes. But his comment makes it clear that the written form did not address the essence of the modes.

> [Just because] a man notes down the Phrygian scale it does not follow that he must know the *essence* of the Phrygian scale. Plainly then notation is not the ultimate limit of our science.[19]

This reminds us of a problem in our modern Church-mathematical notational system. We lack completely symbols for feeling, even though that is the whole point of music. We can imagine one saying, 'We can write music, but the notation does not reveal the *essence* of the music.'

This distinction seems to be intended by Aristoxenus again when he refers to a song 'which is sung to the *Hypodorian scale*,' but is described as 'being in the *Aeolian mode*.'

---

17 *Problemata*, 922b.10.

18 'Concerning Music.' Plutarch clams this mode was introduced by the woman lyric poet, Sappho (ca. 640–550 BC).

19 Ibid., 39.

Second, although it is understood that the names of the Greek modes were originally intended to represent the music of specific peoples, and not music theory, one must imagine that the styles within 'Dorian,' for example, were rather broad and that it was not just one style. Something of this nature seems suggested by a comment of Plutarch,

> Indeed it is much questioned among the Dorians themselves, whether the enharmonic composers be competent judges of the Dorian songs.[20]

It must have been a similar sophistication within the genre which caused additional adjectives such as Aristophanes' expression, a '*soft* Ionian Love song,'[21] not to mention Aeschylus',

> Through me too sorrow runs
> Like a *strange* Ionian Song.[22]

What can 'a *strange* Ionian Song' mean? This adjective also occurs twice in Euripides,

> O Muse, be near me now, and make
> A *strange* song for Ilion's sake.[23]
>
> ......
>
> A lad alone on Ida,
> Playing tunes on his pipe, *strange* melodies,
> Like the melodies Olympus sang.[24]

Aristoxenus mentioned another of these stylistic distinctions when he quoted a passage from Aristotle's *Problems*,

> which justifies the use of the Hypodorian and Hypophrygian modes for the lyrics sung by actors, when realistic action was called for, but not for those of the chorus.[25]

A final example of information within the genre now lost to us is found in a play by Aristophanes and is a representative of ancient Greek humor.

> You also know what a pig's education he has had; his school-fellows can recall that he only liked the Dorian style and would study no other; his music master in displeasure sent him away saying; 'This youth, in matters of harmony, will only learn the Dorian style because it is akin to bribery.'[26]

---

[20] 'Concerning Music.'

[21] *The Ecclesiazusae*, 881.

[22] *The Supplices*, 69, trans. Gilbert Murray, *The Complete Plays of Aeschylus* (London: George Allen, 1952).

[23] *The Trojan Women*, 510.

[24] *Iphigenia in Aulis*, 574.

[25] Quoted in Sir Arthur Pickard-Cambridge, *The Dramatic Festivals of Athens* (Oxford: Clarendon Press, 1953), 263, 265.

[26] *The Knights*, 990.

Today we have no idea why this was funny to the ancient Greeks, but it apparently involved a play on words, the spirit of which one French translator attempted to capture by referring to it as the 'Louis d'or-ian mode.'

There are also some interesting contemporary comments which fall into the realm of performance practice. First, Plutarch mentions a composer named Sacadas,

> who composed a choral ode with the first strophe in Dorian, the second in Phrygian, and the third 'after the Lydian manner; and this style was called Trimeres (or threefold) by reason of the shifting of the modes.'[27]

To the modern reader this would appear to be something on the order of modulation and it may have some relevance to a song by Alkman:

> Sing, O Muse, sing high and clear
> O *polytonal* many-voiced Muse,
> Make a new song for girls to sing.
> About the towered temple of Therapne.

Alkman (ca. 640–600 BC), one of the ancient Greek lyric poets, was a slave and choral conductor. He was admired by Goethe and Aristotle said he suffered terribly from lice. Chamaeleon says Alkman 'led the way as a composer of erotic songs, and was the first to publish a licentious song, being prone in his habits of life to the pursuit of women and to poetry of that kind.'[28]

Second, there is a comment by Aristotle (*Politica,* 1342b) which is very interesting from several viewpoints. One can only wish that Aristotle had gone into his usual detail when he mentioned an instance of a performer who attempted to perform a dithyramb, 'acknowledged to be Phrygian,' in the Dorian and could not do it.

Finally, there are three interesting comments from much later during the Christian Era, when the Church modes, with the same names, had replaced the ancient Greek modes. Today the Church modes are generally taught as scales with differing placements of half- and whole-steps. No theory teacher today uses the kinds of descriptions used by the ancient Greeks, 'noble,' 'majestic,' etc., much less do they recommend to their students that these modes have differing effects on the listener. But these late medieval and Renaissance theorists had some reason for continuing to think of the new Church modes as representing character in the style of the old Greek modes. It is a topic very worthy of reconsideration by today's theorists.

Andreas Ornithoparchus, in his *Musice active micrologus* of 1517 warns that the musician must diligently observe which mode he plays for specific listeners! The men of our time, he says, know how to do this according to the nature of the occasion.

---

[27] Quoted in Plutarch in 'Concerning Music.' Athenaeus (*Deipnosophistae*, xiv, cap. 31) says that Pronomus, the Theban, was the first who played three kinds of music upon one aulos; and that before him players used separate instruments for each.

[28] Chamaeleon, quoted by Archytas of Mytilene, quoted by Athenaeus, in *Deipnosophistae*, XIII, 600.

But our men of a more refined time do use sometimes the Dorian, sometimes the Phrygian, sometimes the Lydian and sometimes other modes, because they judge that according to differing occasions they are to choose differing modes. And that is not without cause, for every habit of the mind is governed by songs. For songs make men sleepy and wakeful, careful and merry, angry and merciful. Songs heal diseases and produce diverse wonderful effects, moving some to vain mirth, some to a devout and holy joy, yes often to godly tears.[29]

Heinrich Glarean in his *Dodecachordon* of 1547, a work devoted to the new Church modes, makes a similar comment which goes beyond mere half- and whole-step descriptions.

On the other hand, I believe that for the last four hundred years [the Ionian mode] has also been so deeply admired by church singers, that, enticed by its sweetness and alluring charm, they have changed many songs of the Lydian mode into this mode.[30]

In another place Glarean discusses this process at more length.

Modes are also changed from one into another but not with equal success. For in some cases the change is scarcely clear even to a perceptive ear, indeed, often with great pleasure to the listener, a fact which we have frequently declared is very common today in changing from the Lydian to the Ionian. Those who play instruments and who know how to sing readily the verses of poets according to a musical play, understand this. Indeed, in this way they are frequently worthy of praise if they do it skillfully, especially if they change the Ionian into Dorian. But in other cases the changing seems rough, and scarcely ever without a grave offense to the ears, as changing from the Dorian to the Phrygian. And so whenever present day organists encounter this difficulty in changing church songs in such a way, if they are not well trained and quick, they often incur the derision of experienced listeners.[31]

The third example comes from the *Harmonie universelle* (1636) by Marin Mersenne (1588–1648). Unfortunately, Mersenne does not give us the basis for the recommendations, but it is clear that he was thinking along the lines of the old Greek character associations when he endorsed Giovanni Doni's[32] suggestions of a correspondence between the modes and the color of specific organ pipes.

The organ can be used to express each mode because of the great number of its stops, of which the one of tin is proper for the Dorian, and the others composed of pipes more or less large at the top than at the bottom, closed and open, for example, the narrow ones are suitable for the Phrygian, and the wider ones for the Lydian; and then he says that the pipes which imitate the block flutes are good to express the Dorian; those which imitate the fife and the flageolet for the Phrygian; and the cornett and the pipes which make the German flute for the Lydian. The boxwood is proper to make the Dorian pipes; the regals are good for the Lydian, and the brass pipes for the Phrygian.[33]

---

[29] Ornithoparchus, *Musicae active mirologus* and Dowland, *Introduction: Containing the Art of Singing* (New York: Dover, 1973), 156.
[30] Glarean, *Dodecachordon*, trans. Clement Miller (American Institute of Musicology, 1965), I, 153.
[31] Ibid., I, 129.
[32] Giovanni Battista Doni, *Compendio del trattato de' generi e de' modi* (Rome, 1635).
[33] *Harmonie universelle*, V, vii, 30.

Another subject which the ancient philosophers took quite seriously was the choice of modes to be used in education. Their interest in the relationship between music and character development followed naturally their assumptions about the varying characters of the modes. The most extended discussion of this topic is found in Plato, who begins with a discussion of the music teacher.

> The teachers of the lyre take similar care that their young disciple is temperate and gets into no mischief; and when they have taught him the use of the lyre, they introduce him to the poems of other excellent poets, who are the lyric poets; and these they set to music, and make their harmonies and rhythms quite familiar to the children's souls, in order that they may learn to be more gentle, and harmonious, and rhythmical, and so more fitted for speech and action; for the life of man in every part has need of harmony and rhythm. Then they send them to the master of gymnastic.[34]

What kind of music is Plato describing here? First, the musical style must be simple and in a single style. More complex 'mixed styles' Plato did not permit in education, although he admits this type of music was more popular with both children and the general public.

> You would agree with me in saying that one [style] is simple and has but slight changes; and that if an author expresses this style in fitting harmony and rhythm, he will find himself, if he does his work well, keeping pretty much within the limits of a single harmony (for the changes are not great), and in like manner he will make a similar choice of rhythm?
> That is quite true, he said.
> Whereas the other requires all sorts of harmonies and all sorts of rhythms if the music and the style are to correspond, because the style has all sorts of changes.
> That is also perfectly true, he replied.
> And do not the two styles, or the mixture of the two, comprehend all poetry and every form of expression in words? No one can say anything except in one or other of them or in both together.
> They include all, he said.
> And shall we receive into our State all the three styles, the one only of the two unmixed styles? Or would you include the mixed?
> I should prefer only to admit the pure imitator of virtue.
> Yes, I said, Adeimantus; and yet the mixed style is also charming: and indeed the opposite style to that chosen by you is by far the most popular with children and their attendants, and with the masses.
> I do not deny it.[35]

In one of the most frequently quoted passages regarding Plato's views on music, we are told the choice of modes is to be strictly limited.

> The harmonies which you mean are the mixed or tenor Lydian, and the full-toned or bass Lydian, and such-like.
> These then, I said, must be banished; even to women who have a character to maintain they are of no use, and much less to men.
> Certainly.

---

34 *Protagoras*, 326b.

35 *Republic*, III, 397c.

> In the next place, drunkenness and softness and indolence are utterly unbecoming the character of our guardians.
>
> Utterly unbecoming.
>
> And which are the soft and convivial harmonies?
>
> The Ionian, he replied, and some of the Lydian which are termed 'relaxed.'
>
> Well, and are these of any use for warlike men?
>
> Quite the reverse, he replied; and if so the Dorian and the Phrygian are the only ones which you have left …
>
> If these and only these are to be used in our songs and melodies, we shall not want multiplicity of strings or a panharmonic scale?
>
> I suppose not.[36]

Aristotle's discussion of this subject is not so extended, but it is clear his views followed those of Plato.

> Even in mere melodies there is an imitation of character, for the musical modes differ essentially from one another, and those who hear them are differently affected by each. Some of them make men sad and grave, like the so-called Mixolydian, others enfeeble the mind, like the relaxed modes, another, again, produces a moderate and settled temper, which appears to be the peculiar effect of the Dorian; the Phrygian inspires enthusiasm. The whole subject has been well treated by philosophical writers on this branch of education, and they confirm their arguments by facts.[37]

Returning to the subject of education, and particularly the aspect of character building, Aristotle limits the appropriate modes.

> But for education the ethical modes should be used, such as Dorian … All men agree that the Dorian music is the gravest and manliest. And whereas we say that the extremes should be avoided and the mean followed, and whereas the Dorian is a mean between the other modes, it is evident that our youth should be taught in the Dorian music.[38]

One of the modern collections of the poetry of the Alexandrian Period of ancient Greece is called, *Last Flowers*.[39] It is an appropriate title, for among the Greeks, these poets are the last link with the style of the old lyric poets who sang their poetry to the accompaniment of lyre or aulos. One of the beautiful poems of this period, 'Elegy on the Death of Bion,' (fl. 105 BC) proclaims that Dorian music itself has died. We do not know the poet who wrote this, although he says he was a student of Bion.

> Ravines and Dorian waters, sigh with me;
> And rivers, mourn for Bion … He is dead;
> The lovely singer lies within the tomb …

---

[36] Ibid., III, 398e. In *Laches*, 188d, Plato remarks that the Dorian is the true Hellenic mode.

[37] *Politica*, 1340a.40. The 'facts' Aristotle refers to here are unknown today.

[38] Ibid., 1342a27 and 1342b.14.

[39] Henry H. Chamberlin, *Last Flowers* (Cambridge: Harvard University Press, 1937).

> No more the pastoral song may Bion sing;
> With him, alas, has died the lyric strain;
> And all the Dorian music has been slain …
>
> He who the herds once charmed will sing no more,
> Sitting in solitude the oaks among
> To make his music. Now he sings before
> Pluto; forgetfulness is all his song …
>
> Bion, your fate Apollo's self bemoans;
> Full many a Satyr and Priapus weeps
> In sable raiment. Pans with sobs and groans
> Bewail your music. From the watery deeps
> Full many a nymph her tearful visage rears;
> The woodland springs are fountains of their tears …
>
> Who now will play your pipes, O thrice bewailed?
> Who on the reedy vents his mouth would place?
> Thus overbold, he little had availed,
> Where still your lips and breath have living grace,
> Where Echo on the reeds your song maintains.
>
> To Pan I bring your pipes; with little zest
> For him, who fears to emulate your strains
> Lest he himself should come off second best,
> Lest far beyond him would your music go …
>
> Dear master, long before I learned from you
> The Dorian mode; to others may belong
> Your wealth; but your sweet music is my due;
> To me the larger heritage will go.[40]

We cannot know if the old Dorian music was indeed dead, but it is clear they all changed dramatically over time. Glarean seems to weaken any argument that the modes still had specific identifiable characters by suggesting they can be changed in character by the composer. Character, it would seem, has given way to function.

> Yet, it cannot be denied that antiquity has changed these modes, but undoubtedly the nature of modes can be turned in another direction, so that a mode which seems light in character can be used with not much difficulty for serious subjects (provided that a propitious talent is at hand), and on the contrary, a serious mode can be used for light subjects.[41]

During the late Middle Ages the old Greek treatises were being discovered and translated and this resulted in what we call Humanism in music, a return to making music express feeling and not mathematics. The passion of the Baroque composers to try and discover how emotions are communicated in music led, among other things, to rethinking the old Greek idea of associating character and tonality.

---

[40] Henry H. Chamberlin, *Last Flowers* (Cambridge: Harvard University Press, 1937), 67ff.

[41] Ibid., I, 164ff.

We will let Johann Mattheson represent this movement. He was one of the first who understood correctly that the emotions are related to melody, not harmony and points out,

> the nature and character of each key, namely whether it is happy, sad, lovely, devout, etc., are actually matters of the science of melody.[42]

In his *Neu-Eröffnete Orchestre*, Mattheson discusses this in more detail, contending that in the key of F-sharp minor, for example, he finds,

> a key characterized by sadness, but a sadness more pensive and lovelorn than tragic and gloomy; it is a key that has about it a certain loneliness, an individuality, a misanthropy.[43]

What teacher of harmony today speaks to his students with language like this when he speaks of individual key centers? Why has the character of specific keys been replaced by the rational memorization of the order of whole- and half-steps? The ancient Roman Church may have seen a vanishing congregation of those believing most of its old dogma, but in our harmony classrooms it has finally won its long battle: Reason triumphs over Humanism!

And yet, in spite of all, there are musicians today who hear a significant difference between the key of F and the key of G. I once knew an orchestral conductor in Europe who was convinced that for a concert to go well it was mandatory that the first composition in the concert be in the key of D. I, when once conducting in a sixteenth-century hall in Europe, by the end of a concert was thoroughly convinced that the hall itself was in the key of E♭.

For most of music history the music came first and was then followed by theorists who felt duty bound to try to explain the music in question. Since the nineteenth century and the growth of music schools now theory comes first and those composers who feel something different are classified as rule-breakers. I wonder if all, or any, of the left-hemisphere, intellectual and rational language of the academic world which attempts to describe Music has anything at all to do with what Music really is?

What Music really is falls in the realm of vibrations and their affect on the human physiology. What music school studies this? A group of physicists in Europe are studying this and their findings are extraordinary. The ancient Greeks, free of our need for intellectual description, may, in their interest in the subjective quality of their modes, have been closer to the true nature of music than we.

---

[42] Johann Mattheson, *Neu-Eroffnete Orchestre* (Hamburg, 1713), I, ix, 47.

[43] Ibid., 231ff.

The View of the Performance of Music in Ancient Societies

A lack of culture is a serious thing.[1]
Thales (640–546 BC)

IN THIS ESSAY WE EXPLORE THE QUESTION of how music was valued in general by Western European society. For the most part, the reader will find music highly valued, and practiced by the upper class, for a period of time and then a decay until it becomes something which is performed by slaves and not by the upper class. Curiously this cycle seems to repeat itself in the sixteenth and seventeenth centuries and in the nineteenth and twentieth centuries.[2]

For the ancient Assyrians (750–606 BC), a fierce and warlike collection of tribes who took their name from the god Ashur, we have little in the way of literature which might help us understand the value they placed on music. We have perhaps an insight in the fact that whenever they put a city to the sword, they spared the musicians who, with the rest of the valuable booty, were sent back to their capital, Nineveh.[3]

In Egypt we can see numerous tomb paintings which show music as a daily part of the life of the aristocracy, but again almost no surviving literature. Athenaeus (200 AD), an important early historian, did find in Alexandria a remarkable knowledge in music which extended to everyone.

> I would have you know that there is no record in history of other people more musical than the Alexandrians, and I am not speaking merely of singing to the harp, for even the humblest layman among us, even one who has never learned his ABC's, is so familiar with that, that he can immediately detect the mistakes which occur in striking the notes; no, even when it comes to wind instruments [pipes], they are most musical.

The Old Testament, as everyone knows, is also a testimonial to the high value which the ancient Hebrews assigned to music. There is a very interesting passage the reader may not know, as it is found in one of the books left out by the redactors of the Old Testament. This passage reminds us of Aristotle's complaint that the musical entertainers at banquets prevented good conversation. Here, however, it is the reverse: don't talk while the music is being performed, for the music is the highpoint of a good banquet.

---

[1] Quoted in Giovanni Reale, *A History of Ancient Philosophy* (Albany: State University of New York Press, 1987), 143.

[2] Sorry, but in our view the members of our major orchestras are treated like slaves.

[3] Henry G. Farmer, 'The Music of Ancient Mesopotamia,' in *The New Oxford History of Music* (London: Oxford University Press, 1966), 237.

> If thou be made the master of a feast, lift not thyself up, but be among them as one of the rest, take diligent care for them, and so sit down.
>
> And when thou hast done all thy office, take thy place, that thou mayest be merry with them, and receive a crown for thy well-ordering of the feast.
>
> Speak, thou that art the elder, for it becometh thee, but with sound judgment; and hinder not the music.
>
> Pour not out words where there is a musician, and [thus] show not forth wisdom out of time.
>
> A concert of music in a banquet of wine is as a signet of carbuncle in gold.
>
> As a signet of an emerald set in a work of gold, so is the melody of music with pleasant wine.[4]

This, 'pour not out words where there is a musician,' meaning don't talk during the musical performance, takes on an even higher level of importance in Xenophon (fourth century BC) where we are told of a messenger running to a site where the leaders were in attendance of a concert by a male chorus with news of a military disaster. He is stopped at the door and told he must wait until the performance is finished before he can enter to announce his news![5]

The Old Testament as we know it today is not so enthusiastic about banquets as those described above from the period of the Old Testament.

> Woe to those ... who tarry late into the evening till wine inflames them!
>
> They have lyre and harp, timbrel and flute and wine at their feasts; but they do not regard the deeds of the Lord.[6]

It is only with ancient Greece and Rome that we have enough relevant literature to consider more fully the present topic. In the most ancient Greek literature, the works of Homer (ca. 800 BC) we can appreciate the value of music to society in the contemplative and concentrated attitudes of the listeners. In the following passage Homer gives us a picture of what we call an epic singer, a famous one he says, whose music is wondrous, but 'woeful.' Homer makes clear, in this case, that the audience is listening in silence, and indeed one is moved to tears and requests music of a lighter character.

> For them the famous minstrel was singing, and they sat in silence listening; and he sang of the return of the Achaeans—the woeful return from Troy which Pallas Athene laid upon them. And from her upper chamber the daughter of Icarius, wise Penelope, heard his wondrous song, and she went down the high stairway from her chamber ... She stood by the doorpost of the well-built hall, holding before her face her shining veil ... Then she burst into tears, and spoke to the divine minstrel:
>
> 'Phemius, many other things thou knowest to charm mortals, deeds of men and gods which minstrels make famous. Sing them one of these, as thou sittest here, and let them drink their wine in silence. But cease from this woeful song which ever harrows the heart in my breast, for upon me above all women has come a sorrow not to be forgotten ...'

---

4   Ecclesiasticus 32:1ff.

5   Xenophon, *A History of My Times*, VI, 16.

6   Isaiah 5:12.

> Then the wise Telemachus answered her: 'My mother, why dost thou begrudge the good minstrel to give pleasure in whatever way his heart is moved? It is not minstrels that are to blame, but Zeus … With this man no one can be wroth if he sings of the evil doom of the Danaans; for men praise that song the most which comes the newest to their ears.'[7]

A short while later, reflecting the ancient association between music and the divine, Telemachus observes, 'This is a good thing; to listen to a minstrel such as this man is, like to the gods in voice.' Somewhat later, when it is time to dance, the character of the music changes and is described as 'gladsome song.'

All indications are that much of both the culture and musical practice of ancient Greece originally came from Egypt, which is helpful in retrospect for helping us know more of Egyptian music. One of the things historians tell us of ancient Egyptian music (which had no notation) was that once the authorities had determined its rules, and were apparently satisfied with its role in society, no further changes in music were permitted for one thousand years! We sense the shadow of this rigid mental attitude in the complaints which are heard when ancient Greek musicians attempted to change the construction of the lyre. Plutarch relates how Terpander (seventh century BC) was punished for this.

> And indeed so great an esteem and veneration had they for the gravity and simplicity of their ancient music, that no one was allowed to recede in the least from the established rules and measures of it, insomuch as the Ephori, upon complaint made to them, laid a severe mulet upon Terpander (a musician of great note and eminency for his incomparable skill and excellency in playing upon the lyre, and who, as he had ever professed a great veneration for antiquity, so ever testified by his eulogiums and commendations the esteem he always had of virtuous and heroic actions), depriving him of his lyre, and (as a peculiar punishment) exposing it to the censure of the people, by fixing it upon a nail, because he had added one string more to his instrument than was the usual and stated number, though done with no other design and advantage than to vary the sound, and to make it more useful and pleasant.[8]

Plutarch also tells of a musician named Phrynis who had a nine string lyre only to have Empreprepes, one of the Ephors, cut out two strings with a hatchet, saying, 'Do not abuse Music!'[9] Artemon tells of a similar story.

> Timotheus of Miletus (446–357 BC) is held by most authorities to have adopted an arrangement of strings with too great a number … wherefore he was even about to be disciplined by the Lacedaemonians for trying to corrupt their ancient music, and some one was on the point of cutting away his superfluous strings when he pointed to a small image of Apollo among them holding a lyre with the same number and arrangement of strings as his own, and so was acquitted.[10]

---

7   *The Odyssey*, trans. A. T. Murray (London: Heinemann, 1960), I, 325ff.
8   Quoted in Plutarch, in *Customs of the Lacedaemonians*.
9   Quoted in Plutarch, in *Laconic Apophthegms*.
10 Quoted in Athenaeus, *Deipnosophistae*, XIV, 636.

The fragments which survive from the sixth century BC lyric poets give clear evidence that music was still very highly prized by the highest society. Pindar (b. ca. 518 BC), the best known of these poets, once referred to his own music as 'the sweet fruit of the mind.'[11] But this does not mean, of course, that their music was also appreciated by the uneducated public. One of these early poets was aware of the irony that art composed for posterity may *not* enjoy wide popularity with the masses.

> And this is what everyone will say: 'These are the words of Theognis of Megara, whose name is known among all mortals,'
> But I am not yet able to please all the townspeople.[12]

These lyric poets were also singers, as most poetry was sung until about the fourteenth century AD. Sometimes they were accompanied by an aulos[13] player and like some double-reed players today we may imagine that the aulos players soon began to be dissatisfied with playing a mere accompaniment role. This might account for an objection by Pratinas, in 500 BC, who reminded his listeners that the Muse had ordained that the song should be the mistress and the aulos the servant, and not the other way around![14]

In the teaching of the great philosopher, Pythagoras (569–475 BC), we find the view that music was of such importance as to be inseparable from life itself. There is no extant literature by Pythagoras, but one of his followers, Euryphamus, found the association of music and health in an analogy with the lyre.

> Human life resembles a properly tuned and cared for lyre. Every lyre requires three things: apparatus, tuning, and musical skill of the player. By apparatus we mean preparation of all the appropriate parts: the strings, the plectrum and other instruments cooperating in the tuning of the instrument. By tuning we mean the adaptation of the sounds to each other. The musical skill is the motion of the player in consideration of the tuning. Human life requires the same three things. Apparatus is the preparation of the physical basis of life, riches, renown, and friends. Tuning is the organizing of these according to virtue and the laws. Musical skill is the mingling of these according to virtue and the laws, virtue sailing with a prosperous wind and no external resistance.[15]

Another disciple of Pythagoras, Diotogenes, in a fragment entitled, 'Concerning a Kingdom,' extends the same analogy to the organization of a city.

> The king should therefore organize the well-legislated city like a lyre, first in himself establishing the justest boundary and order of law, knowing that the people's proper arrangement should be organized according to this interior boundary, the divinity having given him dominion over them.[16]

---

[11] Ode for Diagoras of Rhodes, Winner of the Boxing Match.

[12] Quoted in Gregory Nagy, *Pindar's Homer* (Baltimore: Johns Hopkins University Press, 1982), 375.

[13] An early relative to the oboe; nearly always mistranslated as 'flute' in English.

[14] Richard C. Jebb, *Bacchylides* (Hildesheim, Georg Olms Verlagsbuchhandlung, 1967), 46.

[15] Quoted in Kenneth Guthrie, *The Pythagorean Sourcebook* (Grand Rapids: Phanes Press, 1987), 245.

[16] Ibid., 223.

Pythagoras, as well, believed that since music was an important key to maintaining the balance of health in the individual, so must the same idea must be valid for the larger society. When consulted by Crotonian civic leaders, Iambilichus (250–325 AD) relates that Pythagoras responded as follows.

> His first advice was to build a temple to the Muses, which would preserve the already existing concord. He observed to them that all of these divinities were grouped together by their common names, that they subsisted only in conjunction with each other, that they specially rejoiced in social honors, and that the choir of the Muses subsisted always one and the same. They comprehended symphony, harmony, rhythm, and all things breeding concord. Not only to beautiful theorems does their power extend, but to the general symphonious harmony.[17]

This tendency of the Pythagoreans to turn to music to find the organizing principle of all things resulted in an early satire which suggested that music might also provide the rules for organizing the kitchen!

> A: For myself, I never enter the kitchen.
> B: Why, what do you do?
> A: I sit near by and watch, while others do the work; to them I explain the principles and the result. 'Softly! the mincemeat is seasoned sharp enough.'
> B: You must be a musician, not a cook!
> A: 'Play fortissimo with the fire. Make the tempo even. The first dish is not simmering in tune with the others next to it.'
> B: Save us!
> A: It's beginning to look like an art to you, what? You see, I serve no course without study mingle all in a harmonious scale.
> B: What does that mean?
> A: Some things are related to each other by fourths, by fifths, or by octaves. These I join their own proper intervals, and weave them into a series of appropriate courses.[18]

Following this logic, Plutarch, who may have been serious and not in satire, found in music the justification for the organization of the domestic environment.

> As in musical concords, when the upper strings are so tuned as exactly to accord, the base always gives the tone; so in well-regulated and well-ordered families, all things are carried on with the harmonious consent and agreement of both parties, but the conduct and contrivance chiefly redounds to the reputation and management of the husband.[19]

Plato quotes a parable by Socrates (470–399 BC) about artists reborn as grasshoppers, the point of which was to assure his listeners that music and the other arts were at that time still held in a special relationship by the gods.

---

[17] Iambilichus, in Ibid.
[18] Athenaeus, *Deipnosophistae*, III, 103.
[19] *Conjugal Precepts*.

SOCRATES. A lover of music like yourself ought surely to have heard the story of the grasshoppers, who are said to have been human beings in an age before the Muses. And when the Muses came and song appeared the grasshoppers were ravished with delight; and singing always, never thought of eating and drinking, until at last in their forgetfulness they died. And now they live again in the grasshoppers, who, as a special gift from the Muses, require no nourishment, but from the hour of their birth are always singing, and ever eating and drinking; and when they die they go and inform the Muses in heaven which of us honors one or other of the Muses. They win the love of Terpsichore for the dancers by their report of them; of Erato for the lovers, and of the other Muses for those who do them honor, according to the several ways of honoring them;—and to Calliope the eldest Muse and Urania who is next to her, they make a report of those who honor music of their kind, and spend their time in philosophy; for these are the Muses who are chiefly concerned with the heavens and with reasoning, divine as well as human, and they have the sweetest utterance.[20]

It is quite clear that Socrates had begun to see an evolution from music's noble old purposes to one of merely trying to please the crowd, resulting, as he puts it, in licentiousness.

AN ATHENIAN STRANGER. Let us speak of the laws about music,—that is to say, such music as then existed,—in order that we may trace the growth of the excess of freedom from the beginning. Now music was early divided among us into certain kinds and manners. One sort consisted of prayers to the Gods, which were called hymns; and there was another and opposite sort called lamentations, and another termed paeans, and another, celebrating (I believe) the birth of Dionysus, called 'dithyrambs.' And they used the actual word 'laws' for another kind of song; and to this they added the term 'citharoedic.' All these and others were duly distinguished, nor were the performers allowed to confuse one style of music with another. And the authority which determined and give judgment, and punished the disobedient, was not expressed in a hiss, nor in the most unmusical shouts of the multitude, as in our days, nor in applause and clapping of hands. But the directors of public instruction insisted that the spectators should listen in silence to the end; and boys and their tutors, and the multitude in general, were kept quiet by a hint from a stick. Such was the good order which the multitude were willing to observe; they would never have dared to give judgment by noisy cries. And then, as time went on, the poets themselves introduced the reign of vulgar and lawless innovation. They were men of genius, but they had no perception of what is just and lawful in music; raging like bacchanals and possessed with inordinate delights—mingling lamentations with hymns, and paeans with dithyrambs; imitating the sounds of the aulos or the lyre, and making one general confusion; ignorantly affirming that music has no truth, and, whether good or bad, can only be judged of rightly by the pleasure of the hearer. And by composing such licentious works, and adding to them words as licentious, they have inspired the multitude with lawlessness and boldness, and made them fancy that they can judge for themselves about melody and song. And in this way the theaters from being silent have become vocal, as though they had understanding of good and bad in music and poetry; and instead of an aristocracy, an evil sort of theatrocracy has grown up. For if there had been a democracy in music alone, consisting of free men, no fatal harm would have been done; but in music there first arose the universal conceit of omniscience and general lawlessness;—freedom came following afterwards, and men, fancying that they knew what they did not know, had no longer any fear, and the absence of fear begets shamelessness. For what is this shamelessness, which is so evil a thing, but the insolent refusal to regard the opinion of the better by reason of an over-daring sort of liberty?[21]

---

[20] *Phdaerus*, 259c.

[21] *Laws*, 700ff.

Socrates mentions this fall of music from its former high ideals to goals of mere entertainment again in *Gorgias*.

> SOCRATES. Can you tell me the pursuits which delight mankind—or rather ... which of them belong to the pleasurable class, and which of them not? In the first place, what say you of aulos playing? Does not that appear to be an art which seeks only pleasure, Callicles, and thinks of nothing else?
> CALLICLES. I assent.
> SOCRATES. And is not the same true of all similar arts, as, for example, the art of playing the lyre at festivals?
> CALLICLES. Yes.
> SOCRATES. And what do you say of the choral art and of dithyrambic poetry?—are not they of the same nature? Do you imagine that Cinesias the son of Meles cares about what will tend to the moral improvement of his hearers, or about what will give pleasure to the multitude?
> CALLICLES. There can be no mistake about Cinesias, Socrates.
> SOCRATES. And what do you say of his father, Meles the harp-player? When he sang to the harp, did you suppose that he had his eye on the highest good? Perhaps he indeed could scarcely be said to regard even the greatest pleasure, since his singing was an infliction to his audience? In fact, would you not say that all music of the harp and dithyrambic poetry in general have been invented for the sake of pleasure?
> CALLICLES. I should.

In another place Socrates comments on a similar decline in the goal of Dramatic Tragedy.

> SOCRATES. And as for the Muse of Tragedy, that solemn and august personage—what are her aspirations? Is all her aim and desire only to give pleasure to the spectators, or does she strive to refrain her tongue from all that pleases and charms them but is vicious? To proclaim, in speech and song, truth that is salutary but unpleasant, whether they welcome it or not?—which in your judgment is of the nature of tragic poetry?
> CALLICLES. There can be no doubt, Socrates, that Tragedy has her face turned towards pleasure and the gratification of the audience.
> SOCRATES. And is not that the sort of thing, Callicles, which we were just now describing as flattery?

There is one passage by Plato (427–347 BC) which reveals he had the same concern for the status of music in society. Since he studied in Egypt, as we know from a passage in the *Laws*,[22] it is no surprise that he leaned toward the view that music is so important to society that it should be controlled by the government. Here he goes so far as to suggest that separate controls should apply to men and women. This passage also reveals that Plato had already begun to see the public turning away from art music ('orderly and severe music') toward entertainment music ('sweet and vulgar music'). He does not intend to condemn pleasure, which he points out all music has, but he is clearly concerned about the impact on society, for music can make man better or worse.

---

[22] Ibid., 656d.

> There are many ancient musical compositions and dances which are excellent, and from these it is fair to select what is proper and suitable to the newly-founded city; and they shall choose judges of not less than fifty years of age, who shall make the selection, and any of the old poems which they deem sufficient they shall include; any that are deficient or altogether unsuitable, they shall either utterly throw aside, or examine and amend, taking into their counsel poets and musicians, and making use of their poetical genius; but explaining to them the wishes of the legislator in order that they may regulate dancing, music and all choral strains, according to the mind of the judges; and not allowing them to indulge, except in some few matters, their individual pleasures and fancies. Now the irregular strain of music is always made ten thousand times better by attaining to law and order, and rejecting the honeyed Muse—not however that we mean wholly to exclude pleasure, which is characteristic of all music. And if a man be brought up from childhood to the age of discretion and maturity in the use of the orderly and severe music, when he hears the opposite he detests it, and calls it illiberal; but if trained in the sweet and vulgar music, he deems the severer kind cold and displeasing. So that while he who hears them gains no more pleasure from the one than from the other, the one has the advantage of making those who are trained in it better men, whereas the other makes them worse ...
>
> We must distinguish and determine on some general principle what songs are suitable to women, and what to men, and must assign to them their proper melodies and rhythms. It is shocking for a whole harmony to be inharmonical, or for a rhythm to be unrhythmical, and this will happen when the melody is inappropriate to them. And therefore the legislator must assign to these also their forms. Now both sexes have melodies and rhythms which of necessity belong to them; and those of women are clearly enough indicated by their natural difference. The grand, and that which tends to courage, may be fairly called manly; but that which inclines to moderation and temperance, may be declared both in law and in ordinary speech to be the more womanly quality.[23]

The seeds of decay in the esteem in which music was held by the highest levels of society are first seen in criticism of instrumentalists. As Greece prospered the aristocrats began to turn to a life of leisure and turned the effort of making instrumental music over to their slaves. Once music became associated with slaves it was no longer something an aristocrat could identify with. This same transformation occurred again as the Renaissance evolved into the Baroque Period. At that time Lord Chesterfield, in one of his famous letters to his son, explained that it was alright to listen to and enjoy music, but one should not actually play music. To make his point he used an analogy, 'Eat meat, but don't be your own butcher.'

This is exactly the point Plutarch (46–127 AD) wished to make in his biography of Pericles (495–429 BC):

> Many times ... when we are pleased with the work, we slight and set little by the workman or artist himself, as, for instance, in perfumes and purple dyes, we are taken with the things themselves well enough, but do not think dyers and perfumers otherwise than low and sordid people. It was not said amis by Antisthenes, when people told him that one Ismenias was an excellent aulos player, 'It may be so,' said he, 'but he is but a wretched human being, otherwise he would not have been an excellent aulos player.'[24]

---

23 *Laws*, 802.

24 Plutarch, *Lives*, 'Pericles.'

Plutarch, in his biography of Alcibiades (450–404 BC), makes an even stronger case for the aristocrat not becoming a player of the aulos.

> When he began to study, he obeyed all his other masters fairly well, but refused to learn upon the aulos, as a sordid thing, and not becoming a free citizen; saying, that to play on the lute or harp does not in any way disfigure a man's body or face, but one is hardly to be known by the most intimate friends, when playing on the aulos. Besides, one who plays on the harp may speak or sing at the same time; but the use of the aulos stops the mouth, intercepts the voice, and prevents all articulation. 'Therefore,' said he, 'let the Theban youths pipe, who do not know how to speak, but we Athenians, as our ancestors have told us, have Minerva for our patroness, and Apollo for our protector, one of whom threw away the aulos, and the other stripped the aulos-player of his skin.' Thus, between raillery and good earnest, Alcibiades kept not only himself but others from learning, as it presently became the talk of the young boys, how Alcibiades despised playing on the aulos, and ridiculed those who studied it. In consequence of which, it ceased to be reckoned amongst the liberal accomplishments, and became generally neglected.[25]

One observer of the fifth century BC was even more disconcerted by the aulos players he found on stage accompanying the choirs. Athenaeus records this angry complaint:

> Pratinas of Phlius, when hired aulos players and dancers usurped the dancing places, became indignant at the way in which the aulos players failed to accompany the choruses in the traditional fashion, and choruses now sang a mere accompaniment to the aulos players; ...' What uproar is this? What dances are these? What outrage hath assailed the alter of Dionysus with its loud clatter? ... 'Tis the song that is queen, established by the Pierian Muse; but the aulos must be second in the dance, for he is even a servant; let him be content to be leader in the revel only, in the fist-fights of tipsy youngsters raging at the front door. Beat back him who has the breath of a mottled toad, burn up in flames that spit-wasting, babbling raucous reed, spoiling melody and rhythm in its march, that hireling whose body is fashioned by an auger!'[26]

There is no doubt this attitude of disrespect towards the aulos player was being expressed by some in the fourth century BC. Indeed, there is a story of Philip II, father to Alexander the Great (356–323 BC), who, after hearing his son perform a composition in a charming and skillfully manner, said to him, 'Are you not ashamed, son, to play so well?'[27] We suspect Aristotle (384–322 BC), who was Alexander the Great's teacher, may have poisoned the father's attitude, for Aristotle had the same view.

> Why is it that some men spend their time in pursuits which they have chosen, though these are sometimes mean, rather than in more honorable professions? Why, for example, should a man who chooses to be a conjurer or an actor or an aulos player prefer these callings to that of an astronomer or an orator?[28]

---

[25] Plutarch, *Lives*, 'Alcibiades.'

[26] Athenaeus, *Deipnosophistae*, XIV.

[27] Plutarch, *Lives*.

[28] *Problemata*, 917a.5.

From a somewhat later period, we have a comment by the famous Stoic philosopher, Epictetus (55–135 AD), who also comments on the problem of how can one admire music if one does not admire the player. He seems to advise one to simply overlook the player and enjoy the music.

> Every art, when it is being taught, is tiresome to one who is unskilled and untried in it. The products of the arts indeed show at once the use they are made for, and most of them have an attraction and charm of their own; for though it is no pleasure to be present and follow the process by which a shoemaker learns his art, the shoe itself is useful and a pleasant thing to look at as well. So too the process by which a carpenter learns is very tiresome to the unskilled person who happens to be by, but his work shows the use of his art. This you will see still more in the case of music, for if you are by when a man is being taught you will think the process of all things the most unpleasant, yet the effects of music are pleasant and delightful for unmusical persons to hear.[29]

Returning to the fourth century BC, we also have Aristotle's testimony that by his time music had now fallen to the level of being merely a source of pleasure.

> In our own day men cultivate it for the sake of pleasure, but originally it was included in education, because nature herself, as has been often said, requires that we should be able, not only to work well, but to use leisure well.[30]

The period which begins with the defeat of the Greeks by Philip of Macedonia, in 338 BC, and includes the reign of his son, Alexander the Great, was the beginning of the end of the glory of ancient Greece. Indeed, one might date the rapid decline of the Greek culture from the year 323–322 BC, which saw the death of both Alexander and Aristotle.[31] Chief among the generals who divided up the empire of Alexander was Ptolemy, who became king of Egypt, made Alexandria his capital and built his famous library there. Because he invited important scholars and artists to join him, many of the writers who document the decline of Greece were residents of Alexandria. Athenaeus quotes from the *Chronicles* of one of these writers, Andron of Alexandria, regarding this critical period.

> The Alexandrians were the teachers of all Greeks and barbarians [meaning Macedonians] at a time when the entire system of general education had broken down by reason of the continually recurring disturbances which took place in the period of Alexander's successors. I say, then, a rejuvenation of all culture was again brought about in the reign of the seventh Ptolemy who ruled over Egypt, the king who received from the Alexandrians appropriately the name of Malefactor. For he murdered many of the Alexandrians; not a few he sent into exile, and filled the islands and towns with men who had grown up with his brother—philologians, philosophers, mathematicians, musicians, painters, athletic trainers, physicians, and many other men of skill in their profession.[32]

---

29 *The Discourses of Epictetus*, trans. P. E. Matheson (New York: Random House, 1957), 308.

30 *Politics*, 1337b.28.

31 The decline may have begun somewhat earlier, as Athenaeus, in *Deipnosophistae*, I, 3, cites the comic poet Eupolis (d. 411 BC) as having mentioned that the works of Pindar were already a 'sealed book, because of the decay of popular taste.'

32 Atheanaeus, *Deipnosophistae*, IV, 184.

The great central themes of Greek thought now began to disintegrate into a number of schools of philosophy, from the Cynics, who spoke of virtue and abstinence, to the Epicurians, who said pleasure was the highest good. Music, of course, was not immune to these disturbances. While music was a topic discussed by nearly all important earlier Greek philosophers, it is notable that the philosophers of the Alexandrian Period (with the exception of Aristotle's student, Aristoxenus) rarely mention it at all.

We can best witness the general decline of musical practice in the writings of the writers who followed the Alexandrian Period, chiefly in the work of Athenaeus.

Athenaeus epitomizes the decline of Art Music during this period as a movement from an aim for the noble and beautiful to an aim of merely pleasing the crowd.

> In olden times the feeling for nobility was always maintained in the art of music, and all its elements skilfully retained the orderly beauty appropriate to them. Hence there were aulos peculiarly adapted to every mode, and every player had flutes suited to every mode used in the public contests. But Pronomus of Thebes began the practice of playing all the modes on the same aulos. Today, however, people take up music in a haphazard and irrational manner. In early times popularity with the masses was a sign of bad art; hence, when a certain flute player once received loud applause, Asopodorus of Phlius, who was himself still waiting in the wings, said, 'What's this? Something awful must have happened!' The player evidently could not have won approval with the crowd otherwise. And yet the musicians of our day set as the goal of their art success with their audiences.[33]

This change in attitude can be seen in a lost play by Sotion, called *The Teacher of Profligacy*, of which Athenaeus preserves for us a portion of dialog which mentions the concert hall of Athens, the Odeum. A character says,

> What's this nonsense you are talking, forever babbling, this way and that, of the Lyceum, the Academy, and the Odeum gates—mere sophists' rubbish? There's no good in them. Let's drink, and drink our fill, Let's have a good time while we may still keep the life in our bodies. Whoop it up, Men! There's nothing nicer than the belly.[34]

Athenaeus attributes much of this kind of attitude to Epicurus (who indeed said, 'The beginning and the root of all good is the pleasure of the stomach'[35]) and his followers, 'those who walk with eyebrows uplifted,' whom he says believed that 'pleasure is the highest Good.'[36]

Athenaeus also quotes from a lost book, *Drinking Miscellany*, by Aristoxenus, a student of Aristotle and eyewitness to this period of decline. Aristoxenus had been speaking of the people of Poseidonia, 'who were originally Greeks, but had been completely barbarized, becoming Tuscans or Romans; changing their speech and other practices,' and then adds,

---

33 Ibid., XIV 631.
34 Ibid., VIII, 336. In Book VIII, 339, Athenaeus also mentions a profligate harp player.
35 *Epicurus*, trans. Cyril Bailey (Oxford: Clarendon Press, 1926), 135.
36 Athenaeus, *Deipnosophistae*, VII, 279.

> In like manner we also, now that our theaters have become utterly barbarized and prostituted and music has moved on into a state of grave corruption, will get together by ourselves, few though we be, and recall what the art of music used to be.[37]

There is another passage by Aristoxenus which also documents the decay of the musical practice during the fourth century BC. Although this book is also lost, this passage has been preserved for us by Plutarch.

> For, of those that were contemporary with him, he gives an account of Telesias the Theban, who in his youth was bred up in the noblest excellences of music, and moreover studied the works of the most famous lyric poets, Pindar, Dionysius the Theban, Lamprus, Pratinas, and all the rest who were accounted most eminent; who played also to perfection upon the aulos, and was not a little industrious to furnish himself with all those other accomplishments of learning; but being past the prime of his age, he was so bewitched with the theater's new fangles and the innovations of multiplied notes, that despising those noble precepts and that solid practice to which he had been educated, he betook himself to Philoxenus and Timotheus, and among those delighted chiefly in such as were most depraved with diversity of notes and baneful innovation.[38]

Because Aristoxenus wrote several music treatises, even though only fragments survive, modern writers often make the mistake of quoting him as an authority of the subject. In fact his music books are only a small portion of his output and there is nothing to suggest it was a specialty of his and furthermore he often qualified his expertise. In one of the surviving fragments he is more guarded in his beliefs about the value of music than in the quotation above.

> Some consider Harmonie a sublime science, and expect a course of it to make them musicians; nay some even conceive it will exalt their moral nature. This mistake is due to their having run away with such phrases in our preamble as ... 'one class of musical art is hurtful to the moral character, another improves it'; while they missed completely our qualification of this statement, 'in so far as musical art can improve the moral character.'[39]

Strabo (63 BC–21 AD) attacks the philosophy of the Alexandrian writer Eratosthenes (276–194 BC) for his apparent acceptance of the new role of music to merely entertain.

> Eratosthenes contends that the aim of every poet is to entertain, not to instruct. The ancients assert, on the contrary, that poetry is a kind of elementary philosophy, which, taking us in our very boyhood, introduces us to the art of life and instructs us, with pleasure to ourselves, in character, emotions, and actions ... Why, even the musicians, when they give instruction in singing, in lyre playing, or in aulos playing ... maintain that these studies tend to discipline and correct the character.[40]

---

37 Ibid., XIV, 632. The Greeks used the term 'barbarized' to refer to one who did not speak Greek well.
38 Quoted by Plutarch in 'Concerning Music.'
39 Aristoxenus, *The Elements of Harmony*, 16, trans., Henry S. Macran (Hildesheim: Georg Olms Verlag, 1974), 31.
40 *The Geography of Strabo*, trans. Horace L. Jones (Cambridge: Harvard University Press, 1960), I.2.3.

Toward the end of the ancient Greek civilization it does seem that some philosophers and historians had begun to sense a loss and attempted to educate their readers on the old values of music. No early writer addresses this topic with more heartfelt passion than the historian Polybius (203–120 BC). He departs from his description of the internal wars of the period 220–216 BC to give a fervent testimonial to the role music plays in shaping the character of entire peoples and a plea that the Cynaetheans return to this use of music to save themselves. In the course of his argument he gives us one of the most extraordinary pictures of the educational use of music ('I mean *True* music,' he says) in ancient Greece. Why, Polybius asks, did the savage character of the Cynaethans so far surpass all the other Greeks of that period in cruelty and lawless behavior?

> My own opinion is that they were the first and indeed the only people among the Arcadians to have abandoned an institution which had been nobly conceived by their ancestors, and was studied by all the inhabitants of Arcadia in their relation to their natural conditions. A am referring here to the special attention given to music, and by this I mean true music, which is a blessing to all peoples, but in the case of the Arcadians, a necessity. We should certainly not accept the suggestion of Ephorus, who threw into the preface to his history a sentence that was quite unworthy of him, to the effect that music was introduced among men merely for the purpose of beguiling and deceiving one another. Nor should be imagine that the Cretans and the Lacedaemonians did not have good reason for substituting the use of the aulos and of rhythmic movements in place of the trumpets in their military operations. In the same way the early Arcadians knew what they were about when they gave music such an important place in their public life that not only boys but young men up to the age of thirty were obliged to study it constantly, even though in other respects they lived under the most austere conditions. For it is a fact that is well-attested and familiar to all that Arcadia is almost the only nation in which the boys are taught from their earliest childhood to sing in measure the hymns and paeans in which they commemorate, according to their traditions, the gods and heroes of particular localities.
>
> Later they learn the measures of Philoxenus and Timotheus, and every year in the theater there are keenly contested competitions in choral singing to the accompaniment of professional aulos players, the boys taking part in the events which are suitable to their age and them men in what is called the men's festival.
>
> And in addition to these occasions, it is their custom all through their lives to entertain themselves at their banquets: they do not listen to hired performers but create their own music, each man being called upon for a song in turn. They are not at all ashamed to admit that they are completely ignorant of other studies, but in the case of singing nobody can claim to be untaught because everybody is obliged to learn; nor can they say that they know not how to sing, but excuse themselves from performing, for this would be considered a disgrace among them. Besides this, the young men practice marching melodies on the aulos while they are on parade, perfect themselves in dances, and give annual displays in the theaters, all these activities being carried on through the patronage of the state and at the public expense.
>
> In introducing these practices I do not believe that the ancestors of the Arcadians thought of them as luxuries or extravagances. On the contrary, they saw that personal manual labor was the general lot, that the life of the people was toilsome and hard, and that as a natural consequence of the country's cold and gloomy climate the character of its inhabitants was correspondingly austere. The fact is that as mortal men we adapt ourselves by sheer necessity to climatic influences, and it is this reason and no other which causes separate nations and peoples dwelling widely apart to differ so markedly in their circumstances, their physique and their complexion, as well as in most of their

> customs. So it was with the intention of softening and tempering the stubbornness and harshness of nature that the early Arcadians introduced the practices I have described. Beside this, they inculcated the habit for men and women alike of holding frequent social gatherings, sacrificial ceremonies, and dances performed by young men and girls, and exerted themselves by every possible means to humanize the hardness of the national character through the softening and civilizing influence of such institutions.[41]

Athenaeus (200 AD) confirmed the point Polyibus was making.

> But the people of Cynaetha came at the end to neglect these customs [the use of music in education], although they occupied by far the rudest part of Arcadia in point of topography as well as climate; when they plunged right into friction and rivalry with one another they finally became so brutalized that among them alone occurred the gravest acts of sacrilege.[42]

Athenaeus found that only the Arcadians and the Spartans, the residents of adjacent city-states in the south of Greece, were still practicing the old values and beliefs about music.

> It was not by chance that the earliest Arcadians carried the art of music into their entire social organization, so that they made it obligatory and habitual not only for boys but also for young men up to thirty years of age, although in all other respects they were most austere in their habits of life. It is only among the Arcadians, at any rate, that the boys, from infancy up, are by law practiced in singing hymns and paeans, in which, according to ancestral custom, they celebrate their national heroes and gods. After these they learn the tunes of Timotheus and Philoxenus and dance them annually in the theaters with Dionysiac aulos players, the boys competing in the boys contests, the young men in the contests of adult males. And throughout their whole lives, in their social gatherings they do not pursue methods and practices so much with the aid of imported entertainments as with their own talents, requiring one another to sing each in his turn. As for other branches of training, it is no disgrace to confess that one knows nothing, but it is deemed a disgrace among them to decline to sing. What is more, they practice marching-songs with aulos accompaniment in regular order, and further, they drill themselves in dances, and display them annually in the theaters with elaborate care and at public expense.
>
> All this, therefore, the men of old taught them, not to gratify luxury and wealth, but because they observed the hardness in every one's life and the austerity of their character, which are the natural accompaniment of the coldness of their environment and the gloominess prevailing for the most part in their abodes; for all of us human beings naturally become assimilated to the character of our abode; hence it is also differences in our national position that cause us to differ very greatly from one another in character, in build, and in complexion. In addition to the training just described, their ancestors taught the Arcadian men and women the practice of public assembly and sacrifice, also at the same time choruses of girls and boys, eager as they were to civilize and soften the toughness of their natures by customs regularly organized.[43]

……

---

[41] Polybius (second century BC), *The Rise of the Roman Empire*, IV, 20.

[42] Athenaeus, *Deipnosophistae*, XIV, 626.

[43] Ibid., XIV, 626ff.

> Of all the Greeks the Spartans have most faithfully preserved the art of music, employing it most extensively, and many composers of lyrics have arisen among them. Even to this day they carefully retain the ancient songs, and are very well taught in them and strict in holding to them ... For people [are] glad to turn from the soberness and austerity of life to the solace of music, because the art has the power to charm.[44]

Otherwise, Athenaeus, took a dim view when he summarized the current state of the decline of music and warned his readers of the future implications if the decline were not halted.

> It happened that in ancient times the Greeks were music lovers; but later, with the breakdown of order when practically all the ancient customs fell into decay, this devotion to principle ceased, and debased fashions in music came to light, wherein every one who practiced them substituted effeminacy for gentleness, and license and looseness for moderation. What is more, this fashion will doubtless be carried further if some one does not bring the music of our forebears once more to open practice.[45]

With the ancient Roman civilization the musicians were at first slaves and it was for this reason that the historian Nepos (100–22 BC) wrote that the practice of music and singing was not appropriate to a man of distinction.[46] But the vast number of these slaves made possible some very large performing forces. A procession in the time of Ptolemaeus Philadelphus (283–246 BC), for example, included no fewer than six hundred singers and three hundred kithara players.[47] A similar report by Horace reports numerous aulos and lyres accompanying songs in the temple of Venus.[48] Many of these musicians were Greeks who fled to Rome after the conquest of Macedonia in 167 BC and the destruction of Corinth in 144 BC.[49]

We have a charming story by Cicero (106–43 BC) about one of his own slave-musicians. Cicero in his defense of Milo mentions, in an aside, that the latter 'happened on this occasion to have with him some singing boys of his wife, and a bevy of waiting maids.'[50] Cicero mentions in a letter to Atticus, that his own slave once helped stack a jury.

---

44 Ibid., XIV, 632.

45 Ibid., XIV, 633.

46 Alfred Sendrey, in *Music in the Social and Religious Life of Antiquity* (Rutherford: Fairleigh Dickinson University Press, 1974), 407.

47 Ibid., 411.

48 *Carmina*, IV, 1, 22.

49 Their instruments went with them, but changed names. Marcus Varro, in *On the Latin Language*, VI, 75 and VIII, 61, gives *tuba* for trumpet and *tubicines* for the players (*liticines* and *bucinator* for the other types of trumpet); *cornicines* for 'horn blowers'; *tibiae* for auloi and *tibicines* for the players; and *cithara* for lute.

50 Cicero, *On Behalf of Milo*, 55.

> You know who I mean by Baldhead, my trumpet-blower, whose complimentary speech about me I mentioned to you. Well, he fixed up the whole job in a couple of days with the help of a slave, and a gladiator at that. He sent for people, gave promises, sureties, cash down. He even went so far—God, what a scandal!—as to enhance the bribe to some members of the jury by offering nights with certain ladies and introductions to young men of good family.[51]

But there must be another point of view. To begin with, the relegation of music to the sphere of the utilitarian would not explain the fervent practice of it by some members of the highest level of society. For example, Sulla, though a harsh ruler, was a good singer. The consul Lucius Flaccus (fl. ca. 19 AD) was a diligent trumpet player, practicing daily it would appear.[52] And while we know nothing specific of Julius Caesar's interest in music, perhaps his sympathy for it is reflected in the fact that upon his death and ritual cremation, the musicians of Rome threw their professional clothes onto the fire as an expression of grief.[53]

Cicero tells us of one member of the aristocracy, Chrysogonos, whom he felt supported too much music.

> But what am I to say about his vast household of slaves and the variety of their technical skill? I say nothing about such common trades, such as those of cooks, bakers, litter-bearers: to charm his mind and ears, he has so many artists, that the whole neighborhood rings daily with the sound of vocal music, stringed instruments, and auloi, and with the noise of banquets by night. When a man leads such a life ... can you imagine his daily expenses, his lavish displays, his banquets? Quite respectable, I suppose, in such a house, if that can be called a house rather than a manufactory of wickedness and a lodging house of every sort of crime.[54]

He also mentions a distinguished citizen who walked around with an aulos player following him, as a kind of status symbol. This too, Cicero disapproved of.

> Gaius Duellius, the first Roman to win a naval victory over the Carthaginians, was often seen by me in my childhood, when he was an old man, returning home from dining out, attended, as was his delight, by a torch-bearer and aulos player—an ostentation which as a private citizen he had assumed, though without precedent: but that much license did his glory give him.[55]

Perhaps it was more difficult for women to display their skills as singers, since the singing prostitute was such an institution in antiquity. It is in this perspective that the historian Sallust (86–34 BC) mentioned a court lady that sang more artfully than was suitable for an honorable woman.

---

51 L. P. Wilkinson, *Letters of Cicero* (New York: Norton, 1966), 34.

52 Sendrey, *Music in the Social and Religious Life of Antiquity*, 391.

53 Suetonius, *Lives of the Caesars*, Book I, lxxxiv.

54 Cicero, *Pro Sexto Roscio Amerino*, XLVI, 134.

55 Cicero, *De Senectute*, xiii, 44.

> Among their number was Sempronia, a woman who had committed many crimes that showed her to have the reckless daring of a man. Fortune had favored her abundantly, not only with birth and beauty, but with a good husband and children. Well educated in Greek and Latin literature, she had greater skill in lyre playing and dancing than there is any need for a respectable woman to acquire.[56]

Since music performance was now associated with slaves in ancient Rome, it is no particular surprise that Cicero, in a discussion of the professions, found medicine, architecture, and the teaching of 'respectable subjects'[57] to be respectable, but he places music at the very bottom of a list of professions not to be considered respectable.

> Now the following is the gist of my understanding about professions and trades, those that free men can think of entering and those that are contemptible. First, no one can approve professions that arouse people's dislike, for example, collectors of harbor duties or usurers. Similarly, the work of all hired men who sell their labor and not their talents is servile and contemptible. The reason is that in their case wages actually constitute a payment for slavery. Another disreputable class includes those who buy whole lots from wholesalers to retail immediately. They would not make a profit unless they indulged in misrepresentation, and nothing is more criminal than fraud. All mechanics work in contemptible professions because no one born of free parents would have anything to do with a workshop. The employments lest worthy of approval are those that pander to pleasure: 'Fish-mongers, butchers, cooks, sausage-makers, fishermen,' as Terrence says. Add to this list, if you like, perfume makers, stage dancers, and the whole musical stage.[58]

Only once does Cicero acknowledge that members of the upper class were interested in music, and then he characterizes it as an innocent amusement in the form of rest from more important duties or when they have nothing else to do.

> But just as persons usually engaged in constant daily employment, when debarred from work because of the weather, betake themselves to tennis or gambling or dicing or even devise for themselves some novel game to occupy their leisure, so when the persons in question have been debarred from their work of politics by the circumstances of the time or have chosen to take a vacation, some of them have devoted themselves entirely to poetry, others to mathematics, and others to music.[59]

While ancient Greek civilization progressed from music making by the higher classes to music made by slaves, the Empire Period (14–476 AD) of ancient Rome was just the reverse. Now the music making also became an important part of higher society. As Sendrey reviews this period,

---

[56] *The Conspiracy of Catiline*, 25, 5.

[57] Cicero, *De Officiis*, I, 155, Cicero adds the autobiographical observation, 'What ever useful services I personally rendered to my country, if I performed any worth mentioning, I undertook them after receiving intellectual and literary training for them from the lessons of my teachers. It is not only living contemporaries who instruct and teach those eager to learn, but teachers fulfill the same task after death by their literary records.'

[58] Ibid., I, 151.

[59] Cicero, *De Oratore*, III, xv, 58.

around 50 AD music in Rome was recognized as an art form valued for itself. From then on, it became an essential element in the education of every distinguished Roman, male or female; women especially passed entire days practicing music, singing, and even composing new songs. Even the emperors were affected by the music mania.[60]

......

In the pantomimes, *symphoniae* were inserted, which meant that a choir sang and danced to the accompaniment of a group of instrumentalists. Sometimes an actor sang a solo aria; in other instances a professional singer sang the lyrics, while a mime interpreted the words with gestures and appropriate dances. The pantomimes were frequently presented in gigantic proportions; sometimes 3,000 singers and 3,000 dancers participated in them.

There were numerous instrumental virtuosi, and the number of good average artists was legion. From all parts of the empire musicians converged on Rome, attracted by the gold of the capital of the world. The huge number of musically educated slaves made it possible for their masters to maintain large choirs and orchestras with almost no expense ...[61]

Many wealthy persons had their own permanent music groups. Some had their especially gifted musicians sent to famous teachers for further education.

Professional virtuosi were in great demand and undertook extended concert tours in all parts of the empire. They were highly paid and often became the idols of the audiences. For several of them monuments or statues were erected ... Women of high society adored them and paid large sums for their love; other female admirers fought for the possession of a plectrum the admired artist had used in the concerts; others offered sacrifices to the gods to insure victory for their favorites in the festival contests ... The victors in poetical and musical contests received the coveted oak wreath from the hands of the emperor ...

The honoraria of some of the traveling virtuosi bordered on the fantastic ...

In a fresco of Herculaneum (now in the Naples Museum) a concert is depicted in the home of a wealthy man. It shows a female aulos player ... and accompanied by a kithara player. That it is a real house concert and not merely a private musical entertainment is evident from the large audience depicted in this fresco.[62]

The mention above, of three thousand singers, while extraordinary, only reflects the great number of practicing musicians in Rome. In 284 AD, Carinus presented a series of plays in which he used, among other things, one hundred trumpeters and one hundred horn players.[63] Seneca mentioned that sometimes it seemed that there were more people on the stage than there used to be in the audience.[64]

Some of the more austere philosophers failed to appreciate all this music, especially Seneca the Elder (first century AD) who complained that the noble sciences were being neglected and that the mentality of the masses was being governed by ignoble occupations, such as singing and dancing, which exerted an effeminate influence on youth. Thus he observes,

---

60 Sendrey, *Music in the Social and Religious Life of Antiquity*, 387.

61 Painting, however, was reserved for those of noble birth. Pliny the Elder, in Natural History, XXXV, xxxvi, 78, says slaves were forbidden to be instructed in it and he observes that in both painting and sculpture there were no famous works executed by a slave.

62 Sendrey, *Music in the Social and Religious Life of Antiquity*, 387ff.

63 Ibid., 412.

64 *Epistolae*, 84.10.

> I am always ashamed of humanity, when I enter the school of the philosophers; the Neapolitans are interested in the theater and are eager to find a good bagpiper ... but where a man should receive a good education, there is nobody, there is no interest for such a purpose.[65]

From time to time among the early philosophers one encounters this association between music and the effeminate. An often repeated incident is one first told by the fifth century BC historian, Herodotus. An advisor recommends,

> As for the Lydians, forgive them—but at the same time, if you want to keep them loyal and to prevent any danger from them in future, I suggest you put a veto upon their possession of arms. Make them wear tunics under their cloaks, and high boots, and tell them to teach their sons to play the zither and harp, and to start shopkeeping. If you do that, my lord, you will soon see them turn into women instead of men, and there will be not any more danger of their rebelling against you.[66]

Thucydides, another fifth century BC historian, suggests that effeminacy was also associated with the intelligent class, not just the arts.[67] Likewise, Tacitus sarcastically wonders, in a discussion of festivals,

> Would justice be promoted, or would they serve on the knights' commissions for the honorable office of a judge, because they had listened with critical sagacity to effeminate strains of music and sweet voices?[68]

Thucydides, in his review of the development of civilization, points out in contrast that 'frantic violence became the attribute of manliness.'[69] Clearly, it is against the common violence of the pre-Christian world that the concept of the arts being associated with effeminacy must be understood. Ancient histories are filled with examples of the violence of every day life, but for the reader with little experience in material from this era perhaps a single example will do. Polybius mentions three young women brought naked and riding on horses into a stadium in Egypt.

> All of them were then handed over to the fury of the mob, whereupon some began to tear them with their teeth, others to stab them, others to gouge out their eyes. As soon as any of them fell, the body was torn limb from limb until they had dismembered them all, for the savagery of the Egyptians is truly appalling when their passions have been roused.[70]

Whatever the objections of the philosophers, the arts continued to flourish. In an objection from the fourth century AD, Ammianus Marcellinus reports that,

---

[65] *Controversiae*, I, poem, quoted in Sendrey, *Music in the Social and Religious Life of Antiquity*, 390.
[66] Herodotus, *The Histories*, I, 156.
[67] Thucydides, *The Peloponnesian War*, II, 30.
[68] Tacitus, *The Annals*, XIV, 20.
[69] Ibid., VI, 82.
[70] Polybius, *The Rise of the Roman Empire*, XV, 33.

> the Roman palaces, formerly famous for disseminating sciences, now resound with the singing and playing of instruments. Where formerly the philosophers were welcome, there are now singers and music teachers in their place; everywhere one could hear music, but the libraries, the depositories of knowledge, were silent as the graves.[71]

As a part of this wide spread interest in music it seems that virtually everyone wanted to become a lyric poet. Seneca the Younger complained that lovers of music spend their entire day in singing and composing songs, forcing their voices by artificial means to attain a different character from the natural sound.[72]

Horace complains that while the layman would never dare attempt to engage in other professions, he does not hesitate to think of himself as a musician.

> The fickle public has changed its taste and is fired throughout with a scribbling craze; sons and grave sires sup crowned with leaves and dictate their lines. I myself, who declare that I write no verses, prove to be more of a liar than the Parthians: before sunrise I wake, and call for pen, paper, and writing-case. A man who knows nothing of a ship fears to handle one; no one dares to give southernwood to the sick unless he has learnt its use; doctors undertake a doctor's work; carpenters handle carpenters' tools; but, skilled or unskilled, we scribble poetry, all alike.[73]

We remind the reader that to be a poet meant to be a singer at this time, as is clear, for example, from Propertius' comment that he 'took to the lyre & sang.'[74] Horace was even more specific.

> You have no cause to think that the words which I,
> By far-resounding Aufidus born, *compose*
> *For singing to the lyre*, in meters
> All but unknown before mine, will perish.

Some of the greatest of the early Roman writers contributed to this body of lyric poetry, including Virgil (70–19 BC), Horace (66–8 BC), Tibullus (54–18 BC), Propertius (50–16 BC) and Ovid (43 BC–17 AD). We know that Ovid once sang at a wedding,[75] Propertius played the lyre and sang[76] and Virgil in his youth played and sang shepherd songs.[77]

Although we regard it as being very unlikely, we must report that Horace reserved for himself the credit for introducing the lyric poetry of Greece to the Roman audience.

---

71 Ibid., 391.
72 *De brevitate vitae*, 12, 4, quoted in Sendrey, *Music in the Social and Religious Life of Antiquity*, 390.
73 Horace, *Epistles*, II, 1, 117.
74 Propertius, *Poems*, I, 3.
75 Ovid, *Letters in Exile*, I, 2.
76 Propertius, *Poems*.
77 Virgil, *Georgics*, IV, 564.

I was the first to plant free footsteps on a virgin soil; I walked not where others trod. Who trusts himself will lead and rule the swarm. I was the first to show to Latium the iambics of Paros, following the rhythms and spirit of Archilochus, not the themes or the words that hounded Lycambes. And lest you should crown me with a scantier wreath because I feared to change the measures and form of verse, see how manlike Sappho molds her Muse by the rhythm of Archilochus; how Alcaeus molds his, though in his themes and arrangement he differs, looking for no father-in-law to besmear with deadly verses, and weaving no halter for his bride with defaming rhyme. Him, never before sung by other lips, I, the lyrist of Latium, have made known. It is my joy that I bring things untold before, and am read by the eyes and held in the hands of the gently born.[78]

---

[78] Horace, *Epistles*, I, xix, 34.

PART 2
VIEWS FROM THE CATHEDRAL

Music as Viewed by Medieval Church Philosophers

THE INTENT OF THIS ESSAY is to present the views of music by some of the most important Medieval Church philosophers. Following the extensive commentary by the ancient Greek and Roman philosophers, the discussion of music during the Christian Era is somewhat disappointing. One significant reason for this was the Church, which refused to acknowledge music as a separate art, warning the Christian not to worship art or the artist but rather God who made the artist. In the case of Music the Church neatly eliminated this problem by making Music a branch of mathematics. In addition, of course, the Church controlled literature, a fact which not only further discouraged philosophers from writing about music, but left the impression for later readers that there was less important secular music making than there clearly was.

The status of music, as viewed by philosophers at the beginning of the Christian Era, had suffered from a decay in musical values during the previous three centuries, as had often been documented by the earlier philosophers. Indeed, judging by the very negative views of two important first- and second-century philosophers, one may suppose that music was viewed by the educated class as something which had fallen to a very low state. This conclusion seems clear in a judgment by Sextus Empiricus (second century AD).

> Nor ... ought we to run down the ancient music because the present-day music is hackneyed and effeminate, when the Athenians, who devote great care to temperance, appreciating the dignity of music have handed it down to their descendants as a most necessary branch of learning. A witness to this is the poet of the Old Comedy, who says,
>   I will now relate from the start the life which I have provided for mortals.
>   The first rule was that none should hear from an urchin the sound of a mutter,
>   Next, they must walk in order good on their way to their master of music.
> Hence, even if music now weakens the mind by its effeminate tunes and womanish rhythms, this is no argument against the ancient and virile music.[1]

A similar comparison of the values of pre-Christian and early Christian Era music seems confirmed by comments by Philodemus (first century AD), who wrote that 'music was first approved and then rejected' and that 'possibly others had found music a profitless pursuit even before.'[2] For those of us accustomed to the notion that music is an 'international language,' these are very negative views indeed. Let us consider these two early philosophers at greater length.

---

[1] Sextus Empiricus, 'Against the Musicians,' in *Against the Professors*, trans. R. G. Bury (Cambridge: Harvard University Press, 1949), VI, 14.

[2] Quoted in Warren D. Anderson, *Ethos and Education in Greek Music* (Cambridge: Harvard University Press, 1966), 153.

The discovery in Herculaneum of fragments of a first-century book, *On Music*, by the Epicurean philosopher, Philodemus of Gadara, has provided us with an unusually negative assessment of music. We know of no other early philosopher who maintains, for example, that music lacks even the power to arouse or soothe emotions![3]

Among Philodemus' list of indictments against music are musicians who 'produce pieces which are devoid of significance [such as] instrumental music and trilling'[4] and the fact that such music naturally 'equates with disorderliness and lack of restraint.'[5] Music, he says, has no serious value, 'on the contrary, most of it ends up at dinner parties.'[6] Its function, he continues, must therefore be to give pleasure. But it is only a very simple and low level of pleasure,

> a direct titillation of the ear in which the mind has no share, analogous to the taste of pleasant food and drink.[7]

If there is any value in such a primitive level of pleasure, it would be one appropriate only to the common masses.

> The conclusion that music is profitable does not obtain. If it actually does profit any group, that group is the common people. And the common people are not profited by every kind of music; nor is this true of the quantity of very elaborate music that is heard ... and not by all but some Greeks, and under certain circumstances, and ... now through hired performers.[8]

Certainly, Philodemus contends, a man of the upper class should not spend his time going to hear concerts—they last too long, wasting valuable time, and they are exhausting and cause our attention to wander. And, in addition, there is no point in actually learning to perform music when there are already so many concerts available.

> It is a sign that men are poor-spirited and have nothing worth while with which to occupy themselves—for why should I say, 'make themselves happy?'—if they labor to learn music for the sake of providing pleasure for themselves in the future, and do not realize what a wealth of recitals is provided publicly, and the chance that we have of sharing in them continually in the city, if we wish; and if they fail to consider that when it goes on for long it exhausts our powers and begins to pall, so that often when performances are long drawn out our attention wanders. Not to mention the fact

---

[3] Quoted in L. P. Wilkinson, 'Philodemus in Ethos in Music,' *Classical Quarterly* 32, no. 3–4 (July 1938): 174, doi: 10.1017/S0009838800025878. An extant poem by Philodemus demonstrates that the philosopher was not immune to love. Here he seems to give testimony to the power of romantic music, although he notes he does not understand how it works!

> Xanthippe's touch on the lyre, and her talk, and her speaking eyes, and her singing, and the fire is just alight, will burn thee, my heart, but from what beginning or when or how I know not. [*Greek Anthology*, V, 131.]

[4] Wilkinson, 'Philodemus in Ethos in Music,' 175.

[5] Anderson, *Ethos and Education in Greek Music*, 163.

[6] Ibid., 167.

[7] Wilkinson, 'Philodemus in Ethos in Music,' 179.

[8] Anderson, *Ethos and Education in Greek Music*, 166.

that the pleasure is not necessary, and that the process of learning and practice that our enjoyment involves is laborious, and cuts out the things most important to our well-being; nor the impropriety of singing like any boy or actively playing the lyre.[9]

Philodemus also sees no social value for the educated person in even acquiring an understanding of music. In his opinion, it doesn't even serve to make a good topic for conversation!

> To have something to say and start the ball rolling at parties and other gatherings is not a peculiar gift (of musical knowledge), and it is not, as we decided, a thing valued by all; perhaps it might even provoke laughter if a philosopher were to indulge in it; and the theoretical side is not understood by most people, and, if it is to be mastered, demands trouble, which is a departure from the things that make for happiness.[10]

As a philosopher, Philodemus did make two important observations having to do with the universality of music. First, he seemed to have come to the correct view that there is a genetic aspect of music and he found significance for this in the fact that an infant (presumed to have no Reason) was clearly affected.

> We have an innate affinity with the Muses, one which does not have to be learned. This is clearly shown by the way infants are lulled to sleep with wordless singing.[11]

Second, Philodemus seems to suggest that it was understood that the key to aesthetics lies not with the music itself but with the listener. He observes, 'not everyone will be moved in the same way by the same music.'[12] In another place we find,

> Now with regard to these things it is possible for varying impressions to be received corresponding to predispositions; but with regard to the actual hearing there is no difference whatsoever, all having the same perceptions of the same melody and deriving like pleasure from it; thus both in the case of the Enharmonic and the Chromatic scale people differ, not in respect of the irrational perception, but in respect of their opinions, some, like Diogenes, saying that the Enharmonic is solemn and noble and straightforward and pure, and the Chromatic unmanly and vulgar and mean, while others call the Enharmonic severe and despotic, and the Chromatic mild and persuasive; both sides importing ideas which do not belong to either scale by nature. Whereas the more scientific [modern] thinkers bid us cull from each what pleases the ear, thinking that none of the qualities imputed belongs to either by its nature.[13]

Philodemus draws the wrong conclusion here, assuming that music must not communicate anything real or anything of substance. If it did, he supposes, everyone would receive the same communication.

---

9   Wilkinson, 'Philodemus in Ethos in Music,' 180.
10   Ibid., 181.
11   Anderson, *Ethos and Education in Greek Music*, 173.
12   Ibid., 172.
13   Wilkinson, 'Philodemus in Ethos in Music,' 177.

The main theme of this treatise by Philodemus was a strong attack against the ancient educational idea that music can influence character. Indeed, the very pretext for writing this book seems to have been as a rebuttal to a book by the Stoic philosopher, Diogenes, who had lived a century earlier, and who had contended that the correct use of music, 'will create a disposition which is harmonious and rhythmic in the highest degree.'[14] Regarding this well-known Greek association of music and character, Philodemus quotes an anecdote, for which Diogenes was apparently the source, of a painter who could only capture the correct character of his subject through listening to music as he worked. Perhaps in seeking another opportunity to denounce the ideas of Diogenes, Philodemus pretends to miss the real point.

> Presumably Diogenes did not suppose that music endows men with added technical proficiency. If he did, he was simpleminded.[15]

Philodemus was, in fact, well acquainted with the Greek association of music and character, as the following demonstrates,

> (They have proposed the theory) that every mode has a Tonos which relates to the emotions assumed to be present [in it]. Melodic composition, rhythms, and the rest are dealt with similarly. Therefore, as they maintain, our inner attitudes become familiarized with the modes in a kind of rapture (literally, 'in the manner of one who is *entheos*,' who has the god within him).[16]

For Philodemus these kinds of ideas could not be supported by Reason. This entire body of Greek philosophical claims, he pronounces, is 'filled full of "divine" inspiration and varnishing over, in a way that has no reason or order.'[17] Indeed, he says, they were attempting to credit music with something which only Reason can accomplish.

> As for those who say that music makes us gentle, softening our spirit and taking away its savageness, one must consider them utter fools; for it is only the instruction of reason which accomplishes this.[18]

He is particularly enthusiastic in his denunciation of any notion that music can promote action.

> And therefore the musical specialist who seeks the kind of understanding that will enable him to discern the nature of the various kinds of sense perception is looking for precise knowledge in things which do not have it, and his teaching on this matter is empty of meaning. The fact is that no melody, as melody (that is, with an irrational nature), rouses the soul from immobility and repose

---

[14] Anderson, *Ethos and Education in Greek Music*, 159.

[15] Ibid., 167. A first century poem by Lucilius tells of another painter who had a somewhat similar difficulty, 'Eutychus the painter was the father of twenty sons, but never got a likeness even among his children.' [*Greek Anthology*, IV, 215]. Similarly, Leonardo da Vinci used to tell a story about a good painter who had ugly children. When asked how this was possible, the man answered, 'Well, I make my paintings in daylight but my children at night!'

[16] Ibid., 158.

[17] Ibid., 171.

[18] Ibid., 168.

and brings it toward its natural ethical disposition, any more than it soothes or sets at rest the soul that is carried away by frenzy...Nor does melody have the power to divert the soul from one impulse to another or to cause intensification or lessening of the state in which the soul may find itself. For music is not an imitative thing, as some foolishly claim; nor does it, as Diogenes supposes, contain ethical likenesses that are non-imitative while showing in full all such ethical qualities ... as magnificence and humbleness of spirit, or manliness and its opposite, or orderliness and boldness. This is no more true of music that it would be of cooking.[19]

In a related discussion, Philodemus curiously refuses to believe that even the human face is a reflection of inner emotions. Today, of course, all psychologists are aware that the face not only expresses emotions in man, prenatal man, and even animals, but that the expressions together with their associated emotions are *universal*. But, Philodemus writes,

> Inducing to action means impulse and choice; but melody does not, like reason, impel us rationally or implant a choice. [It is absurd to say that music] somehow affects the disposition not only of the body but of the mind as well. How can it even be claimed that the body is affected? A singer's altered facial expression does not prove this.[20]

In the view of Philodemus, if music could be said to have any effect on man whatsoever, it was not the music itself but the *words* which the music accompanied, particularly in the case of the use of music by the Greeks to inculcate religious attitudes in the young. Philodemus attacks even Diogenes' suggestion that in erotic poetry music has the power to stimulate. It was not the melodies of Ibycus, Anacreon and others who corrupted the young, says, Philodemus, but their words.[21]

From these views the reader will understand that Philodemus could find no independent place in education for music. He would have us believe that his view was widely shared.

> Many say that those who lack natural capacity are not made one whit better by music.[22]

Nevertheless, he proposes that while music itself cannot educate, it can serve as a vehicle to aid rational processes.

> It is not the theoretical knowledge of good and bad or suitable and unsuitable melodies that educates, but philosophy working through literary and musical training.[23]

---

[19] Ibid., 164.

[20] Ibid., 165, the final two sentences being paraphrases by Anderson.

[21] Ibid., 170.

[22] Ibid., 174.

[23] Ibid., 175.

This thought that music has no inherent value for man but can be valued in its ability to illuminate other philosophical ideas was a thought which was much related to the Church's acceptance of music as a branch of mathematics. As repugnant as this philosophy may be to us, we must acknowledge some debt to it for helping music survive the Dark Ages as a member of the Liberal Arts.

The second treatise we have mentioned which is thoroughly negative toward music is *Against the Musicians*, by the second-century philosopher, Sextus Empiricus. Empiricus begins by noting that at his time the term 'Music' was used in three meanings. First, as a science 'dealing with melodies and notes and rhythm-making and similar things.' Second, to connote instrumental skill, 'as when we describe those who use auloi and harps as musicians':

> It is with these significations that the term 'Music' is properly and generally used.

And, finally, as an adjective referring to the other arts. 'Thus we speak of a work as "musical," even though it be a piece of painting.'[24]

Empiricus' plan for this treatise is to first list the characteristics which most people praise in music, the views, he admits, the majority of people hold. He then proposes to prove that each of these views is false. We will summarize the positive characteristics[25] he mentions and then devote more attention to his refutation of them.

First, most people believe that music, like philosophy, helps in 'regulating human life and repressing the passions of the soul.' Here he quotes the often told story that Pythagoras once calmed some youths, who 'were in a state of Bacchic frenzy' from drinking, by having an aulos player perform a 'spondean' melody, whereupon they suddenly became sober.

Second, he notes that 'Music gives sober sense to those lacking in sense and incites the cowards to courage,' as in the use of music in the military. He recalls that ancient literature often mentions that it was for this reason that the heroes, when leaving on a long voyage, left their musicians as the most trustworthy guardians of their wives.

Third is the role of music in education, in forming character. Here he quotes the anecdote of Socrates who began the study of music as an old man. When someone made fun of him, he responded, 'that it was better to be accused of being late-learned than unlearned.'

The fourth concerns the role of music in poetry. We quote his remarks here to remind the reader that most poetry was still sung.

> If poetry is useful for life, and music appears to adorn it by its melodies and by making it fit for singing, then music will be beneficial. And, of course, the poets are called 'tune-makers,' and of old the verses of Homer were sung to the lyre. So likewise were the songs and choral odes of the tragic poets.

The fifth is concerning the use of music in religious ceremonies, to 'incite the mind to emulate the good.'

---

[24] Empiricus, 'Against the Musicians,' VI, 1.
[25] Ibid., VI, 7ff.

The sixth, and last, regards the use of music as 'a consolation to those in grief; and for this reason those who are trying to lighten the grief of mourners sing for them to the aulos.'

Now Empiricus presents his refutation of all these attributions,[26] beginning with the notion that music helps in 'regulating human life and repressing the passions of the soul.' Here he says he does not concede that any melody has, in itself, any particular quality, or 'that some tunes are in their nature stimulating, others repressive.'

> In the case of musical tunes it is not by nature that some are of this kind and others of that kind, but it is we ourselves who suppose them to be such. Thus the same tune serves to excite horses, but not at all to excite men who hear it in a theater.

And, he says, it may not actually excite the horses, only distract them. This becomes his principle refutation, that music only distracts. Thus the drunken youths, in the Pythagoras story, only experienced a momentarily moderating influence of the music, soon thereafter to return to their original state.

> As to Pythagoras, in the first place he was foolish in desiring to render drunkards sober at the wrong moment, instead of quitting the place; and secondly, by trying to reform them in this way he confesses that aulos players have more influence than philosophers for the reforming of morals.

In this regard, he also mentions that this is the reason why men who engage in 'toilsome work' often sing, 'to divert their minds from the distress caused by their work.'

This is the same reason why he rejects any notion that music can supply courage in the soldier, rather, he says, it merely diverts his attention from the realities of battle. Regarding the stories of the heroes leaving their wives with musicians, as 'sober-minded guardians,' this is, he says, 'the fictions of story-tellers.'

With regard to the role of music and poetry, anyone who sees utility in music in this regard is 'simple-minded.' For Empiricus, the fact that poetry has words gives it a substance which cannot be proven in music.

> One can argue that poetry is useless, and prove equally well that while music, being concerned with melody only, naturally serves to give pleasure, poetry which is concerned with thought as well, is able to be of benefit and teach prudence.

Empiricus at this point breaks off with his refutation of the above listed positive characteristics presumed of music and he turns his attention instead to the question: Does the performer benefit more from music than the non-performer who only listens to music? His real concern here is with regard to the reputed ability of music to improve the character, because if this is true, then the performer has a distinct advantage over the non-trained listener. This, again, makes no sense to Empiricus.

---

[26] Ibid., VI, 19ff.

> Firstly, the pleasure felt by ordinary people is not inevitable as are those caused by food, drink and warmth after hunger, thirst and cold; and secondly, even if they are inevitable we can enjoy them without musical skill.

He provides here the example of the infant who is 'lulled to sleep by listening to a tuneful cradle song,' yet obviously has no skill in music.

> And for this reason it may be that, just as we enjoy tasting food or wine though without the art of cooking food or that of wine-tasting, so also, though without the art of music, we take pleasure in hearing a delightful melody; for though the expert musician understands that it is artistically performed better than the ordinary man, he gets from it no greater feeling of pleasure.

From this observation, Empiricus concludes that there is no evidence that music leads one either to wisdom or virtue. Indeed, he believes, music often has the effect of 'making young people easily led into incontinence and debauchery.'

Finally, Empiricus indulges in a bit of circuitous nonsense, the kind of philosophizing which the Christian writers complain about—philosophy which proves nothing. His intent is to prove that music does not even exist. Since this will strike one as absurd, we remind the reader that early philosophers were still very much disturbed, intellectually, by the fact that you cannot *see* music.

First Empiricus surveys the elements of music, notes, intervals, and 'Ethos.'

> Just as every interval in music consists of notes, so also does every 'Ethos' [or 'character']; and it is a certain 'Genus' of melody. For just as of human characters some are gloomy and stubborn, such as those of the ancients are reported to have been, while others yield easily to lusts and debauchery and lamentations and groanings, so a certain kind of melody produces in the soul stately and refined motions, another kind motions that are base and ignoble. Melody of this sort is called, in general, by the Musicians 'Ethos' from the fact that it is productive of 'character'.[27]

If music exists, says Empiricus, everything must be based on the individual note. He then offers the following reasoning illustrating that notes do not exist. The Cyrenaic philosophers say only feelings exist, nothing else. Democritus says sense-objects do not exist, hence neither sound. If sound exists, it must be either incorporeal or corporeal and the Stoics prove it is not the former and the Peripatetics demonstrate it is not the latter. He continues in this vein and finally concludes,

> Now, then, as sound does not exist, neither does the note … and when the note does not exist, neither does the musical interval exist, nor symphony, nor melody, nor the Genera formed by these. Therefore, Music does not exist either.[28]

---

[27] Ibid., VI 48.

[28] Ibid., VI, 58.

But our faithless philosopher is not satisfied by stopping there. Next he offers a series of arguments intended to demonstrate rhythm and time do not exist. Here is his conclusion to the first of these arguments.

> If time is anything, it is either limited or unlimited. But it is not limited, since, if so, we shall be saying that there was once a time when time did not exist, and that there will sometime be a time when time will not exist. Nor is it unlimited; for a part of it is past, a part future, and if each of these does not exist time is limited, and if each does exist, then both the past and the future will exist in the present, which is absurd. Therefore time does not exist.[29]

In another book, 'Outlines of Pyrrhonism,'[30] Empiricus 'proves,' through similar logic that nothing can be taught and that neither teacher nor student exists.

Having considered the views of these two very negative philosophers of the first two centuries of the Christian Era, we now move on to a few comments on the state of music during the fourth century AD by the emperor Julian. First, he confirms that the tradition of the ancient Greek solo singer of epic poetry was still known and flourishing.

> For you are already surfeited with them, your ears are filled with them, and there will always be a supply of composers of such discourses to sing of battles and proclaim victories with a loud clear voice, after the manner of the heralds at the Olympic games.[31]

Reflecting the life of leisure enjoyed by the upper class in ancient Rome, Julian viewed instrumental music as being invented by man for the purpose of pleasure and entertainment.

> It seems likely that myth was originally the invention of men given to pastoral pursuits, and from that day to this the making of myths is still peculiarly cultivated by them, just as they first invented instruments of music, the aulos and the lyre, for their pleasure and entertainment.[32]

From this perspective, Julian considers two kinds of study, subjects related to the body and those related to the emotional part of man. Here he clearly is thinking of music and suggests that noble persons would not want to devote the effort necessary to accomplish the ability to perform, for 'persistent study is disgraceful!'

> And in the next place he will also observe the first principles of certain arts by which the body is assisted to that permanence, for instance, medicine, husbandry and the like. And of such arts as are useless and superfluous he will not be wholly ignorant, since these too have been devised to humor the emotional part of our souls. For though he will avoid the persistent study of these last, because

---

[29] Ibid., VI, 62.

[30] III, 239–273.

[31] Julian, 'The Heroic Deeds off Constantius,' in *The Works of the Emperor Julian*, trans. Wilmer Wright (London: Heinemann, 1913), I, 209.

[32] Julian, 'To the Cynic Heracleios,' in Ibid., II, 77.

> he thinks such persistent study disgraceful, and will avoid what seems to involve hard work in those subjects; nevertheless he will not, generally speaking, remain in ignorance of their apparent nature and what parts of the soul they suit.[33]

In another place, Julian is much more specific in saying that the noble class now considered it degrading to study music, and especially singing.

> The fashion of education that now prevails among the well-born deprives me of the use of the music that consists in song. For in these days men think it more degrading to study music than once in the past they thought it to be rich by dishonest means.[34]

In spite of such comments which come from the rather unique perspective of an emperor, together with the absence of secular literature caused by the Church's control, there are nevertheless a few clues which suggest that others still considered music to be important. There are several poems from the sixth to the eighth century which suggest that even the nobles thought it was good to have a minstrel in the house. One poem observes that, 'It is fitting that men have a good minstrel,'[35] and lists among the attributes of a 'good man,' he that 'sings poems.'[36] However it would only be when the curtain of the Dark Ages rose that literature would be more revealing of society's view of music.

The philosopher Psellus first reports that at the time of Constantine IX (1042–1055) there was still no discernible lifting of the Dark Ages.

> Today, in fact, neither Athens, nor Nicomedia, nor Alexandria in Egypt, nor Phoenicia, nor even the two Romes (the ancient and lesser Rome, and the later, more powerful city[37]), nor any other State glories any longer in literary achievement. The golden streams of the past ... all are blocked and choked up: their damming is complete.[38]

Three decades later, however, Psellus was employed by the Emperor Michael VII (1071–1078) who was in every way a 'Renaissance man.' Psellus describes this ruler as well-read in several areas of science, philosophy and interested in a wide variety of spiritual and literary subjects. He engaged in extemporaneous poetry, which Psellus characterizes, 'if the rhythm is generally defective, at least the sentiments are sound.'[39] There is one intriguing passage, relative to Michael VII, of which we can only wish Psellus had supplied more detail.

> It is agreed that certain standards of behavior, certain manners of speaking are appropriate to an emperor, others to a philosopher, others to an orator, others to a musician.

---

[33] Julian, 'To the Uneducated Cynics,' in Ibid., II, 11.

[34] Julian, 'Misopogon,' in Ibid., II, 421.

[35] 'Gnomic Verses,' *The Greek Anthology*, trans. W. R. Paton (Cambridge: Harvard University Press, 1939), II, xiii, 127.

[36] Ibid., 139.

[37] Constantinople.

[38] Michael Psellus, *Chronographia*, trans. E. R. A. Sewter (Baltimore: Penguin Books, 1966), VI, 43.

[39] Ibid., VII, 4.

We are surprised to find very little discussion of music by the major Scholastic Philosophers of the thirteenth century, especially since we know it was part of the curriculum at the University of Paris.[40] Maybe we should refer to the problem as paradoxical, for this was an atmosphere in which the Liberal Arts were given new impetus and music itself, in so far as performance, was breaking new ground everywhere, in the towns, in the courts and in the Church, yet none of these philosophers wrote extensively on music. It almost seems that music had disappeared from the list of the seven Liberal Arts. Perhaps, in the perspective of these philosophers, that is what happened. While they continue to refer to music as one of the Liberal Arts, perhaps hearing music all around them, and especially the wonderful art music of the troubadours and Minnesingers, they had come to realize that music was somehow no longer a 'science' in the way the other disciplines of the Liberal Arts were and that certainly music was something which could no longer be considered as a branch of mathematics, which was the original reason why it was included among the Liberal Arts. We wonder if perhaps this was one of the deductions anticipated that the reader would make in the allegorical poem, 'The Battle of the Seven Arts' (*La Bataille des. VII Ars*), composed in about 1236 by a trouvère named Henri d'Andeli. In this work he describes a battle between Grammar and Logic. Music is present here, but stands apart and is not a participant in the 'battle.'

> Madam Music, she of the little bells
> And her clerks full of songs
> Carried fiddles and viols,
> Psalteries and small flutes;
> From the sound of the first fa
> The ascended to cc sol fa.
> The sweet tones diatessaron
> Diapente, diapason,
> Are struck in various combinations.
> In groups of four and three
> Through the army they went singing,
> They go enchanting them with their song.
> These do not engage in battle.[41]

There was another characteristic which distinguished music from the other six Liberal Arts—music,[42] alone, could not be *seen*. We would therefore venture to suggest the following possibility. These philosophers, in their enthusiasm to write commentaries on the newly available works of Aristotle and the other ancient Greek philosophers, and subsequently to reconcile these ideas to those of the Church, were drawn immediately to the subjects of Reason, the Intellect, Understanding, and Metaphysics. All these subjects are of the left hemisphere

---

[40] Nan Cooke Carpenter, *Music in the Medieval and Renaissance Universities* (Norman: University of Oklahoma Press, 1954), 48, 115.

[41] Quoted in Carpenter, Ibid., 71.

[42] When we use the term Music we always mean the performance of Music, not the notated representative of it.

domain, a world of writing and language, a world dependent on the eye. Perhaps it should be no surprise that several writers state that the eye is the most important of the senses. And Music, of course, has very little to do with either the eye or Reason.

The one philosopher of the thirteenth century whom we might have expected to write extensively about music was Robert Grosseteste (d. 1253). A contemporary, Matthew Paris, tells us Grosseteste was well-grounded in the *Quadrivium*, which included music. It has always been assumed that he was a great lover of music, perhaps an inaccurate generalization based on some early poetry. In the following, we are told that he listened to music day and night because it gave him solace and sharpened his mind. When asked why he took such delight in music, he answered that the virtue in music protected one against the devil and that good skill in harp playing was closely associated with the Church.

> Y shall you tell as I have herd
> Of the bysshop seynt Roberd;
> His toname is Grosteste,
> Of Lyncolne, so seyth the geste.
> He lovede moche to here the harpe,
> For mans witte it makyth sharpe;
> Next hys chamber, besyde his study,
> Hys harpers chamber was fast the by.
> Many tymes, by nightes and dayes,
> He hadd solace of notes and layes.
> One askede hem the resun why
> He hadde delyte in mynstrelsy:
> He answered hym on thys manere
> Why he helde the harpe so dere:
> 'The virtu of the harpe, thurgh style and ryght
> Wyll destrye the fendys myght;
> And to the cros by gode skeyl
> Ys the harpe lykened weyl.'[43]

But there are no great new philosophical views on music by Grosseteste. In his treatise, *De artibus liberalibus*, he places music at the head of the *Quadrivium*, but there is nothing new here, only the old discussions about the mathematical basis of music, reference to the 'Music of the Spheres,' and so on.[44] His few specific remarks about music reveal an interest more in the practical, such as the use of music in healing.

But it was clearly his interest in music which prompted him to attempt to explain the physics of sound production and the nature of hearing. His explanation was all bound up in numbers and the soul, namely that a sound is understood as a number in the ear, which is then

---

[43] William de Wadington, *Manuel des Peches*, trans. Robert Mannyng, quoted in James McEvoy, *The Philosophy of Robert Grosseteste* (Oxford: Clarendon, 1982), 43.

[44] Some Latin text is quoted in Carpenter, *Music in the Medieval and Renaissance Universities*, 82.

compared to numbers stored in the soul-memory, whereupon it is judged harmonious or dissonant. Music, then, was not just a matter of hearing musical tones, but involved a broad range of faculties dealing with numbers, memory and finally Reason.[45]

The one scholar who did contribute original thought on music at this time was another Englishman, Roger Bacon (b. ca. 1214). Bacon studied at Oxford[46] and at the University of Paris, where he received a doctorate in theology and then joined the Franciscan Order in about 1247. Unlike the gentle patron of his Order, St. Francis, Bacon was very outspoken and many who read or heard him must have felt somewhat insulted. Youth, he says, has no interest in the perfection demanded by science, indeed they take pleasure in their imperfection, and older people, 'with the greatest difficulty climb to perfection in anything.'[47] He was even more outspoken in his disrespect for the masses, the 'unenlightened throng,' the 'ignorant multitude,' whom he says can never rise to the perfection of wisdom. For this reason, he maintains, the wise have always been an elite segment of society, separated from the masses. He found this true in religion ('as with Moses so with Christ the common throng does not ascend the mountain') and well as in the universities.

> We see that such is the case among the professors of philosophy as well as in the truth of our faith. For the wise have always been divided from the multitude, and they have veiled the secrets of wisdom not only from the world at large but also from the rank and file of those devoting themselves to philosophy.[48]

He cites a book by A. Gellius in which the author maintained that the great Greek philosophers had discussions among themselves at night, so as to 'avoid the multitude.'

> In this book he says that it is foolish to feed an ass lettuce when thistles suffice him. He is speaking of the multitude for whom rude, cheap, imperfect food of science is sufficient. Nor ought we to cast pearls before swine.

He was also outspoken about false teaching in the schools and other forms of vice and corruption. One can suppose he did not make many friends and, in fact, was brought to trial in 1278, condemned and thrown into prison for fourteen years.

But, from our perspective today, he reads much more objectively than most philosophers of his day. We admire him for being honest enough to point out that the famous philosophers were sometimes wrong[49] and that none of us can have perfect knowledge, for what we

---

45 McEvoy, *The Philsoophy of Robert Grosseteste*, 258.

46 Bacon is often cited as a student of Grosseteste, but as McEvoy, Ibid., 14, points out, there is no known foundation for this belief.

47 *Opus Majus*, 'Causes of Error,' III, in *The Opus Majus of Roger Bacon*, trans. Robert Burke (New York: Russell & Russell, 1962), 9ff.

48 This discussion is found in Ibid., 'Causes of Error,' IV.

49 Ibid., 'Causes of Error,' VII.

know is far less than what we don't know.[50] And we believe he was right on the mark when he observed that the greatest barriers to truth are the 'submission to faulty and unworthy authority, influence of custom [and] popular prejudice.'[51]

In his discussion of the Liberal Arts, Bacon first comments that while the ancients knew of the various sciences, they only actually used two: astronomy for the calendar, and music for worship.[52] Mathematics, he calls the 'gate and key' for the other Liberal Arts[53] and he specifically recommends that the study of mathematics should come before the study of music.

> The natural road for us is to begin with things which befit the state and nature of childhood, because children begin with facts that are better known by us and that must be acquired first. But of this nature is mathematics, since children are first taught to sing, and in the same way they can learn the method of making figures and of counting, and it would be far easier and more necessary for them to know about numbers before singing, because in the relations of numbers in music the whole theory of numbers is set forth by example, just as the authors on music teach, both in ecclesiastical music and in philosophy.[54]

Sounding very much like those today who attempt to defend music in the schools by suggesting, 'music helps reading,' or 'music helps math,' Bacon gives a strong endorsement for the importance of music in fully understanding another of the Liberal Arts, grammar.

> Now the accidental parts of philosophy are grammar and logic. Alpharabius makes it clear in his book on the sciences that grammar and logic cannot be known without mathematics. For although grammar furnishes children with the facts relating to speech and its properties in prose, meter, and rhythm, nevertheless it does so in a puerile way by means of statement and not through causes or reasons. For it is the function of another science to give the reasons for these things, namely, of that science, which must consider fully the nature of tones, and this alone is music, of which there are numerous varieties and parts. For one deals with prose, a second with meter, a third with rhythm, and a fourth with music in singing. And besides these it has more parts. The part dealing with prose teaches the reasons for all elevations of the voice in prose, as regards differences of accents and as regards colons, commas, periods, and the like. The metrical part teaches all the reasons and causes for feet and meters. The part on rhythm teaches about every modulation and sweet relation in rhythms, because all those are certain kinds of singing, although not so treated as in ordinary singing ... Therefore grammar depends causatively on music.
>
> In the same way logic ... Alpharabius especially teaches this in regard to the poetic argument, the statements of which should be sublime and beautiful, and therefore accompanied with notable adornment in prose, meter, and rhythm ... And therefore the end of logic depends upon music.[55]

---

[50] Ibid., X.

[51] Ibid., I.

[52] Ibid., XIV.

[53] Ibid., 'Mathematics,' I.

[54] Ibid., III. See also XVI for more on the relationship of music to both mathematics and theology.

[55] Ibid., II.

In his discussion of music, as one of the Liberal Arts, Bacon contributes one of the most precise and interesting definitions offered by any philosopher of the thirteenth century. He begins by dividing the world of music into two broad categories, 'one part of music deals with what is audible, the other with what is visible.'[56]

Audible music he recognizes as being of two divisions, vocal music and instrumental music. In vocal music, in turn, Bacon finds four subdivisions.

> For one part concerns melody, as in singing; the second concerns meters, and considers the nature and properties of all songs, meters, and feet; the third concerns rhythm, and considers every variety of relations in rhythms; the fourth concerns prose and considers accents and other aforesaid things in prose discourse. For accent is a kind of singing; whence it is called accent from *accino*, *accinis* [I sing, thou singest], because every syllable has its own proper sound either raised, lowered, or composite, and all syllables of one word are adapted or sung to one syllable on which rests the principal sound. Thus length and shortness and all other things required in correct pronunciation are reduced to music.

This is a very interesting discussion for several reasons. First, these thoughts come at the end of two thousand years, at least, during which poetry was sung. When Bacon says 'every syllable has its own proper sound either raised, lowered, or composite,' we wonder if there was a commonly recognized, but now lost, tradition in the performance of sung poetry. Did the text, perhaps, 'compose' the music? We also find fascinating his statement, 'For accent is a kind of singing.' This comment, seven hundred years before our age, reminds us that among ancient peoples singing preceded language. Can we not see a trace here of that distant period when pitch fluctuation preceded, and perhaps turned into, the sounds we call consonants?

Bacon is not so expansive on instrumental music, noting only that the subject deals with 'the structure of the instruments and their use.' He also adds that the theologian must also know the 'numberless mystical meanings' of the instruments. We wish he had elaborated more, for he has made it clear in previous passages that he takes literally the Old Testament references to instruments, and not metaphorically as did many earlier medieval Church philosophers.

It is Bacon's recognition of a category of music which he calls 'visual music' which is of great significance. The ancient Greek philosophers never discussed this topic at length, but there are sufficient hints in their descriptions of choral performance to suggest that the inevitable movements by the singers were thought of not as a kind of dance, but as the part of music you could see. Indeed, he says dance is a branch of music. One must remember that the Greeks placed considerable significance in the fact that one cannot *see* music and it was for this reason that music was so closely associated with religion (whose principal mysteries also cannot be seen). The significance of Bacon's discussion is that it supplies important insights into this ancient association of music and movement.

---

[56] Ibid., XVI, in *The Opus Majus of Roger Bacon*, I, 259, for this entire discussion.

> Music, moreover, consisting in what is visible, is necessary; and that it is such is evident from the book on the Origin of the Sciences. For whatever can be conformed to sound in similar movements and in corresponding formations, so that our delight may be made complete not only by hearing, but by seeing, belongs to music. Therefore dances and all bendings of bodies are reduced to gesture, which is a branch of music, since these are conformed to sound in similar movements and corresponding formations, as the author of the aforesaid book maintains. Therefore Aristotle says in the seventh book of the Metaphysics that the art of dancing is not complete without another art, that is, without another kind of music to which the art of dancing is conformed.

Bacon mentions the Old Testament reference to the dancing by the sister of Moses and recommends that theologians need to study this aspect of music (dance) in order that in preaching on these passages they might,

> know how to express all their properties, so that they may give utterance to all the spiritual senses of an angelic devotion.

In the end, however, Bacon returns to the old Church position that the Liberal Arts have their real value in bringing one to know God.

> I say, therefore, that one science is the mistress of the others, namely, theology, to which the remaining sciences are vitally necessary, and without which it cannot reach its end.[57]

He adds that whatever cannot be connected with the Gospel is therefore against it and should be shunned by the Christian.

---

[57] Ibid., 'Philosophy,' I.

Boethius on Music

Before the full impact of the Dark Ages had set in, three distinguished thinkers managed to write specialized works on the subject of music. They were Boethius (475–524, AD), Cassiodorus (480–573, AD) and Isidore of Seville (560–636 AD) and the existence of their works in manuscript copies made possible the education of musicians for centuries, not to mention helping to preserve the liberal arts through the Dark Ages. The book by Boethius, *De institutione musica*, was the most influential music treatise of the Middle Ages. This work was still a commonly studied text in the fourteenth century, though as yet unpublished. Further, the reader will recognize the influence of this book on academic thought even today.

Anicius Manlius Severinus Boethius was born in or near Rome and orphaned young. He was brought up in the household of one of the richest and most venerable aristocrats of the time, Symmachus. He married Symmachus' daughter and pursued a typical career for a senatorial scion of the time, alternating between ceremonial public office and private leisure. He was highly educated and was fluent in Greek. The breadth of his education can be appreciated by a survey of it found in a letter written to him by Cassiodorus.

> You have thoroughly imbued yourself with Greek philosophy. You have translated Pythagoras the musician, Ptolemy the astronomer, Nicomachus the arithmetician, Euclid the geometer, Plato the theologian, Aristotle the logician, and have given back the mechanician Archimedes to his own Sicilian countrymen. You know the whole science of Mathematics.[1]

Boethius served as consul and eventually served as *magister officiorum* in the half-Roman regime of the Ostrogothic King Theoderic, who had taken Italy at the behest of the emperors in Constantinople. For reasons no longer clear, Boethius came to be suspected by Theoderic of disloyal sympathies and in 525–526 he was executed.

His philosophical work, *The Consolation of Philosophy*, was written while Boethius was awaiting trial and execution. It is sad to imagine him sitting in his cell, aware that he was likely to lose everything and concluding that Reason is the only happiness in life, for it alone cannot be taken away.

> Therefore I advise thee, that thou learn, that there is no happiness in this present life. But learn that nothing is better in this present life than reason: because man cannot by any means lose it.[2]

He observes further that, 'No man can injure the rational mind, or cause it that it should not be what it is.' He illustrates this with a startling anecdote.

---

[1] Letter to Boethius, in *The Letters of Cassiodorus* (London: Frowde, 1886), 169.

[2] Boethius, *Consolatione Philosophiae*, trans. Samuel Fox (London: George Bell, 1895) XI, ii.

> This is very evidently to be known by a certain Roman nobleman, who was called Liberius. He was put to many torments because he would not inform against his associates, who conspired with him against the king who had with injustice conquered them. When he was led before the enraged king, and he commanded him to say who were his associates who had conspired with him, then bit he off his own tongue, and immediately cast it before the face of the tyrant.[3]

It seems clear that Boethius would have simply concluded that man *is* Reason, were it not for one troublesome problem. He recognized that there was something else to man, something he called the 'spirit,' which did not seem to act according to Reason. He observed the evidence of this primarily in the subsequent dreams when man sleeps.

In one respect Boethius makes a great step forward in embracing the value of individual experience, something the Church had not been able to do while maintaining the position that God determines everything. In spite of his adamant belief in Reason, Boethius proposes that it is through *experience*, together with knowledge, that one learns.

> We very well know that no man doubts of this, that he is powerful in his strength, who is seen to perform laborious work: any more than if he be anything, any one doubts that he is so. Thus the art of music causes the man to be a musician, the medical knowledge to be a physician, and rhetoric causes him to be a rhetorician.[4]

Wisdom, observes Boethius, comes from experience. He illustrates this by pointing out that the wise man understands that he profits from a hard life, and therefore does not wish for an easy life.

> Then replied Wisdom sharply, and said: Therefore no wise man ought to fear or lament, in whatever wise it may happen to him, or whether severe fortune or agreeable may come to him; any more than the brave man ought to lament about this, how often he must fight. His praise is not the less; but the opinion is, that it is the greater. So is also the wise man's reward the greater, if more adverse, and severer fortune comes to him. Therefore no wise man should be desirous of a soft life, if he makes account of any virtues, or any honor here in the world, or of eternal life after this world.[5]

Boethius contends that there are five things which are indispensable to happiness: wealth, power, dignity, renown, and pleasure. These, he says, are like five members of a man, yet all of the same body.[6] Near the end of this same book, he inadvertently admits that music gives pleasure.

> For it is near the time when I had intended to begin other work, and I have not yet finished this: and methinks, too, thou are rather weary, and these long discourses appear to thee too lengthy, so that thou art now desirous of my songs. I know, too, that they give thee pleasure.[7]

---

3   Ibid., XVI, ii.

4   Ibid., XVI, iii.

5   Ibid., XL, iii.

6   Ibid., XXXIII, ii, and XXXIV, vi.

7   Ibid., XXXIX, iv.

Boethius also wrote some poetry while in prison. He reminds us that most early poetry was sung, not recited or read, and makes the interesting observation which touches both on the bicameral mind and its separation of language and feeling. He tells us that while he could freely compose happy poetry and music, when composing in a tragic style he had difficulty finding words to match the emotions of his music.

> The songs [lays] which I, an exile, formerly with delight sung, I shall now mourning sing, and with very unfit words compose. Though I formerly readily invented, yet I now, weeping and sobbing, wander from appropriate words.[8]

One of his extant poems expresses this same theme.

> Lo! I sang cheerily
> In my bright days,
> But now all wearily
> Chaunt I my lays;
> Sorrowing tearfully,
> Saddest of men,
> Can I sing cheerfully,
> As I could then?
>
> Many a verity
> In those glad times
> Of my prosperity
> Taught I in rhymes;
> Now from forgetfulness
> Wanders my tongue,
> Wasting in fretfulness
> Meters unsung.

DE INSTITUTIONE MUSICA

Four centuries after Boethius, a writer commented, 'If there is someone interested in profound and perplexing subtlety, let him read the *De institutione* by Boethius ... and he will be able to test his genius.' And it *is* tough reading, filled to overflowing with sleep-inducing prose such as the following.

> But since the nete synemmenon to the mese (3,456 to 4,608) holds a sesquitertian ratio—that is, a diatessaron—whereas the trite synemmenon to the nete synemmenon (4,374 to 3,456) holds the ratio of two tones ...[9]

---

[8] Ibid., II.

[9] Boethius, *Fundamentals of Music*, trans. Calvin Bower (New Haven: Yale University Press), IV, ix.

With this brief excerpt perhaps the reader will understand and forgive us from passing over the mathematical speculation on music and concentrating instead on the ideas of Boethius which center on the philosophical and aesthetic aspects of music.

True to the spirit of the Greek philosophy, Boethius could not quite justify music without bringing it into the realm of Reason. No doubt from his perspective it was a tribute to music, among the other arts, that it *could* be correlated with Reason. Lacking our modern understanding of the twin hemispheres of the brain, and the full equality of both experiential and conceptual information, Boethius thought music was too important to belong to the senses—it had to be Reason which made the senses understandable.

> Harmonics is the faculty that weighs differences between high and low sounds using the sense of hearing and reason. For sense and reason are, as it were, particular instruments for the faculty of harmonics. The sense perceives a thing as indistinct, yet approximate to that which it is; reason exercises judgment concerning the whole and searches out ultimate differences. So the sense discovers something confused, yet close to the truth, but it receives the whole through reason. Reason itself comes to know the whole, even though it receives an indistinct and approximate likeness of truth. For sense brings nothing whole to itself, but arrives only at an approximation. Reason makes the judgment.[10]

To support his contention that Reason correctly judges where the senses cannot, he offers the following illustration.

> To see how the sense gathers confused information and by no means attains the fullness of reason, let us consider the following. Given a line, it is not difficult for the sense [of vision] to tell what is longer or what is shorter. But if the goal is to determine a measure some precise degree larger or smaller, the first impression of the sense will not be able to do it, but the clever skill of reason will.[11]

The role that Reason, therefore, must play in the perception of music, Boethius summarizes as follows.

> The entire judgment is not to be granted to the sense of hearing; rather, reason must also play a role. Reason should guide and moderate the erring sense, inasmuch as the sense—tottering and failing—should be supported, as it were, by a walking stick.[12]

He is wrong, of course. We understand today that music is its own form of truth and requires no conceptual understanding whatsoever. Were it not so, ordinary people would find no pleasure in music. But Boethius, having the perspective that he does, believes the pleasure we obtain from music also derives in part from Reason.

---

[10] Ibid., V, ii.

[11] Ibid.

[12] Ibid, and I, ix.

> Judgment should be exercised with respect to all these consonances which we have discussed; one ought to decide by the reason, as well as by the ear, which of them is the more pleasing. For as the ear is affected by sound or the eye by a visible form, in the same way the judgment of the mind is affected by numbers or continuous quantity.[13]

Thus, Boethius concludes, the noble in music is personified by the person who understands it as a rational concept, not the composer or the performer. Anyone today who understands the true essence of music would regard the following as an incredible statement, although there are universities in the United States of America who personify this viewpoint.

> Now one should bear in mind that every art and also every discipline considers reason inherently more honorable than a skill which is practiced by the hand and the labor of an artisan. For it is much better and nobler to know about what someone else fashions than to execute that about which someone else knows; in fact, physical skill serves as a slave, while reason, rules like a mistress. Unless the hand acts according to the will of reason, it acts in vain. How much nobler, then, is the study of music as a rational discipline than as composition and performance![14]

Regarding aesthetics, Boethius first ranks types of music into three species, in an apparent descending order of aesthetic importance.[15] The most important, presumably representing God directly, is Cosmic Music, in particular the 'Music of the Spheres.'[16]

Next, in order of importance, is Human Music, by which he is thinking primarily of vocal music.

> Whoever penetrates into his own self perceives human music. For what unites the incorporeal nature of reason with the body if not a certain harmony and, as it were, a careful tuning of low and high pitches as though producing one consonance? What other than this unites the parts of the soul, which, according to Aristotle, is composed of the rational and the irrational? What is it that intermingles the elements of the body or holds together the parts of the body in an established order?

The third kind of music is Instrumental Music, music which he curiously seems to suggest exists in the instruments themselves. Again, for the modern person, the thought that music exists anywhere but in the ear of the listener is quite odd.

> The third kind of music is that which is said to rest in various instruments. This music is governed either by tension, as in strings, or by breath, as in the aulos or those instruments activated by water, or by a certain percussion, as in those which are cast in concave brass, and various sounds are produced from these.

---

[13] Ibid., I, xxxii.

[14] Ibid., I, xxxiv.

[15] Ibid., I, ii.

[16] This is discussed further in I, xxvii.

With regard to consonance and dissonance, one would expect Boethius to present a detailed conceptual description, yet he seems content to observe that consonance is that which falls 'pleasantly' on the ear, while dissonance is heard as 'harsh and unpleasant.'[17]

For the modern reader, perhaps the most important discussion regarding the aesthetics of music by Boethius is found in his discussion of the nature of pleasure in music. Here, finally, he leaves the world of Reason and begins to approach the true essence of music, feeling. He begins, literally in the first sentence of his book, by admitting that our ability to perceive through the senses is innate, it is not the product of reason. Indeed, he correctly observes, the senses are something quite apart from the 'mind.'

> Perception through all the senses is so spontaneously and naturally present in certain living creatures that an animal without them cannot be conceived. But knowledge and clear perception of the senses themselves are not so immediately acquired through inquiry with the mind.[18]

Next, he observes that the first source of pleasure in music is found in the musical materials themselves.

> Now the same can be said with respect to other sensible objects, especially concerning the witness of the ears: the sense of hearing is capable of apprehending sounds in such a way that it not only exercises judgment and identifies their differences, but very often actually finds pleasure if the modes are pleasing and ordered, whereas it is vexed if they are disordered and incoherent.[19]

Boethius, in his most eloquent testimony to the role of feeling in music concludes that this relationship is so strong that we 'cannot be free from it even if we so desired.' He also returns here to the idea that music is innate, observing that even someone who 'cannot sing' nevertheless expresses his emotions in song.

> Why is it that mourners, even though in tears, turn their very lamentations into music? This is most characteristic of women, as though the cause for weeping might be made sweeter through song ...
> Someone who cannot sing well will nevertheless sing something to himself, not because the song that he sings affects him with particular satisfaction, but because those who express a kind of inborn sweetness from the soul—regardless of how it is expressed—find pleasure. Is it not equally evident that the passions of those fighting in battle are roused by the call of trumpets? If it is true that fury and wrath can be brought forth out of a peaceful state of mind, there is no doubt that a more temperate mode can calm the wrath or excessive desire of a troubled mind. How does it come about that when someone voluntarily listens to a song with ears and mind, he is also involuntarily turned toward it in such a way that his body responds with motions somehow similar to the song heard? How does it happen that the mind itself, solely by means of memory, picks out some melody previously heard?

---

[17] Ibid., I, ix.

[18] Ibid., I, i.

[19] Ibid.

> From all these accounts it appears beyond doubt that music is so naturally united with us that we cannot be free from it even if we so desired.[20]

Then, as if surprised that he finds himself so removed from Reason, Boethius immediately follows this by noting that it is not enough for a musician to know *music*, he must know *about* it. It is the tragic flaw of twentieth-century American music education.

> For just as in seeing it does not suffice for the learned to perceive colors and forms without also searching out their properties, so it does not suffice for musicians to find pleasure in melodies without also coming to know how they are structured internally by means of ratio of pitches.

Boethius now goes beyond feeling to the subject of the apparent ability of music to affect character. This entire discussion clearly carries evidence of his knowledge of the ancient Greek philosophers and their beliefs on music. In his review of this subject it is particularly interesting that he clearly separates music from the other 'sciences' of the liberal arts in assigning to music alone an influence on morality. It is also fascinating that he uses the expression, 'that we ourselves are put together in its likeness,' for one of the latest discoveries in physics, in research conducted in England, is that all organs of the body vibrate to specific pitches. One of these physicists has stated that we have evolved to look as we do, due to the combination of these harmonies and gravity. Boethius discusses the effect of music as follows.

> There happen to be four mathematical disciplines [arithmetic, music, geometry, and astronomy], the other three share with music the task of searching for truth; but music is associated not only with speculation but with morality as well. For nothing is more characteristic of human nature than to be soothed by pleasant modes or disturbed by their opposites. This is not peculiar to people in particular endeavors or of particular ages. Indeed, music extends to every endeavor; moreover, youths, as well as the aged are so naturally attuned to musical modes by a kind of voluntary affection that no age at all is excluded from the charm of sweet song. What Plato rightfully said can likewise be understood: the soul of the universe was joined together according to musical concord. For when we hear what is properly and harmoniously united in sound in conjunction with that which is harmoniously coupled and joined together within us and are attracted to it, then we recognize that we ourselves are put together in its likeness. For likeness attracts, whereas unlikeness disgusts and repels.
>   From this cause, radical transformations in character also arise. A lascivious disposition takes pleasure in more lascivious modes or is often made soft and corrupted upon hearing them. On the other hand, a rougher spirit finds pleasure in more exciting modes or becomes aroused when it hears them. This is the reason why musical modes were named after certain peoples, such as 'Lydian' mode and 'Phrygian,' for in whatever a particular people finds pleasure, by that same name the mode itself is designated. A people finds pleasure in modes because of likeness to its own character, for it is not possible for gentle things to be joined with or find pleasure in rough things, nor rough things in gentle. Rather, as has been said, similitude brings about love and pleasure. Thus Plato holds that the greatest care should be exercised lest something be altered in music of good character. He states that there is no greater ruin of morals in a republic than the gradual perversion of chaste and temperate music,

---

[20] Ibid.

for the minds of those listening at first acquiesce. Then they gradually submit, preserving no trace of honesty or justice—whether lascivious modes bring something immodest into the dispositions of the people or rougher ones implant something warlike and savage.

Indeed no path to the mind is as open for instruction as the sense of hearing. Thus, when rhythms and modes reach an intellect through the ears, they doubtless affect and reshape that mind according to their particular character.[21]

He adds that this is exactly what has happened in his own time.

Since the human race has become lascivious and impressionable, it is taken up totally by representational and theatrical modes. Music was indeed chaste and modest when it was performed on simpler instruments. But since it has been squandered in various, promiscuous ways, it has lost its measure of dignity and virtue; and, having almost fallen into a state of disgrace, it preserves nothing of its ancient splendor.

---

[21] Ibid. Recent clinical research demonstrates that the brain actually changes physically according to the music it listens to.

Cassiodorus on Music

CASSIODORUS (480–573 AD) was born to a politically famous family of Southern Italy and he, himself, also held many important public positions and was the immediate successor of Boethius as *magister officiorum* under Theodoric. He eventually became *praetorian prefect* of Italy, caught up in the struggle between Ostrogoth and Byzantine politics.

After Benedict of Nursia founded the Monte Cassino monastery upon the ruins of an ancient temple of Apollo, Cassiodorus was inspired to retire early from public life and built his own monastery of Vivarium on his own estate. Here he not only wrote a now lost *History of the Goths*, and a biography of Boethius, but began collecting manuscripts and having his monks copy works of earlier pagan (ancient Greek and Roman) and Christian writers to preserve such works for future generations. To this end he also wrote treatises for the instruction of his monks in the proper uses of reading and methods of copying ancient texts. And there Cassiodorus remained, still writing at age ninety-three. The wide range of the works he had copied included the Hebrew classic, *Jewish Antiquities*, by Josephus and with regard to ancient Roman works it has been said that were it not for Cassiodorus, no Latin classic except the works of Virgil would have come down to us in complete form.[1]

In fact, Cassiodorus was one of several important Church philosophers who understood the importance of preserving the liberal arts. For Church men such as Cassiodorus, the great value of the liberal arts, including music, was to produce in the Christian the intelligence necessary to understanding the Scriptures.

> Beyond any doubt knowledge of [the liberal arts], as it seemed to our Fathers, is useful and not to be avoided, since one finds this knowledge diffused everywhere in sacred literature, as it were in the origin of universal and perfect wisdom. When these matters have been restored to sacred literature and taught in connection with it, our capacity for understanding will be helped in every way.[2]

In the spirit of the Church's attacks against the pagan writers, among whom were included Plato and Aristotle, there were some, such as Theophilus, Archbishop of Alexandria, who destroyed all the ancient manuscripts he could find.[3] Thus it was so important that there were other individuals who saved ancient manuscripts during those early centuries of turmoil.

We must not take this for granted. One has only to imagine these monks, working in dark cells with poor illumination, no doubt often cold and hungry, to appreciate by how narrow a margin fate has preserved so many works of the ancient world. Standing over the monks were

---

[1] M. R. James, quoted in *Martianus Capella and the Seven Liberal Arts*, trans. William Harris Stahl (New York: Columbia University Press), I, 7, fn. 12.

[2] Cassiodorus, *Divine Letters*, trans. Leslie W. Jones (New York: Octagon Books, 1966), XXVII, 1.

[3] Will Durant, *The Age of Faith* (New York: Simon and Schuster, 1950), 907.

their superiors, one of whom told his scribes that God would forgive one of their sins for each line they copied. One monk, his superior reported, escaped Hell by the margin of a single letter! It is no wonder that we find a scribe has written at the end of one of his volumes,

> This completes the whole;
> For Christ's sake give me a drink!

And another,

> For the work of the pen,
> Let the writer receive a beautiful girl.

We are also indebted to Cassiodorus for his first-hand reports on the state of society during the critical period at the time of the fall of Rome and the beginning of the Dark Ages. The 'Dark Ages,' which are dated from the sixth century, take this name primarily from the general disappearance in Western Europe of secular letters, in particular philosophy, history and science. Consequently Cassiodorus observed already at the beginning of the sixth century,

> Arithmetic, Theoretical Geometry, Astronomy, and Music are discoursed upon to listless audiences, sometimes to empty benches.[4]

In another place, Cassiodorus mentions that teacher's salaries were being cut back and argues that instead they should be increased.

> I have referred disputes involving sons to the senators, that they may take thought for the careers of those affected by the advancement of education at Rome. For it is incredible that you should lack concern for something which brings honors to your offspring, and gives your assembly the counsel that comes from constant reading. Now recently I came to know by discreet reports from various people, that the teachers of eloquence at Rome are not receiving the constituted rewards for their labors, and that the trafficking of certain men has caused the sums assigned to the masters of the schools to be diminished.
>
> Therefore, since it is clear that rewards feed the arts, I have judged it abominable that anything should be stolen from the teachers of youth; they should instead be incited to their noble studies by an increase in their fees.
>
> For the school of grammar has primacy: it is the fairest foundation of learning, the glorious mother of eloquence, which has learnt to aim at praise, to speak without fault. As good morals view an alien crime, so it views a dissonant error in the course of declamation. For, as the musician creates the sweetest song from a choir in harmony, so, by well ordered modulations of sound, the grammarian can recite in meter.
>
> Grammar is the mistress of words, the embellisher of the human race; through the practice of the noble reading of ancient authors, she helps us, we know, by her counsels.[5]

---

4   Letter to 'the Illustrious Consularis,' III, lii, in *Variae*, trans. Thomas Hodgkin (London: Frowde, 1886).

5   Letter to the Senate in Rome, in Ibid., IX, xxi.

The reader has perhaps also noticed here Cassiodorus' reference to a choir singing 'in harmony.' This is six hundred years before traditional music history texts admit to even two-part compositions.

The writings of Cassiodorus fall naturally into the two divisions of his life, his public service and then his private literary years. We, too, shall follow this division. There is a comment on aesthetics which is important because it suggests that the early Church's opposition to art had begun to soften and that for at least some Church thinkers the appreciation of Beauty had not been extinguished. Cassiodorus transforms the ancient phrase, 'Art imitates Nature,' into 'Art conquers Nature.'

> From Art proceeds this gift, which conquers Nature. And thus the discolored surface of the marble is woven into the loveliest variety of pictures; the value of the work, now as always, being increased by the minute labor which has to be expended on the production of the Beautiful.[6]

We have an extraordinary survey of the purposes of music by Cassiodorus in the form of a letter to Boethius. His purpose in writing was to ask Boethius to find a harp player to fulfill a request by Clovis, King of the Franks. He requests Boethius to find someone 'who is skilled in musical knowledge,' who with his 'sweet sound can tame the savage hearts of the barbarians.' Cassiodorus then digresses to compose a tribute to the power of music to move men and to affect their character, even recalling the ancient Greek beliefs on the specific influences of various modes. He also suggests that oratory and poetry achieve their success through their relationship with music and concludes with a reference to the 'Music of the Spheres' and praise of string music. It is an extraordinary testimonial to the recognition of art music in the sixth century.

> For what is more glorious than music, which modulates the heavenly system with its sonorous sweetness, and binds together with its virtue the concord of nature which is scattered everywhere? For any variation there may be in the whole does not depart from the pattern of harmony. Through this we think with efficiency, we speak with elegance, we move with grace. Whenever, by the natural law of its discipline, it reaches our ears, it commands song.
>
> The artist changes men's hearts as they listen; and, when this artful pleasure issues from the secret place of nature as the queen of the senses, in all the glory of its tones, our remaining thoughts take to flight, and it expels all else, that it may delight itself simply in being heard. Harmful melancholy he turns to pleasure; he weakens swelling rage; he makes bloodthirsty cruelty kindly, arouses sleepy sloth from its torpor, restores to the sleepless their wholesome rest, recalls lust-corrupted chastity to its moral resolve, and heals boredom of spirit which is always the enemy of good thoughts. Dangerous hatreds he turns to helpful goodwill, and, in a blessed kind of healing, drives out the passions of the heart by means of sweetest pleasures.
>
> Through bodily means he softens the bodiless soul, and leads it where he wills by hearing only, while unable to control it by speech. In silence, he cries aloud through his hands; he speaks without a mouth; and, by the service of insensible matter, he is strong to govern the senses.

---

[6] Letter to Agapitus, Praefectus Urbis, in Ibid., I, vi.

Among men all this is achieved by means of five modes, each of which is called by the name of the region where it was discovered. Indeed, the divine compassion distributed this favor locally, even while it assuredly made its whole creation something to be praised. The Dorian mode bestows wise self-restraint and establishes chastity; the Phrygian arouses strife, and inflames the will to anger; the Aeolian calms the storms of the soul, and gives sleep to those who are already at peace; the Ionian sharpens the wits of the dull, and, as a worker of good, gratifies the longing for heavenly things among those who are burdened by earthly desire. The Lydian was discovered as a remedy for excessive cares and weariness of the spirit: it restores it by relaxation, and refreshes it by pleasure. This one a corrupt age perverted to cabaret performances, making an immoral invention out of a decent remedy ...

But all this was evidently achieved by the human art of [instrumental] music. Yet, as we know, the living voice has a natural rhythm: it preserves an exquisite melody when it is silent at the right moment, speaks suitably, and steps with careful elocution, on musical feet, down the path of intonation. The sweet and forceful speeches of orators were likewise invented to move men's souls, so that judges would pity the erring, and be enraged with the criminal. Whatever an eloquent man may achieve clearly belongs to the glory of this discipline.

To the poets also, as Terentianus bears witness, two original meters are ascribed: the heroic and iambic, the one devised to arouse, and the other to quieten men. From these, various ways of delighting the souls of an audience have been born; and, as with the tones of an instrument, so in the human voice, the pregnant meters have brought forth different passions of the soul.

The researches of the ancients have revealed that the Sirens sang to a miracle; and, though the waves drove on the sailors, and the wind filled their sails, under the pleasant deception they preferred to run on the rocks, rather than forgo such sweetness. Only the man of Ithaca [Ulysses] escaped, who was quick to stop up the seductive hearing of his crew. Against the poisonous sweetness, that craftiest of men thought up the device of a fortunate deafness: what they could not overcome by their judgment, they conquered instead by insensibility ...

But, that I may follow the example of the wise Ithacan, and pass on, let me speak of that psaltery which came down from heaven, which a man to be sung throughout the world so composed and modulated for the soul's deliverance that, by these hymns, the wounds of the mind might be healed, and God's special grace implored. Let the world wonder at this and believe: David's lyre drove out a devil; its sound commanded the spirits; and, as the cithara played, the king [Saul] whom an inward enemy had evilly enthralled returned to his freedom.

For, although many instruments of this delight have been discovered, nothing has been found more effective to move the soul than the sweet resonance of the hollow cithara. Hence, we suppose that the strings of the instrument were called cords because they easily move the heart [*corda*]. So great is the concord of the diverse notes assembled there that a string, once struck, makes it neighbor vibrate spontaneously, although itself untouched. For such is the power of harmony that it makes a lifeless object move spontaneously because it so happens that its fellow is in motion.

Hence different notes emerge without a tongue; hence some sweet chorus is formed from a variety of sounds: one is high through great tension, another low through a certain slackening of the string, a third mezzo, through a mellow adjustment of the instrument's back. Human beings cannot achieve a unison to equal the social concord that unreasoning objects have attained. For there all notes which are tuneful or flat, harsh or most clear, and so on, are gathered, as it were, into one glory; and, as a diadem delights the eyes by the various light of its gems, so does the cithara delight the ears by the diversity of sound.

> It is the talking loom of the Muses, with speaking wefts and singing warps, on which the plectrum shrilly weaves sweet sounds. Now this instrument Mercury is said to have discovered, modeling it on the mottled tortoise. As the bringer of such benefits, astronomers have believed it should be sought among the stars, urging that music must be heavenly, since they can detect the shape of a lyre placed among the constellations.
>
> Yet, the harmony of heaven cannot be fittingly described by human speech, as nature has not revealed it to human ears, but the soul knows it through reason only. For they say that we should believe that the blessedness of heaven enjoys those pleasures which have no end, and are diminished by no interruption. They maintain, indeed, that things above are absorbed by that same perception, that heavenly beings enjoy those same pleasures, and that those who are engrossed by such contemplations are constantly enfolded in blessed delights.[7]

This letter is particularly important because it seems to confirm the existence of art music at this time which was listened to by contemplative listeners, something for which there is little independent discussion elsewhere. Another letter by Cassiodorus mentions that singers and dancers were rewarded by the Consul[8] and in yet another he mentions a gift to the court of 'musical instruments of ebony,' which were no doubt used for art music.[9]

One letter of Cassiodorus gives a brief history of the theater, and the use of music therein, in the context of his comments on the decline of this art.

> When farmers, on the holidays, celebrated the rites of various deities in groves and villages, the Athenians were the first to raise this rustic beginning into an urban spectacle. To the place where they looked on, they gave the Greek name of theater, since the gathered throng, separated from the bystanders, could look on with no hindrance.
>
> But the back-drop of the theater was called the *scaena* from the deep shade of the grove where, at the start of spring, the shepherds sang various songs. Musical performances flourished there, and the precepts of a wise age. But it gradually came about that the respectable arts, shunning the company of depraved men, withdrew from that venue out of modesty.[10]

Cassiodorus continues with an enlightening and rare description of the use of music in Comedy and Pantomime.

> Comedy ... is where the rustic actors made fun of human doings in merry songs. To these were added the speaking hands of dancers, their fingers that are tongues, their clamorous silence, their silent exposition. The Muse Polymnia is said to have discovered this, showing that humans could declare their meaning even without speech ...
>
> Again, there is the pantomime actor, who derives his name from manifold imitations. When first he comes on stage, lured by applause, bands of musicians, skilled in various instruments, support him. Then the hand of meaning expounds the song to the eyes of melody, and, by a code of gestures, as if by letters, it instructs the spectator's sight; summaries are read in it, and, without writing, it performs what writing has set forth.

---

7 Letter to Boethius, in Ibid., II, xl.
8 Letter to Maximus, Illustris, Consul, in Ibid., V, xlii.
9 Letter to the King of the Vandals, in Ibid., V, i.
10 Letter to the Patrician Symmachus, in Ibid., IV, li.

He makes a very interesting reference to a musical instrument, the *acetabula*,[11] which 'yields such pleasure that, of all the senses, men think their hearing is the highest gift conferred on them,' and concludes by again commenting on the decline of these arts.

> The succeeding age corrupted the inventions of the ancients by mingling obscenities; their headlong minds drove towards bodily lusts an art devised to give decent pleasure.

While Cassidorus bemoans the decline in serious theater, in a letter answering some complaint about the behavior of the audience at entertainment spectacles, he seems much more tolerant (and reminds us we probably should be too).

> As to their complaints of rudeness against the mob, you must distinguish between deliberate insolence and the license of the theater. Who expects seriousness of character at the spectacles? It is not exactly a congregation of Catos that comes together at the circus. The place excuses some excesses.[12]

On the same topic, another letter makes a curious and happy suggestion.

> The Circus, in which the king spends so much money, is meant to be for public delight, not for stirring up wrath. Instead of uttering howls and insults like other nations, whom they have despised for doing so, let them tune their voices, so that their applause shall sound like the notes of some vast organ, and even the brute creation delight to hear it.[13]

Cassiodorus' book, *Institutiones divinarum et humanarum lectionum*, to which we now turn our attention, was a very influential book which includes chapters on all the seven liberal arts, including music. The chapter on music is rather brief, but because the book traveled everywhere in Europe his remarks were well-known.

It is important that we begin by considering his outline of the divisions of philosophy, for music's placement in this organization is, at the same time, an aesthetic comment. Philosophy, he says, is divided into two main branches, Speculative Philosophy and Practical Philosophy. Practical Philosophy, 'is that which seeks to explain advantageous things,' and includes only Moral, Economic and Political subject matters.[14]

Speculative Philosophy 'is that by means of which we surmount visible things and in some degree contemplate things divine and heavenly, surveying them with the mind alone, inasmuch as they rise above corporeal eyes.' This main branch of philosophy is made up of three sub-branches, Natural, Theoretical, and the Divine. Music is found under 'Theoretical,' together with Arithmetic, Geometry, and Astronomy.

---

[11] Presumed by some to be an instrument like the glockenspiel, but with metal cups instead of bars.
[12] Letter to Speciosus, in *Variae*, I, xxvii.
[13] Letter to the Roman People, in Ibid., I, xxxi.
[14] Cassiodorus, 'On Dialectic,' in *An Introduction to Divine and Human Readings*, trans. Leslie Jones (New York, Octagon Books, 1966).

Thus we see he thought of music not as a 'practical,' but as a 'speculative' art, 'something we contemplate with the mind,' and that it is clearly included in the category of mathematical-based disciplines. He, following the Church's position, saw music most closely related to arithmetic, indeed it is together with this subject that he defines it.

> *Arithmetic* is the science of numerable quantity considered in itself. *Music* is the science which treats measure in relation to sound.

This division of philosophy into the speculative and the practical was not followed within the field of Music by Cassiodorus, because Church dogma required him to keep music in the conceptual (speculative) category. However, in practice it must have been obvious to all at the time that Music also had its speculative and practical sides. By Al-Farabi's music treatise, *Ihsa al-ulum*, of ca. 1900 AD, we see Music formally divided into practical and theoretical music and this division has remained with us and is clearly reflected in the philosophy of every university music school.

Cassiodorus' chapter on music is not lengthy and is concerned again with an explanation of music theory. He begins by defining music as being innate to man, related to the organization of the heavens, and fundamental to religion.

> Musical science, then, is diffused through all the acts of our life if we before all else obey the commands of the Creator and observe with pure hearts the rules which he has established. For whatever we say or whatever inward effect is caused by the beating of our pulse is joined by musical rhythms to the power of harmony. Music is indeed the science of proper modulation; and if we observe the good way of life we are always associated with this excellent science. When we sin, however, we no longer have music [we are not 'in harmony']. The sky and the earth and everything which is accomplished in them by the supernal stewardship are not without the science of music; for Pythagoras is witness to the fact that this world was founded through the instrumentality of music and can be governed by it.
>
> Music also freely permeates religion itself: witness the ten-stringed instrument of the Decalogue, the reverberations of the harp, timbrels, the melody of the organ, the sound of cymbals. There is no doubt, moreover, that the Psalter itself was named after a musical instrument because it contains the exceedingly pleasant and agreeable modulation of the heavenly virtues.[15]

Cassiodorus discusses the various modes with respect to their theoretical relationships. It is only regarding Hypodorian, 'the lowest of all,' that he mentions the influence of music on the state of the listener.

> These tones ... have been shown to possess such great usefulness that they calm excited minds and cause even wild animals and serpents and birds and dolphins to approach and listen to their harmony.[16]

---

[15] 'On Music,' in Ibid, 1.

[16] Ibid., 8.

The purpose of music, he says, is to educate and 'to soothe.'

> Most pleasant and useful, then, is the branch of learning which leads our understanding to heavenly things and soothes our ears with sweet harmony.[17]

Isidore, Bishop of Seville, is the only writer known today representing Gothic Spain, and needs to be mentioned together with Boethius and Cassidorus. His twenty-volume *Etymologiarum*, which is really the first encyclopedia, has the goal of presenting all the information a Christian needs to know. Its practical importance lies in the fact that it treats the seven liberal arts, including music, and thus was one more powerful weapon for preserving traditional knowledge throughout the Dark Ages.

We wish to mention here only two interesting passages from his discussion of music. First, he introduces the word *Symphonia*, by which he means harmony in the modern usage. He also maintains that 'melody' comes from the Greek, *mel* [honey] reflecting the 'sweetness' of music.

Second, he presents the most extensive discussion of texture by any early writer to this date, in a catalog of the various qualities of the human voice.

> Sweet voices are fine, full, loud, and high.
> Penetrating voices are those which can hold a note an unusually long time, in such a way that they continuously fill the whole place, like the sound of trumpets.
> A thin voice is one lacking in breath, as the voice of children or women or the sick. This is as it is in string instruments, for the finest strings emit fine, thin sounds.
> In fat voices, as those of men, much breath is emitted at once.
> A sharp voice is high and thin, as we see in strings.
> A hard voice is one which emits sound violently, like thunder, like the sound of an anvil whenever the hammer is stuck against
> the hard iron.
> A harsh voice is a hoarse one, which is broken up by minute, dissimilar impulses.
> A blind voice is one which is choked off as soon as produced, and once silent cannot be prolonged, as in crockery.
> A pretty voice [*vinnola*] is soft and flexible; it is so called from *vinnus*, a soft curling lock of hair.
> The perfect voice is high, sweet, and loud: high, to be adequate to the sublime; loud, to fill the ear; sweet, to soothe the minds of the hearers. If any one of these qualities is absent, the voice is not perfect.[18]

---

[17] Ibid., 10.

[18] *Etymologiarum*, III, xv, trans. W. M. Linsay, quoted in Oliver Strunk, *Source Readings in Music History* (New York: Norton, 1950). This important work, published a dozen times in the fifteenth century, has never been translated into English.

Late Medieval Music Treatises

THE NINTH THROUGH THE ELEVENTH CENTURIES represent one of the most interesting periods in music history. Not only are the first steps toward modern notation taken at this time, but also the first stirrings of Humanism appear, which will eventually bring an end to the Church's classification of music as a branch of mathematics. In this regard we should point out that we make little reference in this essay to the mathematics and 'theory' found in these treatises, as we regard these subjects to be only the 'grammar' of music. Our interest is in the 'music' of music, the ideas which reflect how contemporary people actually heard, valued and used music in their lives.

AURELIAN OF REOME, *MUSICA DISCIPLINA* (CA. 843 AD)

This treatise is valuable for allowing us a brief glimpse into how music was perceived during the height of the Dark Ages, a period during which we have very few contemporary reports of performance. Neither do we know much about the author. He says he had been a member of a monastery near the present town of Moutiers-St. Jean. For an unspecified offense he was dismissed and composed this treatise in an attempt to placate his local bishop. Thus he begins with a poem dedicated to this bishop.

> Whoever reads this, composed in the line of great authority,
> Will know that the most wholesome authors are here;
> Here is the musician Pythagoras, the fountain head of the Greeks;
> Here are the sayings of the Latin fathers.
> I, your Aurelian, have compiled, arranged, and written,
> O Pastor Bernard, this slight gift.[1]

This initial poem might have more properly mentioned Boethius, Cassiodorus, and Isidore of Seville upon whom this work, like nearly all late medieval material on music, draws heavily. In the Preface which follows, also dedicated to Bernard, whom he calls 'the archsinger of the entire Holy Church,' Aurelian makes the interesting observation that present day singers know the rules, but are nevertheless lacking as musicians.

> I know that very noble singers are found, but I confess that I have seen none skilled in this art save you alone; for some of our musicians know many rules of music, yet nowhere, I think, is a musician found like the old ones.[2]

---

[1] Aurelian of Reome, *The Discipline of Music*, trans. Joseph Ponte (Colorado Springs: Colorado College Music Press, 1968), 1.

[2] Ibid., 3.

Following this political dedication, the author next pays his respect to past authorities, pointing out that music should not be neglected, and testifies that music's power is still evident in both secular and sacred usage.

> There is much authority both in the ancient books, that is, those of the heathen,[3] and in the holy books, affirming that the discipline of music should not be disdained, since there are to be found, both among the heathen and our own people, innumerable acts of efficacious through its power.[4]

The foundation for church music he finds both in the Old Testament and in the Church's belief of the existence of choirs of angels. Beyond this, he observes, all of nature seems to be harmoniously organized and man is innately and physically prepared for music.

> Man himself, if he knows that he possesses all the resources customarily associated with this art, will not doubt the great harmony with which he is equipped for this discipline: for in his throat he has a pipe for singing; in his chest, a kind of harp, adorned with strings, as it were, the fibers of the lungs; in the alternations of the beating of his pulse, fluctuating ascents and descents.[5]

Aurelian defines music as, 'the science, applicable to sound and song, of correctly controlling variations of sound.'[6] He remarks that music was associated with one of the daughters of Jupiter, who were also goddesses of memory, 'because this art, unless it is imprinted in the memory, is not retained.'

Following Boethius, Aurelian categorizes music in the order of importance: celestial music, human music and instrumental music.[7] He admits man cannot actually hear the 'music of the spheres,' but finds evidence for it in an apparent mistranslation of a passage from the Old Testament, Job 38:37, '... or who can make the harmony of heaven to sleep.'[8]

With regard to 'human music,' he makes two very unusual contentions for this age. First, he says, it is music which joins 'Reason to the body.' Next he makes an astounding deduction, considering that he could have known nothing physically about the rational left and the irrational right hemispheres of the brain, that it is only music which unites the rational and the irrational.

> What else is it that binds together the parts of the soul and body of man himself, who, as Aristotle is pleased to put it, has been joined together of the rational and the irrational.[9]

---

3   'Heathen' here is the Church's synonym for Plato, Aristotle, et. al.

4   Ibid., I.

5   Ibid., I.

6   Ibid., II.

7   Ibid., III.

8   Modern translations, such as the *Revised Standard Version*, make no inference to music.

> Who has put wisdom in the clouds, or given understanding to the mists?
> Who can number the clouds by wisdom?

9   Ibid., III. The Aristotle reference is apparently to the *Nicomachean Ethics*, I, 13.

It is perhaps from this perspective that he makes a division in the nature of Time. Rhythm he understands to be the mathematical part of music, but Meter he regards as movement genetic to man.

> [Another part] of human music, which is called metrics, although it takes its origin from music, should nevertheless be separated from it, since it is applied to song not so much through reasoning and through the rationality of this art as through natural impulse. But rhythmics, because it is totally based on intellect and reasoning, should be considered proper to music. A musician is one who has the faculty of judging without error with regard to reasoning, purposeful reflection, and musical convention, concerning quantities and rhythms, the kind of relationships of melodies, and the songs of the poets.[10]

He ranks instrumental music lowest in aesthetic value, because this kind of music 'is separated from the science and intellect of music.'[11] This reflects an early view that the 'music' is somehow made by the instrument, not the man or the subsequent vibrations, etc.

Following the lead of nearly all earlier Church philosophers, Aurelian goes to some length to provide a detailed explanation of the role of Reason in good musicianship. These basic thoughts, faulty logic and all, are voiced even today and continue to obscure the fact that the experience of music has nothing to do with Reason. He begins by asking the question, 'What is the difference between a musician and a singer?'

> There is as much difference between a musician and a singer as there is between a grammarian and a mere reader, or between physical skill and intellect. For physical skill obeys like a servant, but reason rules like a mistress, because the hands of the worker labor in vain, unless work grows out of the intellect. Every art and discipline has naturally a more honorable character than a handicraft, which is performed by hand and toil. For it is a much greater thing to know what someone does than to do what someone knows. Thus it is that the intellectual contemplation of work does not stand in need of any act of working, but the works of the hands are nothing unless they are directed by reason. How great the glory of the art of music is can be learned from this: that other craftsmen have received their names not from their discipline, but from the instruments themselves, as the hammerer from the hammer, the cithara player from the cithara, and each one of the others who have received their names from the instrument of their employment. But a musician is one who has with well-weighed intellect attained the science of singing not by the servitude of labor, but by the rule of contemplation. We see this antithesis particularly in the works of buildings and of wars. For buildings are inscribed with, and the triumphs of war are called by, the names not of those by whose toil and servitude they were completed, but by the names of those at whose command and inspiration they were begun: hence, the temple is called Solomon's …
>
> Musician and singer seem to differ as much as teacher and pupil. For example, the former creates poems, the latter analyses them; and the least little thing that the pupil accomplishes with time-consuming labor, the teacher discusses and empties of difficulty in the space of a single moment through the skill of his aptitude. And the singer seems to stand before the musician like a prisoner before the

---

10 Ibid., IV.

11 Ibid., III.

judge. Whoever has any notion of music, however small it may be, can understand this fairly well. As we have said in the foreword, very noble singers are found, yet nowhere, in my opinion, is a musician found like the old ones.[12]

Aurelian discusses the aesthetic quality of the human voice by dividing it into fifteen classes, an expansion of the observation by Isidore of Seville which we have quoted in the previous essay.

> The first of the voices is the hyperlydian kind, which is the newest and the highest; the hypodorian is the second and is the lowest of all.
> The third kind is song and it is an inflection of the voice. The sound is simple and sound precedes song.
> The fourth is arsis, that is, a lifting up of the voice, i.e., a beginning.
> The fifth is thesis, which is a putting down of the voice, i.e., and end.
> The sixth kind is where there are sweet voices. Sweet voices are those that are thin and intense, loud and high.
> The seventh is where there are clear voices, which sustain fairly long, so that they fill all the place around, like a trumpet.
> The eighth is where there are thin voices, as are those in infants or of strings.
> The ninth is fat [*pinguis*], as are the voices of men.
> The tenth is where the voice is sharp, thin, and high, as in strings.
> The eleventh is where there is a hard voice that is emitted violently, like hammers on an anvil.
> The twelfth kind is where the voice is rough; a rough voice is one is hoarse and is dispersed through minute and dissimilar sounds.
> The thirteen kind is that in which the voice is blind; a voice is called blind when it stops as soon as it is emitted.
> The fourteenth kind is where the sound is tremulous [*vinnola*]; a tremulous voice is a flexible voice; it is called *vinnola* from *vinno*, that is, a lock of hair gently curled.
> The fifteenth kind is where the voice is perfect; a perfect voice is high, sweet, and loud. If any of these qualities is lacking, the voice will not be perfect.[13]

In another place, Aurelian again refers to the Church's philosophy that music is a branch of mathematics:

> Music has the greatest correspondence to mathematics and encompasses that part of mathematics that compares one quantity with another.[14]

And, he says if one wishes to become more versed in *music*,

> let him turn his eyes to the harmony of proportions, to the contemplation of intervals, and to the exactitude of mathematics.[15]

---

[12] Ibid., VII.

[13] Ibid., V, 13.

[14] Ibid., VI.

[15] Ibid., X.

Aurelian summarizes the history of modes by saying there were first eight, named for the muses, then Charlemagne added four more and more recent Greeks still another four. He seems to want to discourage anyone who might want to enlarge the concept of tonality in this way, saying it is simply not necessary to do this, and adding the admonition from Proverbs 22:28,

> Remove not the ancient landmark which your fathers have set.

It is in this discussion of the new Greek modes that we see a rare early admission, in a Church treatise, that emotions exist. It will be the seventeenth century before the Church itself can officially accept this fact.

> I asked a certain Greek how they would be translated into Latin. He answered that they were untranslatable, but that among the Greeks they were exclamations of one rejoicing.[16]

There are a few observations by Aurelian about the performance of chant which we must include here. First, a curious maxim which demonstrates that the spirit of the old pagan myths had not completely died.

> We pray the singer to begin concluding all the verses of the nocturnal responses from the fifth syllable before the end; and this is according to the musicians who have maintained that not more than five waves of the sea also remove all storms from the same.[17]

Aurelian finds the one moment of true contemplation for the listener of church music to be the music of Communion.

> So long as the faithful people receive heavenly benediction, their minds may be drawn by the sweet melody and suspended in sublime contemplation.[18]

Although Aurelian's treatise on music is closely tied to Reason, he concludes with an admission which goes well beyond the Church's position with respect to the value of music in expressing emotions.

> The very world and the sky above us, according to the doctrine of philosophers, are said to bear in themselves the sound of music. Music moves the affections of men, stimulates the emotions into a different mood. In war it restores the strength of the combatants; and the stronger the blaring of the trumpet, the braver is the spirit made for battle. It influences beasts also, serpents, birds, and dolphins, at its hearing ... And what more? The art of music surpasses all other arts. If anyone doubts that the angels, too, in the starry sky, render praises to God with the practice of this discipline, he is not a reader of [the book of Revelations].[19]

---

[16] Ibid., IX.

[17] Ibid., XIX.

[18] Ibid., XX.

[19] Ibid.

Hucbald, *De harmonica institutione* (ca. 895 AD)

Hucbald (840–930 AD) taught at several monastic schools and it seems clear that this treatise is intended for instruction in such a school. The functional premise of treatises such as this was to produce a church singer who understood music on a conceptual level and could read music, as opposed to only learning by ear. Hucbald promises such a singer that if he will just study the exercises in this treatise, he,

> may at length be granted entry to the inner regions of this discipline, the darkness being gradually withdrawn from his dull eyes.[20]

But again, Hucbald was aware of something beyond the conceptual in music. We do wish he would have expanded his remarks on the distinction between 'judgment' and 'ear.'

> One will generally find that melodies can close on these notes a fifth above without offending either one's judgment or ear.[21]

Anonymous, *Scholia enchiriadis* (ca. 900 AD)

This treatise, formerly ascribed to Hucbald, is the earliest which deals with the improvisation of a simple counterpoint over a given chant. This author is still thinking of the old Church association of music and mathematics, indeed he says 'Music is the daughter of Arithmetic.' It is in this context that he defines music.

> [Music is] the rational discipline of agreement and discrepancy of sounds according to numbers in their relation to those things which are found in sounds ... Because everything comprehended by these disciplines exists through reason formed of numbers and without numbers can be neither understood nor made known.[22]

This writer clearly believed that the aim of this knowledge was 'delight,' a term he uses repeatedly. However, it appears that 'delight' for him was not aesthetic delight, but the delight of Reason.

> Whatever is delightful in song is brought about by number through the proportioned dimensions of sounds; whatever is excellent in rhythms, or in songs, or in any rhythmic movements you will, is effected wholly by number. Sounds pass quickly away, but numbers, which are obscured by the corporeal element in sounds and movements, remain.[23]

---

[20] Hucbald, 'Melodic Instruction' in *Hucbald, Guido, and John on Music*, trans. Warren Babb (New Haven: Yale University Press, 1978), 104a/16.

[21] Ibid., 119b/1.

[22] Anonymous, 'Of Symphonies,' in Oliver Strunk, *Source Readings in Music History* (New York: Norton, 1950), 135.

[23] Ibid., 137.

AL-FARABI, *IHSA AL-ULUM* (CA. 900 AD)

Abū Nasr Muhammad ibn al-Farakh al-Fārābi (870–950 AD) was an Islamic philosopher and one of the great scientists of his time. After finishing his early school years in Farab and Bukhara, Farabi arrived in Baghdad in 901 to pursue higher studies. He studied under a Christian and remained in Baghdad for more than forty years and acquired mastery over several languages and fields of knowledge.

Although he had a life of hardships, and at one time was the caretaker of a garden, he contributed considerably to science, philosophy, logic, sociology, medicine, mathematics and music. Although many of his books have been lost, 117 are known, out of which 43 are on logic, 11 on metaphysics, 7 on ethics, 7 on political science, 17 on music, medicine and sociology, while 11 are commentaries. Some of his more famous books include the book *Fusus al-Hikam*, which remained a text book of philosophy for several centuries at various centers of learning and is still taught at some of the institutions in the East.

This important treatise was the first to specifically distinguish between 'practical music' and 'theoretical music,' a division of the art which would be observed through nearly all later treatises. While there is now a recognition of both performance and the conceptual form of music, they are by no means equally respected for the conceptual is more highly regarded by all theorists before the sixteenth century. Their prejudices still influence much of the educational world today. Nevertheless, it is this division of the art which makes possible the eventual recognition of the aesthetics of music in performance in the Aristotelian model. Al-Farabi's historic new division reads as follows:

> As for the Science of Music, it comprises, in short, the investigation into the various kinds of melodies, and what they are composed of, and for what they are composed, and how they are composed, and in what forms it is necessary that they should be in order that the performance of them be made more impressive and effective. And that which is known by this name [Music] comprises two sciences. One of them is the science of practical music, and the second is the science of theoretical music.
>
> And as for practical music, its concern is the production of the various kinds of perceptible melodies in the instruments adapted for them either by nature or by artifice …
>
> And the science of theoretical music is divided into [two] major parts. The first of them is the discourse about principles and fundamentals … And the second part is the discourse about the rudiments of this art.[24]

---

[24] Quoted in Henry George Farmer, *Al-Farabi's Writings on Music* (New York: Hinrichsen, 1934), 13ff.

AL-FARABI, *DE ORTU SCIENTIARUM* (CA. 900 AD)

In this Latin treatise we find an important passage which preserves two familiar tenets of Greek philosophy, namely the influence of music on character and the definition of dance as visible music. He concludes with a thought that will be familiar with current American music educators, that the educational purpose of music is to make man 'keener' and to prepare him for other studies.

> [Music's] utility lies in tempering the character of living beings that digress from the mean and in perfecting the fitness of those that have not yet been perfected, and in maintaining those that appear to possess the mean and have not yet gone to any of the extremes. It is also of utility to bodily health whenever the body is weakened by a languid soul and is impeded by the existence of its own impediment. Thus the cure of the body is affected by the cure of the soul through the adjustment of its own constitution, and combining this with its own substance of means of effective sounds, such as concordant sounds.
>
> To this science are three roots—meter, melody, and gesture. Meter was devised to regulate a rational comprehension of diction. Melody was devised to regulate the parts of acuteness and gravity, and to it two roots have been included in the sense of hearing. Gesture has been included in the sense of seeing which, by coincident motions and corresponding proportions, has been arranged to agree with meter and sound. This art, therefore, is included in two particular senses—hearing and seeing.
>
> And in this the educational sciences which are called the dominating sciences are completed. Therefore, it is now manifest whence the art of music emerged, and whence it arose and flowed. And these four sciences are called the dominating because they dominate their investigator, render him keener, and disclose to him the right way to become most accurately acquainted with that which comes after them.[25]

ODO OF CLUNY, *ENCHIRIDION MUSICES* (CA. 935 AD)

Odo of Cluny (878–942 AD) is a saint in the Roman Church. He was born to an aristocratic family, was active in French monastic reform and served in some diplomatic roles. His treatise, the first in which letters are used as symbols for pitch in the modern sense, was also written for the purpose of perfecting the ability of church singers to read. With his system, Odo says he has taught boys in a few days to read 'without fault anything written in music,' something which he states that until now ordinary singers could not do even after fifty years' experience.[26]

Given the purpose of this treatise, we are not surprised to find, when the Disciple asks, 'What is music?,' the Master answers, 'The science of singing correctly.' This, of course, means following the rules of music in so far as it was understood as a science. Singing something merely because it pleases the ear held no justification for Odo.

---

[25] Ibid., 49.

[26] Odo, 'Enchiridion musices,' in Strunk, *Source Readings in Music History*, 104.

Ordinary singers often fall into the greatest error because they scarcely consider the force of tone and semitone and of the other consonances. Each of them chooses what first pleases his ear.[27]

On the other hand, following a discussion of the modes, Odo makes a dramatic departure from previous Church-mathematic theory when he gives as the goal of any change in the music, that it 'sound better.' When he summarizes the selection of modes, his comments reflect not 'science,' but improvisation and even 'trial and error.' Actually, without realizing it, he makes a revolutionary statement when he says the ear must judge where the eye cannot.

> From this it is understood that the musician who lightly and presumptuously emends many melodies is ignorant unless he first goes through all the modes to determine whether the melody may perhaps not stand in one or another, nor should he care as much for its similarity to other melodies as for regular truth. But if it suits no mode, let it be emended according to the one with which it least disagrees. This also should be observed: that the emended melody either sound better or depart little from its previous likeness.[28]

Guido of Arezzo, *Micrologus* (ca. 1026–1028 AD)

Guido (991–1033 AD), a Benedictine monk, was the author of this, the most widely read music treatise of the Middle Ages, save the work by Boethius. This is a treatise famous for the introduction of a staff of lines and spaces for the notation of music, an idea which recent research suggests he found in Muslim tradition.

This treatise is another educational one, directed at the training of church singers. He begins his discussion with a little anagram which refers to the disappearance of music in the schools during the Dark Ages.

> Gone from school are the Muses; there may I hope to induce them,
> Unknown yet to adults, to unveil their light to the young ones!
> Ill will's indiscriminate rage let charity frustrate;
> Dire indeed are the blights that else will ravage our planet,
> Opening letters of these five lines will spell you the author.[29]

In his Prologue, Guido immediately focuses on the importance of the ability to sing at sight. If the singer cannot do this, he says, 'I do not know with what face he can venture to call himself a musician or a singer.'[30] He declares that he will discuss here only those things important to singing and then adds a comment we can only wish he had elaborated on. He says he will omit those comments 'which are said but cannot be understood.'[31] He is appar-

---

[27] Ibid., 110.
[28] Ibid., 111.
[29] Guido of Arezzo, 'Micrologus,' 80, in *Hucbald, Guido, and John on Music*.
[30] Ibid., 85.
[31] Ibid., 86.

ently speaking of those insights which musicians arrive at through experience, but cannot be explained through the old Church-mathematic theories of instruction. This same point he makes in a more positive comment:

> In our times, of all men, singers are the most foolish. For in any art those things which we know of ourselves are much more numerous than those which we learn from a master.[32]

Among his comments on music theory, we find interesting his explanation for why there are seven tones of the scale (they are associated with the seven days of the week).[33] It is also interesting that he gives the origin of the word 'tone' as *intonandus*, 'to be sounded.'[34] That is, the concept came from the experience, whereas in today's world of music education the experience is incorrectly assumed to come from the concept. He takes the opposite view with respect to *musica ficta*, which is clearly an appropriate aesthetic concept which grew out of experience. This apparently violated his goal of accurate sight-singing.

> False notes also creep in through inaccuracy in singing; sometimes performers deviate from well-tuned notes, lowering or raising them slightly, as is done by untrue human voices.[35]

Guido's discussion of cadences includes a very curious statement. It strikes our attention especially as so many earlier Church philosophers had commented on the fact that music disappears after it is performed, suggesting that music exists only in its precise moment of performance. Guido presents here a thought which is quite different psychologically.

> The previous notes, as is evident to trained musicians only, are so adjusted to the last one so that in an amazing way they seem to draw a certain semblance of color from it.[36]

His actual explanation of the importance of the cadence he draws from grammar, a place where ancient philosophers often sought relationships with music.

> It is no wonder that music bases its rules on the last note, since in the elements of language, too, we almost everywhere see the real force of the meaning in the final letters or syllables, in regard to cases, numbers, persons, and tenses.[37]

Turning to the affect of music on man, Guido finds it natural that it is similar, in this regard, to the other senses.

---

[32] Quoted in Strunck, *Source Readings in Music History*, 117.

[33] 'Micrologus,' in *Hucbald, Guido, and John on Music*, 116. The number '7' was a very special number in Old Testament mythology.

[34] Ibid., 116.

[35] Ibid., 134.

[36] Ibid., 139.

[37] Ibid., 145.

> Nor is it any wonder if the hearing is charmed by a variety of sounds, since the sight rejoices in a variety of colors, the sense of smell is gratified by a variety of odors, and the palate delights in changing flavors. For thus through the windows of the body the sweetness of apt things enters wondrously into the recesses of the heart.[38]

He provides an illustration of the ability of music to affect character in an anecdote not found elsewhere. As to the explanation how music does this, he offers that this is known only to Divine Wisdom.

> Another man was roused by the sound of the cithara to such lust that, in his madness, he sought to break into the bedchamber of a girl, but, when the cithara player quickly changed the mode, was brought to feel remorse for his libidinousness and to retreat abashed.[39]

Guido makes some interesting aesthetic observations in the course of a discussion of composition. First, it is clear that rhythm, for him, is still something bound to the ancient Greek poetic textual rhythms.

> For just as lyric poets join now one kind of foot, now another, so composers reasonably juxtapose different and various neumes. Diversity is reasonable if it creates a measured variety of neumes and phrases, yet in such a way that neumes answer harmoniously to neumes and phrases, with always a certain resemblance.[40]

What is much more important, especially coming from a Church philosopher, is that he stresses that the composer must create in music emotions which match the emotions of the text. It is particularly interesting here, unless he was simply using 'nueme' as a synonym for 'music,' that he seems to suggest that the neumes in some way characterized feelings whereas in the later Church notational systems there are no longer any symbols for emotions at all.

> Let the effect of the song express what is going on in the text, so that for sad things the neumes are grave, for serene ones they are cheerful, and for auspicious texts exultant, and so forth.[41]

Regarding the emotions in performance, Guido makes a curious and very interesting psychological observation.

> We often place an acute or grave accent above the notes, because we often utter them with more or less stress, so much so that the repetition of the same note often seems to be a raising or lowering.[42]

Another curious suggestion has to do with the psychological relationship of the speed of notes at the cadence.

---

[38] Ibid., 159.
[39] Ibid., 160.
[40] Ibid., 172.
[41] Ibid., 174.
[42] Ibid.

> Towards the ends of phrases the notes should always be more widely spaced as they approach the breathing place, like a galloping horse, so that they arrive at the pause, as it were, weary and heavily.[43]

He concludes this discussion with the aesthetic rule that, in the end, taste must rule.

> Do everything that we have said neither too rarely nor too unremittingly, but with taste.[44]

We know today that music communicates on both a general, genetically understood, level and on an individual level where it is heard in a personal interpretation. Guido apparently failed to perceive the universal aspects of music.

> In accordance with the diversity of people and minds, what displeases one is cherished by another; and, anon, things that blend together delight this man, whereas that one prefers variety; one seeks a homogeneity and blandness in keeping with his pleasure-loving mind; another, since he is serious-minded, is pleased by staider strains; while another, as if distracted, feeds on studied and intricate contortions; and each proclaims that music as much the better sounding which suits the innate character of his own mind.[45]

When Guido writes that ancient men could not have understood music on any rational level he was apparently thinking of the fact that earlier music in Greece and Egypt had no notational form. It is a characteristic of his time that the obvious conclusion did not occur to him, that music is not rational.

> In ancient times there were instruments that we are not clear about and also a multitude of singers who were, however, in the dark, for no man could by any train of thought reason out the differences between notes or a description of music.[46]

JOHN, *ON MUSIC* (CA. 1100 AD)

This author, formerly known as 'John Cotton,' has also written a treatise intended for a choir school. His viewpoint is again primarily a conceptual one and he clearly states that it is knowledge, the ability to judge music, which is the highest accomplishment—not the creation of that pleasing music played by uneducated jongleurs!

> Music is one of the seven liberal arts—and a natural one, as are the others. Thus we sometimes see jongleurs and actors who are absolutely illiterate composing pleasant-sounding songs. But just as grammar, dialectic, and the other arts would be considered vague and chaotic if they were not committed to writing and made clear by precepts, so it is with music …

---

43 Ibid., 175.

44 Ibid., 177.

45 Ibid., 194.

46 Ibid., 288.

> For whoever devotes unremitting labor to it, and perseveres without pausing or wearying, can gain from it this reward, that he will know how to judge the quality of song—whether it is refined or commonplace, true or false—and how to correct the faulty and compose the new.[47]

Indeed, he says, it is knowledge which distinguishes a musician from a mere singer, someone who equates with a 'drunk.'

> Nor, it seems, should we omit that the musician and the singer differ not a little from one another. Whereas the musician always proceeds correctly and by calculation, the singer holds the right road intermittently, merely through habit. To whom then should I better compare the singer than to a drunken man who does indeed get home but does not in the least know by what path he returns.[48]

He attempts to strengthen this viewpoint by quoting Guido, that a musician who does not know what he is doing is a 'beast!'

> From the musician to the singer how immense the distance is;
> The latter's voice, the former's mind will show what music's nature is;
> But he who does, he knows not what, a beast by definition is.[49]

In another place he goes even further, refusing to accept performance traditions which derive from that talent which nature provides has an aesthetic value—even if it sounds correct and is agreeable!

> We said 'having a knowledge of music' because even if one unversed in the subject does what he does correctly, still, because he does it unwittingly, he is little esteemed, especially since both actors and precentors of dancing choruses for the most part sing agreeably, which is granted to them not by art but by nature.[50]

John begins his principal discussion of music by admitting that he does not know where the name 'music' actually derives from. If the reader knows, he does not begrudge him, for 'as Paul says, the Holy Ghost apportions to individuals as he sees fit.'[51] He finds two kinds of music, the first being natural and artificial music made by man and the second the 'music of the spheres,' which he says we know only through philosophers.[52]

His principal instrument for teaching pitch was the monochord, an instrument through which he believed true pitch could be achieved. This was a goal he apparently found to be not universally appreciated.

---

47 John, 'On Music,' 51, in *Hucbald, Guido, and John on Music.*
48 Ibid., 52.
49 John gives the source as the 'Micrologus,' but it actually comes from the beginning of Guido's 'Regulae rhythmicae.'
50 'On Music,' 77.
51 1 Corinthians 12:11.
52 'On Music,' 57.

> For there are indeed a great many clerics and monks who neither understand this discipline nor wish to understand it, and, what is worse, who avoid and abhor those that do.
>
> If, as sometimes happens, a musician takes them to task about a chant which they perform either inaccurately or crudely, they get angry and make a shameless uproar and are unwilling to admit the truth, but defend their error with the greatest effort …
>
> The monochord serves to silence their wrong-headedness, so that those who will not trust the words of a musician are refuted by the testimony of the sound itself.[53]

In discussing cadences, unlike Guido who found confirmation of his logic in grammar, John curiously finds his analogy in business.

> Musicians of judgment have not unreasonably decided to base the decision as to modes on the endings, since in business affairs a singleminded regard for the outcome distinguishes the wise from the heedless.[54]

Regarding the modes, John rejects the expansion of their ranges, which he admits some composers do for aesthetic reasons, 'to tickle the ears.'[55]

In his reflection on performances which he has heard, he makes a statement which is remarkably similar to Mahler's famous definition of 'tradition' as being 'the last bad performance.'

> We do know most assuredly that a chant is often distorted by the ignorance of men, so that we could now enumerate many corrupted ones. These were really not produced by the composers originally in the way that they are now sung in churches, but wrong pitches, by men who followed the promptings of their own minds, have distorted what was composed correctly and perpetuated what was distorted in an incorrigible tradition, so that by now the worst usage is clung to as authentic.[56]

He also has observed that the physical state of the singer can affect the performance, pointing to 'singers weighed down by weariness' singing flat and those of 'high spirits' singing sharp.[57]

John's discussion of the effect which music has on the emotions is quite unlike that of any other philosopher. He begins, like Guido, by pointing out that everyone has different tastes in music.

---

[53] Ibid., 65ff.
[54] Ibid., 82.
[55] Ibid., 96.
[56] Ibid., 104.
[57] Ibid.

> Nor should it seem surprising to anyone that we say different men are attracted by different things, for by nature itself men are so endowed that not everyone's senses cherish the same desire. Thus, it often happens that while to one man what is being sung appears most delightful, by another it is pronounced ill-sounding and utterly formless. Indeed I myself remember singing a number of chants for some people, and what one praised to the heights another disliked profoundly.[58]

Therefore, in his view it is not the mode which affects man, rather it is the natural emotional affinity of the man which is attracted to a particular mode—thus, each man likes a different mode. We are much more attracted to his unusual description of the aesthetic character of the various modes than we are to his logic.

> Some are pleased by the slow and ceremonious peregrinations of the first, some are taken by the hoarse profundity of the second, some are delighted by the austere and almost haughty prancing of the third, some are attracted by the ingratiating sound of the fourth, some are stirred by the well-bred high spirits and the sudden fall to the final in the fifth, some are melted by the tearful voice of the sixth, some like to hear the spectacular leaps of the seventh, and some favor the staid and almost matronly strains of the eighth.

These differences he finds are so pronounced that a musician recognizes the mode immediately by its character, as one does in the case of national characteristics.

> The modes have individual qualities of sound, differing from each other, so that they prompt spontaneous recognition by an attentive musician or even by a practiced singer. Just as someone who has studied the manners and appearances of various peoples distinguishes expertly the nationality of any man he sees, noting, for instance, that this one is a Greek and that one a German, but that one a Spaniard and that one a Frenchman.

The object of the composer, then, is to fit the character of the music to the character of the listener. How the composer does this, not to mention what one does in the case of a large congregation of assorted personalities, he does not say.

> Therefore, in composing chants, the duly circumspect musician should plan to use in the most fitting way the mode by which he sees those are most attracted whom he wishes his chant to please.

Later in this same treatise, John returns to the ancient Greek view that it is the music itself which affects character. He begins by rhapsodizing on the wide range of purpose available in music.

> It should not pass unmentioned that chant has great power of stirring the souls of its hearers, in that it delights the ears, uplifts the mind, arouses fighters to warfare, revives the prostrate and despairing, strengthens wayfarers, disarms bandits, assuages the wrathful, gladdens the sorrowful and distressed, pacifies those at strife, dispels idle thoughts, and allays the frenzy of the demented …

---

58 This discussion is found in Ibid., 109ff.

> Music has different powers according to the different modes. Thus, you can by one kind of singing rouse someone to lustfulness and by another kind bring the same man as quickly as possible to repentance and recall him to himself.[59]

John concludes this subject by arguing in favor of two ideas which were at this time contrary to the teachings of the Church. He was in favor of instrumental music and he saw no reason to restrict chant to the Gregorian repertoire.[60]

John now addresses himself to the subject of the composition of chant and begins by listing some specific aesthetic goals. First the composer must fit the music to the meaning of the words, as well as to the occasion which may range from frivolity to grief.[61] As an example of the latter, he recommends the Hypolydian for lamentations because of its 'doleful sound.'

Speaking of rhythmic notation, one must have variety and 'not abuse one neume by unduly harping on it.' He also appears to discourage melodic repetition, although he says 'we do not find fault if now and then some appropriate melodic figures are repeated just once.'

Finally, we find a curious observation on the relationship of the character of the singing voice with scale-steps. It is a regret the he does not elaborate on this idea which he calls 'obvious.'

> It is obvious that men with harsh and intractable voices avoid semitones as much as possible, while those who have flexible voices relish them greatly—so much so that they sometimes produce them even where they should not be made.[62]

---

[59] Ibid., 114ff.
[60] Ibid., 115.
[61] Ibid., 117ff.
[62] Ibid., 137.

PART 3
EARLY DISCUSSIONS ON PERFORMANCE PRACTICE

Early Reflections on Repertoire

IN THE OLDEST EXTANT LITERATURE of ancient Greece, the works of Homer (eighth century BC), one can see that the concept of good and bad musical repertoire was already recognized. So clear was this distinction, that some of the Greek philosophers emphasized the importance of the choice. In the following passage Homer presents the myth of the god, Hermes, giving the gift of music to Apollo. And as is true today, Homer emphasizes that the choice of repertoire is everything. He begins by charging Apollo to approach with honor this noble art.

> You may choose to learn whatever you desire,
> but since your heart is so eager to play the lyre,
> sing and play the lyre and minister to gay festivities,
> receiving this skill from me and, friend, grant me glory.
> Sing well with this clear-voiced mistress in your arms,
> since you have the gift of beautiful and proper speech.
> From now on in carefree spirit bring it to the well-provided feast,
> the lovely dance, and the revel where men vie for glory,
> as a fountain of good cheer day and night.

As regards the choice to be made, Homer places the critical distinction in the attitude with which the player approaches the art. If one approaches music with seriousness of purpose, music, in turn, will teach one a great deal.

> Whoever with skill and wisdom expertly asks, to him
> it will speak and teach him all manner of things
> joyful to the mind, being played with a gentle touch,
> for it shuns toilsome practice.

But if one approaches music in ignorance, it will never be more than sensory gibberish.

> But if anyone should in ignorance question it at first with rudeness,
> to him in vain it will chatter high-flown gibberish forever.

And then Homer once again poses the choice:

> You may choose to learn whatever you desire.[1]

For the interest of the reader, we pass on an observation made by the translator of the above passage:

---

[1] Homer, *The Homeric Hymns*, trans. Apostolos N. Athanassakis (Baltimore: Johns Hopkins University Press, 1976), 474–489.

> The artistic sensitivity and the truly genteel nature of the advice that Hermes gives Apollo are remarkable. It is small wonder that the best practitioners of the art of singing and playing the lyre were called *theioi* (divine).

And indeed, the choice is everything. The first of the great ancient Greek playwrights, Aristophanes (448–385 BC), makes a point which is just as valid today as it was two thousand five hundred years ago. A character in his *The Thesmophoriazusae*, tells us that one's choice of music reveals one's character.

> Answer me. But you keep silent. Oh! just as you choose; your songs display your character quite sufficiently.[2]

How very true this is! An autobiographical poem by the Baroque poet, Antonio Abbatini, describes the gathering of educated and noble gentlemen in one of the Italian academies. He tells us that during the course of the evening the members themselves would take turns performing, *for the purpose of demonstrating their character*.

> Then to the harpsichord the company transfers,
> And each man takes upon himself to show, with song
> And sound, his virtue, which binds the heart and soul.[3]

The early Church fathers were well aware of the power of music and it is no surprise that the Bishop of Milan, St. Ambroise (339–397 AD), placed his concern, regarding the issue of choice of repertoire, on the affect on the listener. He therefore calls for musicians to be responsible for their choice of repertoire.

> Therefore play what is honorable, that your sympathetic consciousness of others may be honorable. For one who sees is much affected by what he sees, and one who hears by what he hears.[4]

A later churchman, Calvin (1509–1564), whom some writers believe had more influence on future American life than any other church figure, shares the concern of St. Ambroise in warning of music's 'secret and almost incredible power,'

> We must be the more careful not to abuse [music], for fear of soiling and contaminating it, converting it to our condemnation when it has been dedicated to our profit and welfare. Were there no other consideration than this alone, it might well move us to moderate the use of music to make it serve all that is of good repute and that it should not be the occasion of our giving free rein to dissoluteness or of our making ourselves effeminate with disordered pleasures and that it should not become the instrument of lasciviousness or of any shamelessness. But there is still more, for there is hardly any-

---

[2] Lines, 143.

[3] Quoted in Lorenzo Bianconi, *Music in the Seventeenth Century*, trans. David Bryand (Cambridge: Cambridge University Press, 1989), 290ff.

[4] Saint Ambrose, 'Death as a Good,' in *Seven Exegetical Works*, trans. Michael P. McHugh (Washington, D.C.: The Catholic University of America Press), 89.

thing in the world with more power to turn or bend, this way and that, the morals of men, as Plato has prudently considered. And in fact we find by experience that it has a secret and almost incredible power to move our hearts in one way or another.[5]

Later, he continues with even stronger language:

> The early doctors of the Church often complain that the people of their times are addicted to dishonest and shameless songs, which not without reason they call mortal and Satanic poison for the corruption of the world. Now in speaking of music I understand two parts, namely, the letter, or subject and matter, and the song, or melody. It is true that, as Saint Paul says, every evil word corrupts good manners, but when it has the melody with it, it pierces the heart much more strongly and enters within; as wine is poured into the cask with a funnel, so venom and corruption are distilled to the very depths of the heart by melody.

What, then, is good repertoire? For the ancient Greek philosophers this question was embedded in their philosophy of Truth versus Imitation. In a lengthy discussion in the *Republic*,[6] Plato considers the aspect of imitation in art, a topic which is not only fundamental to an understanding of his view of the arts, but one which will be discussed by every writer on aesthetics ever after. Here we find the conclusion that painting, drama and poetry—even that of the greatest Greek poet of them all, Homer—will not be allowed in the utopia which much of the *Republic* describes. They are rejected because they are imitations and not Truth.

What does he mean by this? Plato quotes Socrates as providing the answer to this question by using a common table as an illustration. The table, he says, is an idea. The maker of a table makes not the idea, but an imitation of the idea. The painter is yet another degree removed from truth, because he only paints a picture of an imitation of an idea.

> SOCRATES. Then the imitator is a long way off the truth, and can reproduce all things because he lightly touches on a small part of them, and that part an image. For example, a painter will paint a cobbler, carpenter, or any other artisan, though he knows nothing of their arts; and, if he is a good painter, he may deceive children or simple persons when he shows them his picture of a carpenter from a distance, and they will fancy that they are looking at a real carpenter.

It is very important to notice that while diminishing the value of poetry, painting and the drama, because they are only imitations, Plato never mentions music. We are confident that Plato and the other ancient Greek philosophers understood perfectly well that music is different. Music is not an imitation of anything at all, it is a direct form of Truth between composer (and/or performer) and listener. This is why, in another place, Plato says music is 'Truth,'[7] and also why he notes that experienced singers will immediately know if a composition is good or

---

[5] Jean Calvin, *Geneva Psalter*, quoted in Oliver Strunk, *Source Readings in Music History* (New York: Norton, 1950), 346ff.

[6] *Republic*, X, 595b – 602b. It is generally understood that the works of Plato speak for Socrates.

[7] *Laws*, 668b.

bad.⁸ We might add that the same is true for composers. No matter how unique a composer is, due to the universality of music he will always be judged against the common experience. Such a case was mentioned, without amplification, by Voltaire:

> We have seen a musician die mad, because his music did not appear good enough.⁹

We believe it is fair to say that one of the chief reasons why the ancient Greek philosophers were so critical of entertainment music was because it did not speak directly of Truth, largely because it became distracted with function. This is the very point made by Euripides, in *Iphigenia in Aulis*:

> Not only the idle song
> Of a singer laughing at Truth.¹⁰

In the discussion of imitation, from which we quoted above, Socrates explains his sense of pity that an artist should elect to deal in imitation, rather than in Truth.

> Now do you suppose that if a person were able to make the original as well as the image, he would seriously devote himself to the image-making branch? Would he allow imitation to be the ruling principle of his life, as if he had nothing higher in him?

And this expressed well the dismay which Euripides felt toward entertainment music in its most popular venue, the banquet. Why, he wonders, when musicians have the potential for doing so much good ('to heal men's wounds by music's spell'), do they waste their talents on entertaining at a banquet, when the banquet itself is sufficient entertainment?

> Wert thou to call the men of old time rude uncultured boors thou wouldst not err, seeing that they devised their hymns for festive occasions, for banquets, and to grace the board, a pleasure to catch the ear, shed o'er our life, but no man hath found a way to allay hated grief by music and the minstrel's varied strain, whence arise slaughters and fell strokes of fate to o'erthrow the homes of men. And yet these were surely a gain, to heal men's wounds by music's spell, but why tune they their idle song where rich banquets are spread? For of itself doth the rich banquet, set before them, afford to men delight.¹¹

It is because good music deals with Truth that Socrates reconsidered his position on poetry. Socrates singled out those poets who sang, because with the addition of music he felt they now were dealing in Truth. In fact, he goes so far as to say *only* these poets can use the name, 'poet,' as we read in the *Symposium*:

---

8   Ibid., 812b ff.
9   'The Ignorant Philosopher,' in *The Works of Voltaire* (New York: St. Hubert Guild, 1901), XXXV, 284.
10 Lines, 793.
11 *Medea*, 179.

They are not all called poets, but have other names; only that one portion of creative activity which is separated off from the rest, and is concerned with music and meter, is called by the name of the whole and is termed poetry, and they who possess poetry in this sense of the word are called poets.[12]

And again,

> SOCRATES. Well now, suppose that we strip all poetry of melody and rhythm and meter, there will remain [only] speech?
> CALLICLES. To be sure.[13]

The real point made by Socrates is found in Plato's *Laws*:

> AN ATHENIAN STRANGER. For poets are a divine race, and often in their strains, by the aid of the Muses and the Graces, they attain Truth.[14]

And in this work we find the usual tribute to the Gods for the gift of music.

> AN ATHENIAN STRANGER. And did we not say that the sense of harmony and rhythm spring from this beginning among men, and that Apollo and the Muses and Dionysus were the Gods whom we had to thank for them?
> CLEINIAS. Certainly.

It is also in the book, *Laws*, that Socrates provides us with a little history of music during what he would have called, 'the best years.'

> AN ATHENIAN STRANGER. Let us speak of the laws about music,—that is to say, such music as then existed,—in order that we may trace the growth of the excess of freedom from the beginning. Now music was early divided among us into certain kinds and manners. One sort consisted of prayers to the Gods, which were called hymns; and there was another and opposite sort called lamentations, and another termed paeans, and another, celebrating (I believe) the birth of Dionysus, called 'dithyrambs.' And they used the actual word 'laws' for another kind of song; and to this they added the term 'citharoedic.' All these and others were duly distinguished, nor were the performers allowed to confuse one style of music with another. And the authority which determined and give judgment, and punished the disobedient, was not expressed in a hiss, nor in the most unmusical shouts of the multitude, as in our days, nor in applause and clapping of hands. But the directors of public instruction insisted that the spectators should listen in silence to the end; and boys and their tutors, and the multitude in general, were kept quiet by a hint from a stick. Such was the good order which the multitude were willing to observe; they would never have dared to give judgment by noisy cries.

---

[12] *Symposium*, 205c. In 196e Plato quotes from a fragment of *Sthenoboea* by Euripides, which mentions one Eryximachus who could by his touch create poets of someone, 'even though he had no music in him before.'

[13] *Gorgias*, 502c.

[14] *Laws*, 682.

But then Socrates sadly observes that a decline in the practice of music occurred. Music began to be aimed at the lowest of society, rather than at the educated upper class. He held this change responsible for a consequent decay in society.

> And then, as time went on, the poets themselves introduced the reign of vulgar and lawless innovation. They were men of genius, but they had no perception of what is just and lawful in music; raging like bacchanals and possessed with inordinate delights—mingling lamentations with hymns, and paeans with dithyrambs; imitating the sounds of the flute on the lyre, and making one general confusion; ignorantly affirming that music has no Truth, and, whether good or bad, can only be judged of rightly by the pleasure of the hearer. And by composing such licentious works, and adding to them words as licentious, they have inspired the multitude with lawlessness and boldness, and made them fancy that they can judge for themselves about melody and song.[15]

The last sentence might as well describe the general music culture today.

There are two more definitions of good music by early Greek philosophers which we should mention in passing. Athenaeus (fl. ca. 200 AD) quotes the philosopher, Eupolis (446–411 BC), as saying that 'Music is a matter deep and intricate.'[16] Athenaeus himself observed that, 'It is plain to me that music should be the subject of philosophic reflection.'[17] We certainly agree, if there is no contemplative listener it cannot be art music.

Before leaving the period of Socrates and Plato, there is one more comment about the difference between good and bad repertoire which we must report. Conductors today are familiar with a discussion by the late, great Bruno Walter, in which he points out that a poor composition cannot be made better in rehearsal, but instead only becomes more and more poor. The reason, as he pointed out, is that the rehearsal process only tends to clarify and bring into sharper focus the elements of the composition which make it a poor work in the first place. We were reminded of this in a passage in Plato's *Phaedo*.[18] His point here seems to be that when something is beautiful it can only be explained as being what it is. No analysis, in other words, can explain why something is beautiful. Plato resists such efforts,

> and if a person says to me that the bloom of color, or form, or any such thing is a source of beauty, I dismiss all that, which is only confusing to me.

Shortly after this discussion comes the lines which reminded us of Walter:

> And that by greatness great things become great and greater, and by smallness the less become less?
> True.

This same principle was also discussed several times by Erasmus (1466–1536). The first is evident in the name of the proverb he discusses, 'Beauty bears repeating.'

---

[15] Ibid., 700ff.

[16] Athenaeus, *The Deipnosophists*, trans. Charles Burton Guilick (Cambridge: Harvard University Press, 1951), XIV, 623.

[17] Ibid., XIV, 632.

[18] Lines 100b.

> In general, there is such a power in excellent things that the more often and the more closely they are examined the more they please ... On the other hand, things which are falsely colored or commonplace sometimes have a charm to begin with, through sheer novelty, but soon grow ugly on repetition.[19]

Erasmus mentions this definition again in a letter to the Archbishop of Canterbury when discussing painting.

> A picture of moderate quality is quite attractive on first inspection; if you study it more often, more closely, and more at leisure, it gradually loses its attraction. On the other hand, a painting by a distinguished artist becomes more and more admirable the more often and more attentively you look at it.[20]

In other words, something can never be more than it is. This was also expressed very nicely by Erasmus' German contemporary, the writer Sebastian Brant (1457–1521):

> A potter fashions out of earth
> A pot, to some of little worth,
> A jar, a jug of any style
> For any liquid good or vile.
> No pot will say to the potter's face:
> 'I should have been a lordly vase!'[21]

The decay in music traditions which had been reported by Socrates, as the reader has seen above, continued throughout the ancient Greek period. It is one of the reasons why Aristotle devoted relatively little attention to music. Another reason was that actual performance was now being done by slaves, which meant that the educated philosopher had to take a position of admiring music, but not the performers. This was Aristotle's (384–322 BC) dilemma when he wrote,

> Every art and every inquiry, and similarly every action and pursuit, is thought to aim at some good; and for this reason the good has rightly been declared to be that at which all things aim. But a certain difference is found among ends; some are activities, others are products apart from the activities that produce them. Where there are ends apart from the actions, it is the nature of the products to be better than the activities.[22]

This is a reflection of the way many people at the top of Greek society thought at this time. When Plutarch states this view very vividly in his biography of Pericles, one can see how very far things have progressed since the time of the lyric poets.

---

[19] 'Adages,' in *The Collected Works of Erasmus* (Toronto: University of Toronto Press, 1992), XXXI, 191. This quotation describes much of the education publications for the wind band. A colleague calls this repertoire 'paper plate' music—you use it once and throw it away.

[20] Letter to William Warham, Archbishop of Canterbury [1524], in Ibid., X, 276.

[21] Sebastian Brant, *The Ship of Fools*, trans. Edwin Zeydel (New York: Columbia University Press, 1944), 57.

[22] *Ethica Nicomachea*, 1094a.

> Many times ... when we are pleased with the work, we slight and set little by the workman or artist himself, as, for instance, in perfumes and purple dyes, we are taken with the things themselves well enough, but do not think dyers and perfumers otherwise than low and sordid people. It was not said amiss by Antisthenes, when people told him that one Ismenias was an excellent aulos player, 'It may be so,' said he, 'but he is but a wretched human being, otherwise he would not have been an excellent aulos player.'[23]

There is no question that Aristotle shared this view.

> Why is it that some men spend their time in pursuits which they have chosen, though these are sometimes mean, rather than in more honorable professions? Why, for example, should a man who chooses to be a conjurer or an actor or an aulos player prefer these callings to that of an astronomer or an orator?[24]

This problem aside, there are only two places where Aristotle hints at what his concept of high art might have been with respect to the actual musical literature. The first is his observation that we get the most pleasure in hearing music which is 'expressive of meaning.'[25] The second is his judgment that 'a woeful and quiet character and type of music' is 'more human.'[26]

In a more general sense, Aristotle writes of good art that it must be 'good,' in the sense of virtue, it must be morally good, the standard by which Aristotle measures everything.

> We must see that every science and art has an end, and that too a good one; for no science or art exists for the sake of evil. Since then in all the arts the end is good, it is plain that the end of the best art will be the best good.[27]

Aristotle gives us an illustration of this with respect to music, and at the same time a definition of 'a musical man.'

> A good man is one that delights in virtuous actions and is vexed at vicious ones, as a musical man enjoys beautiful melodies but is pained at bad ones.[28]

Finally, in a general definition which has been often quoted, Aristotle defines *good art* as that art in which 'it is not possible either to take away or to add anything.'[29] Marcus Aurelius (121–180 AD) draws on this idea when he writes,

---

[23] Plutarch, *Lives*, 'Pericles.'
[24] *Problemata*, 917a.5.
[25] Ibid., 918a.33.
[26] Ibid., 922b.20.
[27] *Magna Moralia*, 1182a.33.
[28] *Ethica Nicomachea*, 1170a.9.
[29] Ibid., 1106b.8.

> Everything which is in any way beautiful is beautiful in itself, and terminates in itself, not having praise as part of itself. Neither worse then nor better is a thing made by being praised. I affirm this also of the things which are called beautiful by the vulgar; for example, material things and works of art. That which is really beautiful has no need of anything; not more than law, not more than truth, not more than benevolence or modesty. Which of these things is beautiful because it is praised, or spoiled by being blamed?[30]

In thinking of repertoire in the sense of program planning, there was one characteristic which a number of early philosophers pointed to as necessary and that is variety. Marcus Aurelius, for example wrote,

> As it happens to you in the amphitheater and such places, that the continual sight of the same things and the uniformity makes the spectacle wearisome.[31]

The poet Juvenal found formal oration on stage to be particularly lacking in variety.

> Must I *always* be stuck in the audience at these poetry-readings, never
> Up on the platform myself, taking it out on Cordus
> For the times he's bored me to death with ranting speeches …
> The stale themes are bellowed daily.[32]

Pliny the Younger also mentions a similar concern regarding the need for variety.

> Nothing, in my opinion, gives a more amiable and becoming grace to our studies, as well as manners, than to temper the serious with the gay, lest the former should degenerate into melancholy, and the latter run up into levity. Upon this plan it is that I diversify my graver works with compositions of a lighter nature.[33]

Philosophers well into the Christian Era continued to speak of the need for variety. Ausonius (310–395 AD) believed that a characteristic of good poetry is that it has a variety of moods and that even serious poetry should have lighter moments.

> I have mingled grave with gay, each to give pleasure at its season. Life wears not one hue, nor has my verse one reader only; each page has its due season; mitred Venus approves this, helmed Minerva that; the Stoic loves this part, Epicurus that.[34]

And in Chaucer we find in one place he observes that even the best harpist alive, with the best sounding harp and the most pointed plectrum, would never play on just one string or play just one song, for everyone's 'ears would grow dull.'[35]

---

[30] Marcus Aurelius, *Meditations*, IV, 20.

[31] Ibid., VI, 46.

[32] Juvenal, *Satire I*.

[33] Letter XCIV, to Arrianus.

[34] *Ausonius*, trans. Hugh G. Evelyn White (London: Heinemann, 1921), II, 169.

[35] 'Troilus and Criseyde,' II, 1030.

We hasten to point out that these calls for variety are not meant to mean mixing entertainment music with art music. A good example might be Mahler's *Third Symphony* which contains two movements of rather rural and innocent music surrounded by very serious music.

There is some evidence that both new compositions and the tradition of older ones were honored. In this regard it is curious to find in a discussion relative to war, that Xenophon (427–355 BC) mentions in passing the fact that musicians of his experience were both performing older compositions and creating new ones.

> However, my son, since you are desirous of learning all these matters, you must not only utilize what you may learn from others, but you must yourself also be an inventor of stratagems against the enemy, just as musicians render not only those compositions which they have learned but try to compose others also that are new. Now if in music that which is new and fresh wins applause, new stratagems in warfare also win far greater applause, for such can deceive the enemy even more successfully.[36]

Given the close relationship between the dramatic choruses and earlier choral odes, together with the frequent mention as late as Aristophanes (448–385 BC) of actual lyric poets, we have every reason to suppose that older choral repertoire works were still known and performed during the fifth century. A line in Euripides (480–406 BC) confirms that this was the case.

> For I sing this day to Dionysus
> The song that is appointed from of old.[37]

On the other hand, the old tradition of singing of the glories of men and battles of the past is satirized in one of the plays by Aristophanes. In the following scene,[38] a boy has come to sing after a banquet. Every time he begins one of these historical songs he is interrupted by a guest who is impatient with this old style of song.

> TRYGAEUS. Hi! child! what do you reckon to sing? Stand there and give me the opening line.
> BOY. 'Glory to the young warriors ...'
> TRYGAEUS. Oh! leave off about your young warriors, you little wretch; we are at peace and you are an idiot and a rascal.
> BOY. 'The skirmish begins, the hollow bucklers clash against each other.'
> TRYGAEUS. Bucklers! Leave me in peace with your bucklers.
> BOY. 'And then there came groanings and shouts of victory.'
> TRYGAEUS. Groanings! ah! by Bacchus! look out for yourself, you cursed squaller, if you start wearying us again with your groanings and hollow bucklers.
> BOY. Then what should I sing? Tell me what pleases you.
> TRYGAEUS. 'Tis thus they feasted on the flesh of oxen,' or something similar, as, for instance, 'Everything that could tickle the palate was placed on the table.'
> BOY. 'Tis thus they feasted on the flesh of oxen and, tired of warfare, unharnessed their foaming steeds.'

---

36 'Cyropaedia,' I, *Cyropaedia*, trans. Walter Miller (Cambridge: Harvard University Press, 1960).

37 *The Bacchae*, 70.

38 *Peace*, 1268ff.

TRYGAEUS. That's splendid; tired of warfare, they seat themselves at table; sing to us how they still go on eating after they are satiated.
BOY. 'The meal over, they girded themselves ...'
TRYGAEUS. With good wine, no doubt?
BOY. '... with armor and rushed forth from the towers, and a terrible shout arose.'
TRYGAEUS. Get you gone, you little scapegrace, you and your battles! You sing of nothing but warfare.

Again, because of the decay in culture there were some who insisted on newly composed music to reflect the contemporary day. Athenaeus quotes a play called *The Helots*, produced in the fifth century BC, in which a character says,

> To sing the songs of Stesichorus, of Alkman, and Simonides is out of date. Rather, Gnesippus is the one to hear, for he has invented serenades for adulterers, with iambuca and triangle in hand, to sing and lure their ladies with.[39]

A reference from the eleventh century mentions contemporary music in a very literal sense. The philosopher, Psellus, makes an interesting reference to choral music in this style, during the reign of the empress, Theodora of Constantinople, in 1042 AD.

> Some made thanks-offerings to God for their deliverance, others acclaimed the new empress, while the common folk and the loungers in the market joined in dancing. The revolution was dramatized and they composed choral songs inspired by the events that had taken place before their eyes.[40]

During the Middle Ages there was still music from ancient Greece being performed. A third-century poet-singer, named Plato of all things, is remembered in an eulogy.

> When Orpheus departed, perchance some Muse survived, but at thy death, Plato, the lyre ceased to sound. For in thy mind and in thy fingers there yet survived some little fragment at least of ancient music.[41]

Perhaps it was even such repertoire sung by a court poet described in the twelfth-century English work, 'Beowulf.'

> From time to time, a thane of the king,
> who had made many vaunts, and was mindful of verses,
> stored with sagas and songs of old,
> bound word to word in well-knit rime,
> welded his lay.[42]

---

39 Athenaeus, *Deipnosophistae*, XIV, 638.
40 Michael Psellus, *Chronographia*, trans. E. R. A. Sewter (Baltimore: Penguin Books, 1966), V, 39.
41 Leontius Scholasticus, *Greek Anthology*, VII, 571.
42 'Beowulf,' trans. Francis Gummere in *Epic and Saga*, vol. 49, *The Harvard Classics* (New York: Collier), XIII.

The fundamental issues of concern in the above quotations by early philosophers remain with us today. It is difficult to blame the publishers of the artificial 'music' which they produce for their only goal is money. Can the students have an authentic musical experience performing artificial music? Clearly not. The only protection the educational institution has is a conductor who is sophisticated enough to separate the real from the false. This very point was made in 1945 by Archibald T. Davison, conductor of the famed Harvard Glee Club. He would only be surprised that the revolt has not yet happened.

> The most serious demand is for teachers whose knowledge and experience of music is wide enough to guarantee a sound musical taste. Only when there is intelligent revolt against much educational material that now passes for music will there be hope for a productive music education in this country.[43]

---

43 Quoted in Willi Apel, *Harvard Dictionary of Music* (Cambridge: Harvard University Press, 1947), 472.

Early Reflections on Acoustics and the Perception of Music

Music represented a formidable problem for early philosophers, because they could not see it. They could hear music, of course, and observe it impact on listeners, but since they could not see it, it did not lend itself to correspondence with the rational world they sought to explain. It was due in large part to the power of music and its invisible state that they often associated music with religion rather than the other arts.

The great break-through came with the findings which history credits Pythagoras (582–507 BC), that the lower portion of the overtone series could be represented by numbers. If one could think of music as mathematics, then one could make music rational. But many problems remained, in particular the exact nature of vibrations and how we hear them, accounting for the fact that different people hear music differently (whereas everyone agrees in math) and the results of their observations of how the sound of music is influenced by its surroundings. Their search for answers to these questions is the subject for the present essay.

In addition to the early work in defining the lower part of the overtone series, one of the members of the Pythagorean School, Archytas (428–350 BC), correctly (if circuitously) arrived at the observation that higher frequencies travel with more energy.

> Of the sounds that fall within the range of our senses, some—those that come quickly from the bodies struck—seem shrill; those that arrive slowly and feebly, seem of low pitch. In fact, when one agitates some object slowly and feebly, the shock produces a low pitch; if the waving is done quickly, and with energy, the sound is shrill. This is not the only proof of the fact, which we can prove when we speak or sing; when we wish to speak loud and high, we use a great force of breath. So also with something thrown; if you throw them hard, they go far; if you throw them without energy, they fall near, for the air yields more to bodies moved with much force, than to those thrown with little. This phenomenon is also reproduced in the sound of the voice, for the sounds produced by an energetic breath are shrill, while those produced by a feeble breath are weak and low in pitch. This same observation can be seen in the force of a signal given from any place: if you pronounce it loud, it can be heard far; if you pronounce the same signal low, we do not hear it even when near. So also in the aulos, the breath emitted by the mouth and which presents itself to the holes nearest the mouthpiece, produces a shriller sound, because the impulsive force is greater; farther down, they are of lower pitch. It is therefore evident that the swiftness of the movement produces shrillness, and slowness, lower pitch.[1]

Awareness of the nature of the overtones seems evident in a comment by Plotinus (204–270 AD), when he says the soul can hear what the senses cannot and gives this example:

> Harmonies unheard in sound create the harmonies we hear and wake the Soul to the consciousness of beauty.[2]

---

[1] Fragment 15, quoted in Kenneth Guthrie, *The Pythagorean Sourcebook* (Grand Rapids: Phanes Press, 1987), 184.

[2] Plotinus, *The Enneads*, trans. Stephen MacKenna (London: Faber and Faber, 1962), 59.

The reference above by Archytas of the 'shrill' and 'impulsive force' of the aulos is undoubtedly related to a certain aesthetic prejudice toward this instrument, in spite of the fact that it was the primary melodic instrument in use in ancient Greece. We see this prejudice in the telling of the myth of a goddess who threw the aulos away when she discovered, upon seeing her reflection in a pond while she was playing, that the exertion of playing disfigured her face. Still another prejudice, arising from a misunderstanding of the nature of sound production of the aulos and what we actually hear (only air vibrations), is related by Aristides (530–468 BC), quoting something of Pythagoras which is not found elsewhere.

> This was also the sense of the advice Pythagoras is said to have given his disciples: that if they heard the aulos they should wash out their ears because the breath had defiled them,[3] but that they should use well-omened melodies sung to the lyra to cleanse their souls of irrational impulses. The aulos, he said, serves the thing that is master of our worse part, while the lyra is loved and enjoyed by that which cares for our rational nature.[4]

Aristides concludes this discussion, his essay on music education, by projecting this idea to cosmic proportions.

> Learned men of all nations also bear witness for me that it is not our souls alone that are constituted in this way, but also the soul of the whole universe. Some of them worship the region below the moon, which is full of breaths and has a moist constitution, and yet derives its activity from the life of the region of aether: these people make propitiation to it with both kinds of instruments, wind and stringed. Others worship the pure and aetherial region: they reject all wind instruments as defiling the soul and tempting it towards earthly things, and sing their hymns and praises with the kithara and lyra alone, because these are purer. Wise men imitate and emulate the aetherial region.[5]

One of the early Greek references to acoustics is by Plutarch (46–127 AD), in his essay, 'According to Epicurus.' He poses a series of interesting questions about music, among them,

> Why also, if you scatter chaff or dust about the orchestra of a theater, will the sound be softened?— Why, when one would have set up a bronze statue of Alexander for a frontispiece to a stage at Pella, did the architect advise to the contrary, because it would spoil the actors' voices?[6]

Among the ancient Romans one the most interesting discussions of the perception of music is found in a reflection by Cicero (106–43 BC) admiring the distribution and design of the senses, relative to the body, and for the 'lavishness and splendor of [these] gifts bestowed by the gods on men.'

---

[3] Many philosophers at the time of Pythagoras considered the player himself to be of the lower class, 'sordid persons,' as Plutarch called them. The suggestion here may be that it is the breath of the aulos player, rather than sound waves, which travels through space to the ear of the listener, hence 'defiling them.'

[4] The old, ever present prejudice against wind music, as opposed to string music, may date from ancient philosophies such as this.

[5] Andrew Barker, *Greek Musical Writings* (Cambridge: Cambridge University Press, 1989). Aristides also mentions the myth of the goddess playing the aulos.

[6] He also asks, 'Why, of the several kinds of music, will the chromatic diffuse and the harmonic compose the mind?'

> The senses, posted in the citadel of the head as the reporters and messengers of the outer world, both in structure and position are marvelously adapted to their necessary services. The eyes as the watchmen have the highest station, to give them the widest outlook for the performance of their function. The ears also, having the duty of perceiving sound, the nature of which is to rise, are rightly placed in the upper part of the body. The nostrils likewise are rightly placed high inasmuch as all smells travel upwards, but also, because they have much to do with discriminating food and drink, they have with good reason been brought into the neighborhood of the mouth. Taste, which as the function of distinguishing the flavors of our various viands, is situated in that part of the face where nature has made an aperture for the passage of food and drink. The sense of touch is evenly diffused over all the body, to enable us to perceive all sorts of contacts and even the minutest impacts of both cold and heat. And just as architects relegate the drains of houses to the rear, away from the eyes and nose of the masters, since otherwise they would inevitably be somewhat offensive, so nature has banished the corresponding organs of the body far away from the neighborhood of the senses.
>
> Again what artificer but nature, who is unsurpassed in her cunning, could have attained such skillfulness in the construction of the senses? …
>
> The organ of hearing … is always open, since we require this sense even when asleep, and when it receives a sound, we are aroused even from sleep. The auditory passage is winding, to prevent anything from being able to enter, as it might if the passage were clear and straight; it has further been provided that even the tiniest insect that may attempt to intrude may be caught in the sticky wax of the ears. On the outside project the organs which we call ears, which are constructed both to cover and protect the sense-organ and to prevent the sounds that reach them from sliding past and being lost before they strike the sense. The apertures of the ears are hard and gristly, and much convoluted, because things with these qualities reflect and amplify sound; this is why tortoise-shell or horn gives resonance to a lyre, and also why winding passages and enclosures have an echo which is louder than the original sound.[7]

Cicero concludes this discussion by remarking on how these senses excel those of the lower animals. With respect to hearing, he adds,

> The ears are likewise marvelously skillful organs of discrimination; they judge differences of tone, of pitch and of key in the music of the voice and of wind and stringed instruments, and many different qualities of voice, sonorous and dull, smooth and rough, bass and treble, flexible and hard, distinctions discriminated by the human ear alone.[8]

In another treatise, Cicero seems amazed, yet at a loss to explain, how we absorb such a wide range of information through our senses. He includes an interesting reference, in passing, to hearing,

> for instance, our ears convey to us a number of perceptions which, while consisting in sounds that give us pleasure, are nevertheless frequently so different from one another that you think the one you hear last the most agreeable.[9]

---

7 Cicero, *De Natura Deorum*, II, lvi, 140ff.

8 Ibid., lviii.

9 Cicero, *De Oratore*, III, vii.

From our perspective it seems odd that Cicero did not make the leap and realize it was the brain and not the ears which account for his observations. Similarly it seems that Pliny the Elder (23–79 AD) should have concluded that the changes were due to the acoustics of the room and not in the objects he mentions when he observed that the voice is absorbed by 'sawdust or sand that is thrown down on the floor of the theater orchestras, and similarly in a place surrounded by rough walls, and it is also deadened by empty casks.'[10]

Considering the fact that the Church created an environment of faith and not science, medieval comments dealing with acoustical matters often have an almost supernatural character. One of the aspects of the physical nature of music which most intrigued ancient philosophers was their observations relative to sympathetic vibrations between strings. A work by Agathias Scholasticus (536–594 AD) contributes a little weird science on the subject.

> Some one questioned the musician Androtion, skilled in what concerns the lyre, on a curious piece of instrumental lore. 'When you set the highest string on the right in motion with the plectrum, the lowest on the left quivers of its own accord with a slight twang, and is made to whisper reciprocally when its own highest string is struck; so that I marvel how nature made sympathetic to each other lifeless strings in a state of tension.' But he swore that Aristoxenus, with his admirable knowledge of plectra, did not know the theoretical explanation of this. 'The solution,' he said, 'is as follows. The strings are all made of sheep's gut dried all together. So they are sisters and sound together as if related, sharing each other's family voice. For they are all legitimate children, being the issue of one belly, and they inherit those reciprocal noises. Just so does the right eye, when injured, often convey its own pain to the left eye.'[11]

This same line of thinking resulted in an interesting observation by Albertus Magnus (1193–1280):

> The animosity between the wolf and sheep is so strong its influence extends to all of their anatomical parts; thus, musical strings made of sheep gut do not resonate in harmony with strings made of wolf gut.[12]

Several early commentators on sound refer to vibrations as 'broken air.' We find this, for example, in some observations by the early Renaissance composer and writer, Chaucer (1343–1400 AD), in his poem, 'The House of Fame.' Sound, he says, is nothing but broken air, thus all speech is nothing but air.[13] Similarly, when a player strikes the harp strings, whether hard or lightly, 'the air breaks apart with the stroke.' When a pipe is blown 'sharp' [strongly?], what we hear is the air 'twisted and rent with violence.' And, lastly, all sound tends to rise.

We have an interesting discussion on the perception of music by Erasmus (1466–1536), who, as was very much his nature in general, still thought of music as a branch of mathematics. In a discussion of the Greek proverb, 'Double diapason,' Erasmus gets carried away, admit-

---

[10] Pliny the Elder, *Natural History*, XI, cxii, 270.
[11] *The Greek Anthology*, trans. W. R. Paton (Cambridge: Harvard University Press, 1939), IV, 352.
[12] *De Animalibus*, trans. James Scanlan (Binghamton, NY: Medieval & Renaissance Texts, 1987), 158.
[13] 'The House of Fame,' II, 765ff.

ting 'I have rashly—and as it were forgetting myself—gone further into musical matters than the nature of the work undertaken required.' While he rarely writes of music in detail, these pages clearly reflect his knowledge of the old Church Scholastic mathematics-based theories of music, as well as the principal earlier treatises such as Boethius. Erasmus defines the common usage of this proverb to mean any two things very far apart. In the course of his musical discussion he seeks to make the principal point that the range of two octaves is a kind of natural furthermost limit, with respect to the ear hearing the mathematical proportions in music. Clearly concerned that he was sticking his neck out, he tells us that as he was writing, a famous philosopher, Ambrogio Leone of Nola, just happened to walk in and thus he attributes to this man the remainder of the discussion. Leone finds two reasons for calling the double octave the natural limit. First, he has observed that the [male] voice cannot reach beyond the fifteenth without becoming forced and artificial. The second argument is because Reason and the senses must work together. While Reason can comprehend numbers of any size, hence, for example, the possibility of a distance of a thousand octaves, the senses do not distinguish relationships beyond two octaves.

> But the physical senses have had their own limits prescribed for them by nature, and if they transgress these, they gradually become misty and wandering, and can no longer judge with certainty as they used to do, but through a cloud, as they say, or in a dream. It was not fitting that principles of art should be drawn from an uncertainty of judgment. But since the ancients understood that beyond the fifteenth note of the scale the judgment of the ears began to fail, they decided to fix the bounds of harmony there, so that no one could have any reason to bring up that adage of yours, 'unheard music is useless.'[14]

We suspect that it was this association with mathematics which caused Erasmus to think of music as being somewhat exclusive. In a series of objections to a treatise by Latomus, Erasmus adds, for example, that 'mathematics, metaphysics and music' are not needed by everyone, as for instance the baker and the tailor.[15]

Erasmus on two occasions seems to connect music with the divine. In one case Erasmus writes that he found in the works of Augustine a reference (which cannot be identified today) which mentions the Greek philosopher, Zeno, saying that the soul itself is a 'self-moving harmony, and for this reason can be caught up and carried away by harmonious things.' Erasmus adds a comment which seems to suggest a divinely implanted, or genetic, understanding of music.

> [This is its nature] just as children too are affected by the modes of music through some natural affinity, even when they have no idea what music is.[16]

---

[14] 'Adages,' in *The Collected Works of Erasmus* (Toronto: University of Toronto Press, 1992), XXXI, 202ff. Erasmus discusses the last phrase in a discussion of the proverb, 'Hidden music has no listeners [and is thus worthless].' [Ibid., XXXII, 117ff.]

[15] 'Apology Refuting Rumors and Suspicions ... by Latomus,' in Ibid., LXXI, 47.

[16] 'Adages,' in Ibid., XXXI, 167.

For us, one of the most interesting writers on music of seventeenth-century Italy was Athanasius Kircher (1601–1680), a German born scholar who spent most of his adult life in Rome. His greatest work was the *Musurgia Universalis* (Rome, 1650), a virtual encyclopedia of music. Book Nine he calls, 'The Magic of Consonance and Dissonance,' in which 'the secrets of all the science of music are brought into the light by countless experiments.' Indeed, we find here many curious and interesting things.

First, he is credited with being the person who originated the idea of playing music on drinking glasses, which was the result of his experimentation in observing the effects of the tones produced by glasses filled with wine, water, sea-water and oil, etc. This led him to acoustics in general, in the course of which he concluded that the biblical account of the fall of the walls of Jericho was not due to the sound of the trumpets, but some other physical cause.

Kircher also devotes considerable space in Book Nine to echoes, beginning with a lovely anecdote.

> A certain friend of mine having set out on a journey, had a river to cross, and not knowing the stream, cried out *Oh*, to which an echo answered *Oh*; he imagining it to be a man, called out in Italian, *Onde devo passar?* it answered *passa*; and when he asked *qui?* it replied *qui*; but as the waters formed a deep whirlpool there, and made a great noise, he was terrified, and again asked *Devo passar qui?* The echo returns *passa qui*. He repeated the same question often, and still had the same answer. Terrified with the fear of being obliged to swim in case he attempted to pass there, and it being a dark and tempestuous night, he concluded that his respondent was some evil spirit that wanted to entice him into the torrent.

In the course of this discussion, Kircher cites a building in Pavia which would return an echo thirty times.

Marin Mersenne (1588–1648) studied mathematics, physics, the classics and metaphysics at the Jesuit College of Le Mans and later at the college at La Fleche, where one of his classmates, and life-long friend, was René Descartes. After becoming a Jesuit priest, and a member of the Minorite friars, Mersenne began teaching Hebrew, philosophy and theology at the Sorbonne in Paris in 1619. His residence became a required stopping place for every intellectual visiting Paris.

His studies and experimentation in music resulted in his *Harmonie universelle* (1636), a work of encyclopedia proportion organized in five treatises: on the nature of sound, on mechanics, on the voice and singing, on theory and on instruments.

Mersenne includes among his general comments on instruments some discussion of the aesthetic qualities of the various families of instruments.[17] How does one establish which instruments have the most agreeable sound? This, says Mersenne, is a very difficult question and he finds professional musicians have a great diversity of opinion. For one thing, no one has heard all the instruments, especially those in foreign countries. Another reason has to do with the temperament of the observer.

---

[17] *Harmonie universelle*, V, i, 4.

The difference of temperaments which are found in men similarly causes the sound of some to seem more agreeable to that one than the others, so that these reasons ... can hinder the sincerity of the judgment.

Familiarity also affects the judgment, thus,

soldiers and those who have a warlike temperament and stirring blood find the sound of the trumpet more agreeable than that of the lute or the other instruments, and hunters are more fond of the sound the horn makes than of the others, because they are accustomed to hear it; for what is familiar to us often pleases us more.

Well, says Mersenne, these kinds of difficulties are found in all worldly things, but man must exercise his Reason and make judgments. Therefore he generalizes that the sound of the lute is most charming; the German flute is more agreeable than other flutes and that the violin is the most ravishing of the strings. More interesting to us are some of his comments which reflect on ensemble quality.

As to those which are produced by the wind, one can say in general that all the tones which are made by interrupted air alone are sweeter than the tone of the other wind instruments and any other which could be produced by the string, but they are not so agreeable as those which are made by the vibration of a reed, for although they seem rough, they have a natural gaiety which makes them preferable to the dismal and somber sweetness of the flute, although the gloomy sounds produce a concert of many parts more agreeable than that which is made of gayer tones.

Now in speaking of sounds more generally, we can say that the sweet ones are gloomy, choked and shut up, like those of the stopped flutes, and that the gay ones are more open, like those of the reeds and of flutes that the organ makers call in resonance. The tones are almost all the same provided that they are not so weak that the ear cannot perceive them or so violent that it would be offensive. What makes them more pleasant is the variety with which one embellishes them, either successively or simultaneously with other sounds.

In conclusion, Mersenne offers three additional aesthetic principles with regard to judging the various instruments. First, he concludes that variety is an important factor for the listener.

Choose whatever tone you wish and listen continually: it will put you to sleep or give you a headache. The tone of a flute, placed on a windchest, being continued is amazingly tiresome and displeasing, and that of a lute will be even more ... Then it is the variety that makes the tone agreeable; and if it is not varied, it deserves mostly to be called noise rather than harmonic sound.

Second, he concludes the judgment of individual instruments will depend in part on the 'temperament' of the listener.

If the sound of the flutes, among which can be placed the trumpet, has more power over the mind, it is because of the greater impression it makes in the air, or because of its particular quality. And actually in addition to that reason, experience shows that those who have a more delicate ear and more refined and subtle minds, are pleased more in the sounds of the string instruments. And those with grosser and heavier spirits take a greater pleasure in the sound of the trumpet and flutes, although this may not perhaps be so general that the contrary cannot occur.

Finally, Mersenne recognizes an analogy with color, with the single instrument being like a simple color such as black or white and a concert being like a colored painting. This, in turn, has a relationship with acoustics.

> Some [paintings] are made of such skill that they must be seen in the distance and the others close by, since the pictures which have the thickest colors which are cracked, as the painters say, who have much more skill, demand to be seen from the distance, are loved, cherished, and esteemed by the sons of Art. The others on the contrary, which are very much softened and finished, require to be viewed from very close, and are much esteemed by those who are nearsighted and who are unable to consider of what skill consists. In the same way, the music of the lutes is for those who do not wish to hear the music so much as the voice, and that of the viols is for those who by pushing farther away prefer to hear rather than to see. Now this resemblance will make us note in passing that the low tone, which approaches silence is comparable to black, and the higher to white.

Turning to the string instrument family, Mersenne finds the violin has the greatest 'effect on the passions and affections of the body and soul' of any string instrument, for reasons of 'the great tension of their strings and their high sounds.'

> Those who have heard the Twenty-four Violins of the King avow that they have never heard anything more ravishing or more powerful. Thus it comes that this instrument is the most proper of all for playing for dancing as is experienced in the ballet and everywhere else.[18]

Later, he observes,

> Now the violin has this above all the other instruments aside from the song of animals, both winged and terrestrial, that it imitates and counterfeits all sorts of instruments, such as the voice, the organ, the hurdy-gurdy, the bagpipe, the fife, etc., so that it can suggest the sadness, as the lute does, and can become animated like the trumpet.[19]

Above all, Mersenne seems to place a high aesthetic value on the string instruments in part because of the ease with which one can hear their overtones. While he could not offer the correct explanation of what the overtones were, physically,[20] he could find in them a metaphor for moral action.

---

[18] V, iv, 1, replacing the wind band of the sixteenth century. In IV, iv, he gives the instrumentation of the famous Twenty-four Violins of the King as 6 treble, 6 bass, 4 contratenors, 4 alto and 4 'of a fifth part.'

[19] IV, iv.

[20] Even though Mersenne understood the tones of the natural trumpet corresponded to the overtone principle, he did not understand that the sounds heard above a string tone were based on the same principle. His best guess: 'It is more probable that these different sounds come from the different movements of the exterior air.'

> If the tone of each string is more harmonious and agreeable as it makes a greater number of different tones heard in the same time, and if one may be permitted to compare moral actions to natural, and to translate Physics into human actions, one can say that each action is as much more agreeable and harmonious to God, as it is accompanied by a greater number of motives, provided that they all be good.[21]

Regarding the brass instrument family, Mersenne was most fascinated by the trumpet, in part by its range, which in his time exceeded even the organ!

> As to the range of the trumpet, it is marvelously great ... It surpasses all the keyboards of the spinets and organs.[22]

As Mersenne, above, suggests it was more pleasant to hear a viol consort from some distance, so Roger North, the great English critic of the Baroque, agrees with this acoustic principle when listening to contrapuntal music. This idea occurs to him as he is objecting to the difficulty the listener has in hearing fast, multi-part instrumental works such as fugues, or fugal allegros.

> Perhaps an ear placed in the middle of the performers may distinguish somewhat, but at a decent position, the sum is a musical din, and no better; and music, like pictures, ought to have a just distance, or else the parts it consists of, which in all entertainments ought to be perceptible, will blend as in a mist.[23]

The Reverend Joseph Hall (1574–1656), a bishop in the Church of England, writes in several places of the special solace on hearing music at night

> How sweetly doth this music sound in this dead season! In the daytime it would not, it could not so much affect the ear. All harmonious sounds are advanced by a silent darkness.

Hall finds a parallel in the glad tidings of salvation in the 'night of persecution of our private affliction.'[24] He expands on this idea in another work called 'Songs in the Night.'

> There is no time wherein [songs of praise] can be unseasonable: yea, rather, as all our artificial melody is wont to sound sweetest in the dark, so those songs are most pleasing to thee which we sing in the saddest night of our affliction ...
> The night is a dismal season, attended with solitude and horror, and an aggravation of those pains and cares whereof the day is in any sort guilty ... Songs in the night, are not, cannot be of nature's making, but are the sole gift of the heavenly Comforter.

---

[21] V, iv, 10.

[22] V, v, 11.

[23] Quoted in John Wilson, *Roger North on Music* (London: Novello, 1959), 189.

[24] 'Occasional Meditations,' in *The Works of Joseph Hall, D. D.*, ed. Philip Wynter (New York: AMS Press, 1969), X, 142.

> And if we, out of the strength of our moral powers, shall be setting songs to ourselves in the night of our utmost disconsolation, woe is me, how miserably out of tune they are! how harsh, how misaccented, how discordous even to the sense of our own souls, much more in the ears of the Almighty, in whom dwells nothing beneath an infinite perfection!
>
> But the songs that thou, O God, puttest into the mouths of thy servants in the night of their tribulation are so exquisitely harmonious, as that thine angels rejoice to hear them, and disdain not to match them with their hallelujahs in heaven.[25]

In still another treatise, Hall recommends for those who 'howl in the night of their affliction,' singing at night.[26] He mentions here again his contention that music sounds best in the night.

Francis Bacon (1561–1626) has been called, 'the greatest and proudest intellect of the age.'[27] His quest for knowledge through scientific experimentation finally caused his death when his attempt to forestall putrefaction in a fowl with ice led to a fever.

Bacon, son of a high government official, served in Parliament, was a successful lawyer and eventually held important government posts himself. But he was also prone to accepting bribes, participating in corruption and was eventually sent to prison in the Tower.

Unfortunately, much of Bacon's speculation on the nature of sound and music is based on a faulty understanding of the physics of sound, as, indeed, the conclusions of most early writers were. The most fundamental misunderstanding was with regard to the nature of sound itself. Bacon states 'The sound is not created between the bow and the string; but between the string and the air.' He believed the musical instrument set in motion something he called 'local motion,' and it was here the sound was created. His clearest explanation reads,

> It would be extreme grossness to think that the sound in strings is made or produced between the hand and the strings, or the quill and the string, or the bow and the string, for those are but *vehicula motus*, passages to the creation of the sound; the sound being produced between the string and the air; and that not by any impulsion of the air from the first motion of the string, by the return or result of the string, which was strained by the touch, to his former place; which motion of result is quick and sharp; whereas the first motion is soft and dull. So the bow tortures the string continually, and therefore holds it in a continual trepidation.[28]

From this Bacon was led to a number of curious conclusions. Since he regarded that the sound is created in the air immediately surrounding the instrument, it seemed to him that particular force was necessary to set this air in motion, as one could clearly see in wind players.

> For as for other wind instruments, they require a forcible breath; as trumpets, cornets, hunters' horns, etc., which appeareth by the blown cheeks of him that windeth them.[29]

---

[25] 'Souls in the Night,' in Ibid., VII, 326.

[26] 'The Breathings of the Devout Soul,' in Ibid., VIII, , 18ff.

[27] Will Durant, *The Age of Reason Begins* (New York: Simon and Schuster, 1961), 169, 183.

[28] *Natural History* in *The Works of Francis Bacon* (Cambridge: Cambridge University Press, 1869), V, Section 137.

[29] Ibid., Section 116.

He also misunderstood, in this regard, the physical action of the wind player and the resultant sound. All pipes, he says, have 'a blast, as well as a sound.' Even speech, he concluded, results from the 'expulsion of a little breath.'[30] This explosion of air which he associates with tone production leads him to observe,

> It hath been anciently reported, and is still received, that extreme applause and shouting of people assembled in great multitudes, have so rarefied and broken the air, that birds flying over have fallen down, the air being not able to support them.[31]

Since Bacon understood music to be created in the air, and not in the vibrations, he was at a loss to explain why vibrating tongs set in water seem to produce sounds under water where there is no air present.[32]

He also appears to have been somewhat mystified by the existence of echoes. If it were a real [corporeal] sound, then the echo would have to have been produced in a similar fashion as the original sound, that is by a violin string, a trumpet tone, etc. Since this is obviously not the case, Bacon took the echo to be 'a great argument for the spiritual essence of sounds.'[33]

Failing to understand the nature of vibrations led to a number of other curious conclusions. To his ear, the bass was generally stronger than the treble. From this perception he makes this conclusion.

> In harmony, if there be not a discord to the bass, it doth not disturb the harmony though there be a discord to the higher parts … And the cause is, for that the bass striking more air, doth overcome and drown the treble (unless the discord be very odious); and so hideth a small imperfection.[34]

Similarly, he adds, but cannot explain, that stopping high on a string not only produces a high pitch, but a dull sound.[35] His failure to understand vibrations leads him to strange explanations for dynamics.

> The loudness and softness of sounds is a thing distinct from the magnitude and exility of sounds; for a bass string, though softly struck, gives the greater sound; but a treble string, if hard struck, will be heard much further off. And the cause is, for that the bass string strikes more air; and the treble less air, but with a sharper percussion.[36]

On the subject of acoustics, Bacon finds the explanation in everything except the materials of the instruments themselves.

---

[30] Ibid., Section 125.
[31] Ibid., Section 127.
[32] Ibid., Section 133.
[33] Ibid., Section 287.
[34] Ibid., Section 109.
[35] Ibid., Section 156.
[36] Ibid., Section 163.

> All instruments that have either returns, as trumpets; or flexions, as cornets; or are drawn up and put from, as sackbuts; have a purling sound: but the recorder or flute, that have none of these inequalities, give a clear sound. Nevertheless, the recorder itself, or pipe, moistened a little in the inside, sounds more solemnly, and with a little purling or hissing.[37]

Bacon touches on acoustics again in his fictional, *New Atlantis*. Among his descriptions of various civic buildings in this utopian town it is rather extraordinary to find his call for a kind of experimental acoustic studio.

> We have also sound-houses, where we practice and demonstrate all sounds and their generation. We have harmony which you have not, of quarter-sounds and lesser slides of sounds. Diverse instruments of music likewise to you unknown, some sweeter than any you have; with bells and rings that are dainty and sweet. We represent small sounds as great and deep, likewise great sounds extenuate and sharp; we make diverse tremblings and warblings of sounds, which in their original are entire. We represent and imitate all articulate sounds and letters, and the voices and notes of beasts and birds. We have certain helps which, set to the ear, do further the hearing greatly; we have also diverse strange and artificial echoes, reflecting the voice many times, and, as it were, tossing it; and some that give back the voice louder than it came, some shriller and some deeper, yea some rendering the voice, differing in the letters or articulate sound from that they receive. We have all means to convey sounds in trunks and pipes, in strange lines and distances.[38]

In an attempt to explain what aesthetic principles result in the 'pleasing' quality in music, Bacon looked for correspondence with the sense of sight. In his *Natural History*, the element of 'pleasing' in sight, he found, is in that which has equality, good proportion or correspondence and these he considered identical with music. In addition, he clearly prefers the use of vibrato.

> The division and quavering, which please so much in music, have an agreement with the glittering of light; as the moon-beams playing upon a wave.[39]

Bacon also mentions some problems in acoustics. First, he notes that the eye sees a vast panorama of objects, keeping them all separate, whereas this is not pleasing with respect to sound.

> The sweetest and best harmony is, when every part or instrument is not heard by itself, but a conflation of them all; which requires one to stand some distance off.[40]

Bacon also observes that 'some consorts of instruments are sweeter than others,' but this is, he says, 'a thing not sufficiently yet observed.'[41]

---

37 Ibid., Section 170.

38 *New Atlantis*, in *The Works of Francis Bacon*, V, 407.

39 *Natural History*, Section III, 113.

40 Ibid., Section 224ff.

41 Ibid., Section 278.

Next Bacon offers a variety of observations regarding the most pleasing sounds obtainable from various instruments. A pipe, he maintains, if moist inside, but without actual drops of water, sounds 'a more solemn sweet' than if dry.[42] Music sounds better indoors during frosty weather. If one sings into the hole of a drum, it makes the singing sweeter.

> And so I conceive it would, if it were a song in parts, sung into several drums; and for the handsomeness and strangeness sake, it would not be amiss to have a curtain between the place where the drums are and the listeners.

Bacon observes that sounds are better if one's mind is concentrated on only one sense, hearing. Therefore he suggests that music sounds better at night than during the day.[43] We would guess that this is the reason why, even today, we still listen to classical music in the dark.

Bacon made several brief references to the 'music of the spheres' and in a catalog of projected histories, he includes a 'History of Sounds in the upper region (if there be any).'[44]

John Locke (1632–1704) studied ancient languages, rhetoric, logic and ethics at Oxford and eventually earned a degree in medicine. He held various government positions of largely clerical nature. This experience produced a philosopher who seemed only aware of the faculties of the left hemisphere of the brain. He wrote very little on the emotions, the individual senses or any of the arts. When discussing time, for example, unlike previous philosophers, music is never mentioned.

When Locke considers perception, it pertains to the information of one of the senses and it is inseparable from the mind's concentration on that sense. While Locke not only knew nothing of the specific functions of the separate hemispheres of the brain, and was in addition the epitome of the left-brain man, it is interesting that he had observed that when one is 'intently employed' on some idea and there is music playing, one does not hear it.

> A sufficient impulse there may be on the organ; but if not reaching the observation of the mind, there follows no perception; and though the motion that uses to produce the idea of sound be made in the ear, yet no sound is heard.[45]

In this discussion of the senses, Locke contends that God purposely gave man limited ability in his senses.[46] By way of illustration he proposes that if our sense of hearing were a thousand times stronger we would be distracted by perpetual noise.

---

[42] Ibid., Section 230ff. In his 'Physiological Remains,' however, Bacon says of bells,

> It is probable that it is the dryness of the metal that helps the clearness of the sound, and the moistness that dulls it. [Ibid., VII, 389]

[43] Bacon also mentions in passing [Ibid., Section 241] the subject of 'counterfeiting the distance of voices.' But he sees no purpose for this, other than for 'imposture, in counterfeiting ghosts or spirits.'

[44] 'Catalog of Particular Histories,' in Ibid., VIII, 374.

[45] 'Essay on Human Understanding,' in *The Works of John Locke* (London, 1823; reprinted in Aalen: Scientia Verlag, 1963, II, ix, 4.

[46] Ibid., II, xxiii, 12.

> We should in the quietest retirement be less able to sleep or meditate, than in the middle of a sea-fight.

He was, however, one of the first philosophers who understood correctly the physics of sound.

> That which is conveyed into the brain by the ear is called sound; though, in truth, till it come to reach and affect the perceptive part, it be nothing by motion.
> The motion, which produces in us the perception of sound, is a vibration of the air, caused by an exceeding short, but quick, tremulous motion of the body from which it is propagated; and therefore we consider and denominate them as bodies sounding.
> That sound is the effect of such a short, brisk, vibrating motion of bodies form which it is propagated, may be known from what is observed and felt in the strings of instruments ... as long as we perceive any sound come from them; for as soon as that vibration is stopped, or ceases in them, the perception ceases also.[47]

Isaac Newton (1642–1727) was, without any doubt, the greatest mind ever born to England. He was truly a natural scientist, interested in everything which passed his eye. While all the world knows of his immense contributions to optics and gravitation, one is staggered at the thought of the time he spent on less productive efforts. The rough estimate based on one sale catalog, the Portsmouth Collection, Cambridge, indicates a million and a half words on theology and chronology; half a million on alchemy and one hundred and fifty thousand words on problems of coinage and the Mint. And he also wrote on mathematics, chemistry, astronomy and of course philosophy. It is comforting to read he was a poor student in school.

One of Newton's great contributions to science, and to optics in particular, was his paper of 1672, 'New Theory about Light and Colors.' Always hesitant to publish, this paper formulated his discovery in 1666 that sunlight is not a simple white, but a compound of red, orange, yellow, green, blue, indigo and violet, which emerge when light is passed through a prism. Always, by his own nature, looking for fundamental laws, Newton was at the same time obsessed with finding a correspondence between the rays of light and the vibrations of sound. His earliest extant, and most complete, discussion of this is found in a letter of 7 December 1675, to Henry Oldenburg, secretary of the Royal Society.[48]

> Thus much of refraction, reflection, transparency & opacity. And now to explain colors; I suppose, that as bodies of various sizes, densities, or tensions, do by percussion or other action excite sounds of various tones & consequently vibrations in the Air of various bigness so when the rays of light, by impinging on the stiff refracting superficies excite vibrations in the aether, those rays, whatever they be, as they happen to differ in magnitude, strength or vigor, excite vibrations of various bigness; the biggest, strongest or most potent rays, the largest vibrations & others shorter, according to their bigness strength or power.

---

47 'Elements of Natural Philosophy,' in *The Works of Locke*, III, 325ff.

48 *The Correspondence of Isaac Newton* (Cambridge: University Press, 1959–), I, 376ff.

After an explanation of the physical process of the eye, Newton continues,

> and there I suppose, affect the sense with various colors, reds & yellows; the least with the weakest, blues & violets; the middle with green, and a confusion of all, with white, much after the manner, that in the sense of hearing Nature makes use of aerial vibrations of several bignesses to generate sounds of diverse tones, for the analogy of Nature is to be observed. And further, as the harmony & discord of sounds proceed from the proportions of the aereall vibrations; so may the harmony of some colors, as of a golden & blue, & the discord of others, as of red & blue proceed from the proportions of the aethereall. And possible color may be distinguished into its principal degrees, red, orange, yellow, green, blue, indigo, and deep violet, on the same ground, that sound within an eighth is graduated into tones.

With this letter, Newton enclosed a graph,[49] showing the correlation of the basic colors with their relative notes of music. Regrettably, although he discusses in detail the relationships of the colors relative to this graph, he does not offer here a precise description of their correspondence to music. Nevertheless, Newton remained interested in this topic and he discusses it again in the publication of his *Opticks* in 1704.[50] Whatever was Newton's private understanding on this subject remains in some doubt. To his correspondents who wanted more information, he would sometimes apologize that with regard to music, 'I have not so much skill in that science as to understand it well.'[51]

This seems such a reasonable idea, that there should be some correspondence between the vibrations of light waves and the vibrations of sound, but as yet none has been established. The reader will perhaps recall that Schumann once observed, in a letter to Clara Wieck of 23 May 1833, that 'sound, after all, is only sounding light.'

From his studies of optics, Newton had made important discoveries relative to light waves, establishing their speed and that they moved in straight lines. We may assume that he was at least casually thinking of the correspondence of these laws with musical sound waves as well, or so a letter to John North in 1677 suggests.[52] North had sent Newton a new treatise on music by his elder brother, Francis, for review and Newton makes extensive corrections regarding the nature and direction of sound waves, as well as on the relationships between vibrating strings. At length, Newton evidently tired and signed off.

> The discourse also about breaking of tones into higher notes seems very ingenious and judicious, but I lack experience to discern whether altogether solid, & much follows about Tunes, the scale of Music, & consorts; this requiring a combination of musical & mathematical skill, & therefore I shall content myself with having thus far animadverted upon the author.

---

49 Reproduced in Ibid., I, 377.

50 See *Opticks*, Book I, Part ii, Prop. 3 and in Book II, Part i, Ops. 14, and in Part iii, Prop. 16. Newton refers to the correspondence between music and light waves again in a letter to Dr. William Briggs in April, 1685. [Ibid., II, 418].

51 Letter, February 1676, to Oldenburg regarding a 'Mr. Berchhenshaw's scale of Musick,' in Ibid., I, 420.

52 Ibid., II, 205ff.

A letter to Oldenburg in June 1672 is concerned with Newton's answering objections by Robert Hooke to some of his theories. One sentence is of particular interest, as it demonstrates that Newton correctly understood that music is in the vibrations, not in the instrument—a topic still much under discussion by some writers.

> But when Mr. Hooke would insinuate a difficulty in these things by alluding to sounds in the *string* of a musical instrument before percussion, or in the *Air* of an *Organ bellows* before its arrival at the pipes, I must confess I understand it as little as if he had spoken of light in a piece of wood before it be set on fire.[53]

George Berkeley (1685–1753), Ireland's contribution to philosophy of this period, became absorbed with the writings of Locke at an early age. He appears to us to have become obsessed with the growing emphasis on materialism, which as a facet of the Enlightenment distracted man's thoughts from God. His answer was *Of the Principles of Human Knowledge* which argued that no matter exists apart from its perception in the mind. Contemporaries found this concept difficult to challenge, although in a famous anecdote Samuel Johnson, discussing this with Boswell, kicked a large stone and said, 'I refute it thus!'

Berkeley in his famous *Of the Principles of Human Knowledge* does not bother to argue here whether mind is different from spirit, soul, or oneself. However one regards the essence of mind, he concludes, what exists there is *all* that exists.

> Neither our thoughts, nor passions, nor ideas formed by the imagination, exist without the mind, is what everybody will admit. And it seems no less evident that the various sensations or ideas imprinted on the sense, however blended or combined together (that is, whatever objects they compose) cannot exist otherwise than in a mind perceiving them.[54]

His real point can be made clear by considering what he writes in another place about sound.[55] Sound, he correctly maintains, is simply vibrations in the air. When we call it 'sound,' we are really referring to our sense of hearing. In other words, to use an old riddle, Berkeley would say of a tree falling in the woods where there was no one to hear, that it would produce vibrations in the air, but no sound.

> PHILONOUS. Can any sensation exist without the mind?
> HYLAS. No certainly.
> PHILONOUS. How then can sound, being a sensation exist in the air, if by the *air* you mean a senseless substance existing without the mind?
> HYLAS. You must distinguish, Philonous, between sound as it is perceived by us, and as it is in itself; or (which is the same thing) between the sound we immediately perceive, and that which exists without us. The former indeed is a particular kind of sensation, but the latter is merely a vibrative or undulatory motion in the air.

---

53 Ibid., I, 177.

54 *Of the Principles of Human Knowledge*, in *The Works of George Berkeley, Bishop of Cloyne*, ed. A. Luce (London: Nelson, 1964), II, 42.

55 'First Dialogue between Hylas and Philonous,' in Ibid., II, 181ff.

In conclusion, there are a few observations on acoustics by the great composers which are little known and are worthy of mention. First, the great Bohemian composer, and friend of Beethoven, Anton Reicha composed in 1815 a symphony for three military bands. In the autograph score he has left four pages of performance instructions in his own hand. After warning to be sure you have a good conductor, he makes two interesting comments on acoustics:

> The place selected for the performance must be large and open (uncovered) and that the orchestra must be a distance of 50 steps from the audience …
> The musicians must not be too close to each other, so that the sound gets more widely spread.

This last observation is extremely important for wind instrument players. String instruments, with their sympathetic vibrating wooden boxes, seemingly can almost sit on each other's lap without ill effect on the ensemble sound. On the other hand, each wind instrument has a unique and differing envelope of space around the player where the sound must form before leaving toward the audience. If the players are sitting or standing too close, their bodies and clothing absorb overtones, especially lower ones, and result in an inferior sound. It seems likely that Berlioz heard this problem discussed when he studied with Reicha in Paris, for in a discussion of outdoor acoustics he writes,

> the musicians were all placed horizontally in the arena, and in quite close ranks, stifling amongst themselves the sounds, and one knows that there are no mutes comparable to sand, to clothing, and to human bodies.[56]

In general Berlioz was opposed to the performance of music out-of-doors. Of his many references to this, perhaps the most thoughtful is found in one of his newspapers articles.

> There is no music possible out doors, for a thousand and one reasons, the least of which would be that one cannot hear. No, one cannot hear! One can hear neither details nor nuances, not even a single clean, vibrant chord. There, harmony lacks force and power, the melody is without expression, without vital warmth; every poetic idea is inaudible, or becomes a ridiculous non-essential.
> Doubtless, people have not forgotten the famous monster concert of the July holidays, where three hundred voices and two hundred fifty wind instruments, backed up to the Tuileries, produced such a miserable result.
> The example of military music that resounds with brilliance in the streets proves nothing against what I maintain: far from it, I would cite it, rather, in defense of my opinion. The streets are bordered right and left by houses that serve as amplifiers, one cannot therefore consider what one hears there as open air music. And the proof is that the higher the houses, the greater the echo of the sounds emitted in the street, and if the leading regiment, at the head of which march the musicians, comes along, leaving a street, and entering a plain bare of trees and buildings, the music loses its color instantly, or to put it better, there is no longer any music.

---

[56] 'Military Festival,' *Journal des Debats*, July 29, 1846. Franz Liszt, refers to this problem in a letter of August 10, 1862, to Franz Brendel, when he cautions the conductor to spread the orchestra out as far as possible and not submit to the usual 'limited space.'

> Moreover, as popular concerts always take place in the summer, the heat of the atmosphere is still a real obstacle to musical effect. The rarification of the air by the heat deprives it of as much sonority as its condensation by a dry cold gives to it.[57]

There was one occasion when Berlioz heard music in the out-of-doors and was moved. The reader may recall Chaucer's very accurate observation, above, that sounds rise. It was this effect which Berlioz heard from the hills near Baden.

> I stayed there with no thoughts, listening to the Hymn of the Austrian Emperor, played at some great distance in the Kiosque of the Conversation [Hall], by a Prussian military band, and which the wind brought me from the depths of the valley. Oh, but that melody of the good Haydn is touching! How one feels a sort of religious affection! It is truly the song of a people who love their king ... Of course Haydn was a good man, and not an ordinary man. The proof of this is that he had an insufferable wife and he never beat her ...
> But, we had to return, night having fallen ... I went back via the pine forest full of sounds—and a better sound than most of our concert halls. String quartets could play here ... But when one has the inclination to listen to music in the forest, it always follows a lunch of pate and one only hears fanfares of French horns, hunting horns, waking only the ideas of dogs, thieves and wine merchants.[58]

The most extensive discussion of indoor acoustics is one in which he focuses on the resultant sound of various percussion instruments according to where in the pit they are placed. In particular he was interested in his ability to hear specific pitches in the timpani, as well as the large bass drum which had recently been introduced into the opera orchestra by Rossini.

> Before him, on the rare occasions when the bass drum had been employed, it had not dared to sound except from the depths of a hallway; it had not yet acquired its civil rights.[59]

Only in the hall of the Conservatoire, where the timpani were placed against the curved, rear wall, did Berlioz find 'the softest notes travel to the furthermost points in the hall.' In normal circumstances, Berlioz found that so little attention was given to acoustics that,

> often negligent timpanists dispense with changing the pitch, and play boldly in a piece written in F with timpani tuned in E minor, without anyone being aware of it.

---

57 *Journal des Debats*, July 21, 1835. Berlioz discusses outdoor acoustic problems again in this paper in the issue of Sept. 3, 1845, and in his *Treatise on Instrumentation*.

58 *Journal des Debats*, Sept. 12, 1861.

59 *Journal des Debats*, July 21, 1835. We once made a professional recording in Europe where the timpani were placed in a different room from the orchestra!

There are several extant letters by Mendelssohn which discuss the acoustics in St. Peter's Cathedral in Rome. He found the Papal Choir rather poor, but that their repertoire of polyphonic music sounded rather well, even with additional dissonances resulting from the echoes of the building ('but they had better not sing Bach!').[60] He was, however, quite taken by the effect of the music floating around this vast empty structure.

> The sounds are reflected from above and from every corner, they mingle, die away, and produce the most wonderful music. One chord melts into the other, and what no musician would dare, St. Peter's Church achieves.[61]

---

[60] Letter to Carl Zelter, Dec. 1, 1830.

[61] Letter to Carl Zelter, Dec. 18, 1830.

Early Experience with the 'Pyramid Principle'

As in musical concords, when the upper strings are so tuned as exactly to accord, the base always gives the tone; so in well-regulated and well-ordered families, all things are carried on with the harmonious consent and agreement of both parties, but the conduct and contrivance chiefly redounds to the reputation and management of the husband.[1]

Plutarch (46–127 AD)

BY THE TIME PLUTARCH, a great early philosopher and historian, wrote the lines above, the relationships of at least the lower portion of the overtone series had been understood for about five centuries. The analogy between marriage and harmony by Plutarch, therefore, is one in which the lowest, fundamental pitch governs music as should the husband govern the family. We must also point out the significance of Plutarch's reference here to at least three lines of music. There are no surviving examples of multi-part music from this date and music history texts pretend everything was one-line music until ninth-century organum. Nevertheless there are a number of references in Greek literature to music in more than one part and here Plutarch also implies experience in hearing multi-parts.

But there is another basic principle he may well have been thinking of,[2] which relates to how we hear music. This is not a natural principle precisely, but one resulting through adaptation. In the case of music which lies approximately in the octave above third-space C in the treble clef, our brain seems to alter what we hear by making these tones seem to us louder then they really are. This is almost surely a result of adaptation, the purpose being to make more distinct the higher pitched sounds of consonants used in ordinary speech.

We don't read about this phenomenon until the Renaissance, but then immediately one notices that conductors have learned how to overcome this phenomenon. We call this technique by a name given it in the nineteenth century, the 'pyramid principle.' In practical terms it means ensemble music, both vocal and instrumental, must be artificially balanced by making the lowest tones louder and the highest tones softer. If done carefully the result is that what the listener hears corresponds with what the composer wrote on paper. In a word, we fool the brain of the listener into thinking they hear what the composer wrote.

Marchetto of Padua, a singer and choirmaster at the cathedral of Padua during the first decade of the fourteenth century is a case in point. In an aesthetic discussion of what we hear in music, during which he speaks of consonance and dissonance, calling the first 'amicable' and

---

[1] 'Of the Procreation of the Soul.'

[2] Plutarch does not provide quite enough information to know.

the second 'hateful,'[3] he mentions the pyramid principle. In working with church choirs he found that by pyramiding octaves he could achieve the impression of a a single tone with the upper octave being an overtone of the fundamental.

> If one [the lower pitch] is sung by men, the other by boys, they present to the ear one and the same pitch, as it were.[4]

The next reference to the pyramid principle is found in an important early treatise on singing, the *De modo bene cantandi* (1474) by Conrad von Zabern, who was associated with Heidelberg University. The following discussion by Conrad, on the subject of singing too loud in the upper register, is a clear discussion of the problem and its correct accommodation.

> Another fault which is more obvious than the others is singing high notes with an unstintingly full and powerful voice. This is even more careless than what we have cited above, as will soon become evident. When this shouting is done by individuals with resonant and trumpet-like voices it disturbs and confuses the singing of the entire choir, just as if the voices of cattle were heard among the singers. In a certain eminent collegiate establishment I once heard singers with these trumpet-like voices singing with all their strength in the highest register as if they wished to break the windows of the choir, or at least to shake them. As I marveled not a little at their coarseness, I was moved to make up this rhyme:
>
> *In choir you bellow*
> *Like cows in the meadow!*
>
> I use this jingle in an informal fashion in my efforts and teaching regarding the art of good singing in order to ridicule all those presuming to sing loudly in the high register, to the end that they might recognize their careless crudeness and, after recognizing, zealously desist from it.
> In order to recognize this error completely it must be realized that whoever wishes to sing well and clearly must employ his voice in three ways: resonantly and trumpet-like for low notes, moderately in the middle range and more delicately for the high notes—the more so the higher the chant ascends.

Desiderius Erasmus (1469–1536) was the greatest humanist, scholar and writer of prose of the sixteenth century. He was born near Rotterdam and left an orphan while still a teenager. The executor of his parents estate, in order obtain everything for himself, gave Erasmus over to a monastic career. While he became a very important philosopher, his lack of personal experience in music unfortunately resulted in relatively little important discussion on this subject. Perhaps based on his own observations in the realm of speech, he provides an interesting application for solving the discrepancy in how we hear high versus lower pitches. He suggests that the solution may be achieved through playing *longer* tones in the bass. But, of course, in ensemble performance usually it is difficult to have various parts singing or playing differ-

---

3   Marchetto of Padua, *Lucidarium*, trans. Jan W. Herlinger (Chicago: University of Chicago Press, 1985), treatise 5, I, 1, xi.
4   Ibid., treatise 6, I, 4, xxv.

ing lengths of the same rhythmic symbol, although it is a useful technique when applied to cadences, as we will see in a comment of Praetorius, below. Nevertheless, we find interesting the natural examples he supplies to illustrate this phenomenon.

> BEAR. Some people are so insensitive that they cannot distinguish accent from quantity, even though they are altogether different things. Striking a high note is not the same as holding a note, nor is stressing a sound the same as prolonging it …
>> Yet anyone with a smattering of music can distinguish without any trouble the difference between long and short on the one hand and high and low on the other. And after all speaking is just an articulated sequence of vocal sound. Metrical principles exist in prose as well as in verse, even though the rules are less restrictive and definite. But if they are disregarded speech will no more be speech than singing would be singing if high and low, long and short, were indiscriminately muddled up. The accent can justifiably be called, as it was by some ancient grammarians, the soul of the word … I think you play the guitar?
> LION. After a fashion.
> BEAR. Do you not often find yourself making a low note long or a high note short as well as the other way round?
> LION. Yes. Though the contrast is still more marked with wind instruments.
> BEAR. So why should we be so crude and unmusical when we talk, making every syllable that is accented high long and all the others short? Even donkeys could have taught us better. When they bray they take longer over the low note than over the high one.
> LION. The cuckoo does much the same.[5]

Is there something to what Erasmus says? Maybe so. Think of saying two words: 'Well, no.' If you utter and lengthen the word, 'Well' on a lower pitch, followed by uttering 'No' as a short syllable on a higher pitch, the communication is one of the nature of 'Of course the answer is No.' But, on the other hand, if you utter and lengthen the word 'Well' on a higher pitch followed by a brief 'No' on a lower pitch, the communication is different. Now the speaker implies a certain thought process before deciding 'No.' The psychological implications of this, say in the construction of melody, may well be worth further thought.

With the arrival of the sixteenth century the technology of instrument manufacture finally is able to produce true bass instruments. This in turn results in the consort principle which became so popular in that century. Having now four-part instrumental music, with a true bass, the problem of hearing too much from the upper voices became acute and there was correspondingly more attention given to the pyramid principle.

Heinrich Glarean (1488–1563) of Switzerland was a mathematician; noted singer[6] and an author who had the unfortunate timing of writing the best book, *Dodecachordon* (1547), on the church modes at the moment everyone was moving away from them. In the fictitious, satirical 'Letters of Obscure Men,' of 1515, by Crotus Rubeanus and Ulrich von Hutten, Glarean is described as,

---

5 'The Right Way of Speaking Latin and Greek,' [1528] in *The Collected Works of Erasmus* (Toronto: University of Toronto Press, 1992), XXVI, 422ff.

6 Maximilian I made him 'poet laureate' after hearing him sing.

a very headstrong man ... A terrible man, a choleric, for ever threatening fights—and he must be possessed of a devil.[7]

In any case, Glarean understood the aesthetic problem in hearing the upper voices out of proportion to the other voices and he knew the correct solution:

> There is no song more pleasing than one in which the lowest voice resounds strongly, even if the highest voice caresses the ear more sweetly; for all the upper voices turn completely into chattering if they are deprived of the strength of the lowest voice.[8]

The single book which provides the most important insights into what sixteenth-century music was *really* like, that is to say its breadth in media, styles and practice, has never to this date, so far as we know, been published[9] in any modern language, much less English. Music historians have long been interested in, and have translated and published in modern editions, the first two volumes of Michael Praetorius' *Syntagma Musicum*, which deal basically with theory and physical descriptions of instruments, but not the third volume, which deals with performance practice.

Although he published his book in 1619, it is a description of late Renaissance style and not Baroque, for it is clear that Praetorius, in 1619, could see no evidence of what we call the Baroque on the horizon. In the preface to Volume III, he writes,

> I have included the most important facts a music director and practical musicians will need to know, especially at this time when music has reached such a high level that any further advance would seem inconceivable.[10]

In several places, especially relative to the bass line in consorts, Praetorius emphasizes the importance of the listener hearing the lowest voice. It is, however, in a discussion of cadences[11] that we find his most interesting comment. Moreover, he switches his text from German into Latin for this discussion, making us wonder if he intended this as exclusive information only for those music directors who were formally educated. He recommends a kind of third dimension application of the pyramid principle, whereby instead of the ensemble ending together, the lowest voice extends *beyond* the point where everyone else stops.

---

[7] Letter of 'Demetrius Phalerius to Ortwin Gratius,' in Francis Stokes, trans., *On the Eve of the Reformation* (New York: Harper & Row, 1909), 183.

[8] Glarean, *Dodecachordon*, trans. Clement Miller (American Institute of Musicology, 1965), I, 122.

[9] We hasten to add that this volume has been translated into English by Hans Lampl, as part of a doctoral program at the University of Southern California some thirty years ago, and a copy may be found in their music library. However, at the time we first wanted to examine this translation, this institution would neither provide xerox copies, microfilm, permit the work to circulate through interlibrary loan, nor did they participate in the Ann Arbor Dissertation collection. We are grateful to Dr. Lampl for the donation of a copy of an early draft for our use. Since this chapter was first written we have heard rumors that Volume III has finally been published, but we have not had the opportunity to study its translation.

[10] A facsimile of the original German publication has been printed by Bärenreiter Kassel, 1958. The page numbers we cite, therefore, are from the original print, in this case from the preface pages, which are unnumbered.

[11] Ibid., 80.

> As a piece is brought to a close, all the remaining voices should stop simultaneously at the sign of the conductor or choir master. The tenors should not prolong their tone, a fifth above the bass or lowest voice … after the bass has stopped. But if the bass continues to sound a little longer, for another two or four *tactus*, it lends charm and beauty to the music [*Cantilenae*], which no one can deny.

This, in fact, is a very important principle of performance. When an ensemble, either vocal or instrumental, ends precisely, abruptly together the ear of the listener will hear, above the highest voice, a small acoustic 'tag.' This phenomenon does not actually exist, that is you cannot see it on an oscilloscope. It exists only in the brain of the listener and represents an attempt by the brain to hang on to the upper partials, another aspect of the brain preferring to hear the upper voices. Experienced conductors eliminate this by staggered exits of the various parts, with the lowest voice being the last to be heard. Nevertheless, one cannot quite imagine having the lowest voice last four beats longer than the rest of the ensemble, as Praetorius recommends, although in a vast empty cathedral it might in fact be quite effective.

Another application of the pyramid principle is for tuning an ensemble. Everyone can generally easily tune, in a tutti, to the lowest voice, for the ear is genetically adapted to hearing according to the parameters of the overtone series. On the other hand, two instrumentalists, such as a flute and an oboe, tuning to the *same* pitch will find it very difficult to tune, even if they are professionals.[12] It is in this context that Benedetto Marcello (b. 1686) writes that 'the double basses must be used for tuning.'[13]

Marin Mersenne (1588–1648) studied mathematics, physics, the classics and metaphysics at the Jesuit College of Le Mans and later at the college at La Fleche, where one of his classmates, and life-long friend, was René Descartes. Meresenne's studies and experimentation in music resulted in his *Harmonie universelle* (1636), a work of encyclopedia proportion organized in five treatises. Mersenne considers the perception of pitch in terms of high and low and finds that it is the highest voice which is most prominently perceived. For this he finds a 'natural' example in the peasant.

> Experience shows us that nature without artistry does not ordinarily use a bass at all, for peasants and shepherds sing only the treble or the tenor whenever they sing.[14]

Given his conclusion that this is a natural phenomenon, that is to say Nature created this aesthetic state, he labors to explain why it must be most pleasing to hear music in which the upper voices predominate. He does conclude, however, by noting that there is a role which the lowest note plays in making the result a pleasurable one for the listener.

---

[12] Due to the confusion in one's concentration caused by the relative strength and weakness of the overtones in the dissimilar instruments.

[13] Benedetto Marcello, *Il treatro alla moda*, quoted in Oliver Strunk, *Source Readings in Music History* (New York: Norton, 1950), 530.

[14] *Harmonie universelle*, IV, iv, 3.

> We experience that the trebles in concerts, as much vocal as instrumental, awaken the attention best and are very much more agreeable, as if approaching more nearly to heaven and life, than the basses. Now we take more pleasure in drawing to us those who are more perfect and more full of life than those who are more imperfect and nearer to death. Thus it happens that we love and caress infants more than old people who are like great and weighty sounds and like winter, just as children are like spring and summer and heat or fire. Bass voices are like gloom, sought after only by owls and goblins; but high voices are like light and day, serving as ornaments to nature as high sounds do to music which loses all her charm when she does not have good trebles. Bass voices serve almost as nothing more than to make the high sounds perceptible, and to make them enter the ear and the mind with more diversity and pleasure.[15]

Moreover, he warns that hearing those piercing upper partials during a long concert can be very fatiguing.

> Although the high may be more agreeable, nevertheless the intensity and the work necessary to produce this voice withdraws and diminishes the pleasures of the ear, for when the pleasure does not surpass the pain, it cannot be great.

René Descartes (1596–1650) also appears to have been aware of the necessary pyramid restructuring necessary to overcome the brain's tendency to hear the highest voices as the most important. In a comment regarding the bass voice he writes, 'it must strike the ear more forcibly in order to be heard distinctly.'[16]

With the movement toward the more homophonic style of music of the coming Classical Period, there followed a new interest in the quality of ensemble sound. In particular, one frequently reads of the necessity for hearing the lower voices, to balance the ear's natural tendency to focus on the highest part. A typical comment is found in the writings of the great English theorist, Thomas Mace.

> You may add to your press a pair of violins, to be in readiness for any extraordinary jolly or jocund consort occasion; but never use them but with this proviso, viz., be sure you make an equal provision for them, by the addition and strength of basses, so that they may not out-cry the rest of the musick, the basses especially; to which end it will be requisite you store your press with a pair of lusty, full-sized Theorboes, always to strike in with your consorts or vocal musick, to which that instrument is most naturally proper.[17]

Even the grim old Puritan, John Bunyan, in his *Pilgrim's Progress*, includes a passage which discusses the importance of the lowest voice. The reader will note as well his passing reference to musicians tuning to the lowest voice. After a characterization of the music of the trombone consort as 'doleful,' a description found in other literature of the sixteenth and seventeenth centuries in England, Bunyan speaks through the character, Great-heart.

---

[15] III, i,17.

[16] 'Compendium of Music,' trans. Walter Robert (American Institute of Musicology, 1961), 48.

[17] Quoted in John Hawkins, *A General History of the Science and Practice of Music* [1776] (New York: Dover Reprint, 1963), II, 732.

The wise God will have it so; some must pipe, and some must weep. Now Mr. Fearing was one that played upon his bass; he and his fellows sound the sackbut, whose notes are more doleful[18] than the notes of other music are; though, indeed, some say the bass is the ground of music. And, for my part, I care not at all for that profession that begins not in heaviness of mind. The first string that the musician usually touches is the bass, when he intends to put all in tune. God also plays upon this string first, when he sets the soul in tune for himself. Only here was the imperfection of Mr. Fearing, he could play upon no other music but this, till towards his latter end.

I make bold to talk thus metaphorically, for the ripening of the wits of young readers; and because, in the book of Revelations, the saved are compared to a company of musicians that play upon their trumpets and harps, and sing their songs before the throne.[19]

In the early nineteenth century we have a clear presentation of the accommodation of this hearing problem by the man who coined the term, 'acoustic pyramid.' Wilhelm Wieprecht was the most influential man in the reorganization of Prussian military music.[20] He corresponded with composers such as Berlioz, Meyerbeer, Spontini and Vieuxtemps and was personally requested by both Liszt and Mendelssohn to arrange their music for military band. As part of his interest in the instrumentation of the military band, he invented the modern tuba.

On 28 June 1845, Wieprecht published in a Berlin newspaper his proposed new concept for the instrumentation of Prussian military bands. His plan was based on his 'acoustic pyramid' principle, as his labels make very clear. He recommended the following:

Piercing Register, to be played lightly
    Flutes, large and small
    Clarinets in A♭ or G
    Clarinets in E♭ or D
    Clarinets in B♭ or A
    Oboes
    Bassoons
    Batyphons

Middle Register, to be played stronger
    Cornets in B♭ or A
    Cornets in E♭ or D
    Tenorhorns in B♭ or A
    Bass horns (Baryton) in B♭ or A
    Bass horns in F or E♭

Low Register, to be played very strong
    Trumpets in E♭ or D
    Trombones in B♭ or A
    Bass trombones in F or E♭
    Bass tuba in F or E♭
    Percussion

---

18 'Doleful' was a frequent sixteenth-century English synonym for an ensemble of trombones.

19 *Pilgrim's Progress* in *The Works of John Bunyan*, ed. George Offor (London: Blackie and Son, 1853), III, 215. For the 'pipe' reference, see Matthew 11:16. For the Revelations passages, see 8:2 and 14:2.

20 Hans von Bulow called him the 'l'etat c'est moi of Prussian military music.'

This phenomena of our brain giving unusual attention to the higher pitches, which is such a fundamental problem in ensemble performance, in all likelihood represents some adaptation long before speech and perhaps long before music. It is clearly the most significant influence in the development of advanced speech, which is to say the delineation of the consonants. Thus, upon reflection, one can think of many things far afield which seem to carry an echo of this principle. For example in the Hebrew Old Testament, 'and one rises up at the voice of a bird, and all the daughters of song are brought low; they are afraid also of what is high.'[21]

And while not for a moment wishing to minimize the principle of gravity in the construction of buildings, does this, 'thus one went up from the lowest story to the top story, through the middle story,'[22] not sound like the spelling of a chord?

---

[21] Ecclesiastes 12:4.

[22] Ezekiel 41:7.

Early Thoughts on Tempi

> *Just as there is a difference between grammar and speech,*
> *so there is an infinitely greater one between musical theory and the art of fine playing.*[1]
>
> Couperin (1668–1733)

During the countless centuries of music history before notation, tempo must have been a subject of concern only with regard to dance music. All other solo performance would no doubt have always consisted of performance dictated by feeling. One can imagine that feeling also determined dance tempi until such time as there were known and repeatable dances which would have tended toward a narrow range of recognizable tempi.

We have no way of knowing much about tempo with respect to the medieval two- and three-part scores, that is in the sense of individual performances. But, given the Church's role in turning music into a branch of mathematics, it would seem reasonable to guess that the notation did not anticipate internal tempo changes, such as rubato, no matter how much 'feeling' the clerical singers were attempting to add to the music. In fact we may suppose it was their frustration in trying to be musical in a rigid mathematical system which led to the extensive improvisation in church music.

This aspect of tempo must have become even more problematic in Renaissance church music as it became notated for four, five and more parts. Certainly with proportions, in which the music rapidly became, through diminution, faster (smaller note values), the very mathematical complexity must have made tempo as we use the term irrelevant after the beginning. In some extant examples there quickly accumulate so many ligatures that it seems impossible to believe anyone could have actually sung the music. Some consider these to be mere 'educational examples' of the mathematics in question and not intended to be sung. But some music of this kind was sung and it was a real concern for working church music directors like Praetorius. He feared the conductor might end up beating so fast that,

> we make the spectators laugh and offend the listeners with incessant hand and arm movements and give the crowd an opportunity for raillery and mockery.[2]

By the sixteenth century a change was in the atmosphere and it came from Italy. Certainly we can hear the desire to write with stronger feeling in the music of di Rore and Gesualdo. No doubt this was responsible for the Italians beginning to break down the regimentation of tempi, at least this seems clear in Praetorius' *Syntagma Musicum* (1619), which he wrote as a kind

---

[1] François Couperin, *L'Art de toucher* (Paris, 1717, reprinted Wiesbaden: Breitkopf & Härtel, 1933).

[2] *Syntagma Musicum*, III, 74. A facsimile of the original German publication has been printed by Bärenreiter Kassel, 1958. The page numbers we cite, therefore, are from the original print.

of introductory treatise for the purpose of introducing the Italian style to Germany. When discussing various signatures at the beginning of compositions, Praetorius finds there is no longer agreement among the Italians. He suggests that the slower common time signature is used in madrigals and the faster alla breve sign is used in motets.[3] However, he has noticed that in *all* the compositions of Gabrieli, he uses only the alla breve sign. In the works of Viadana, he finds the alla breve sign in compositions with text and the common time sign in instrumental works. His own opinion, agreeing with what he has found in the works of Lassus and Marenzio, was that,

> the common time sign should be used for those motets and other sacred compositions which have many black notes, in order to show that the beat is to be taken more slowly … Anyone, however, may reflect upon such matters himself and decide, on the basis of text and music, where the beat has to be slow and where fast.

His last sentence is revolutionary, for we can see that the question of tempo has now passed from the composer to the performer.

In concerti, where madrigal and motet *styles* are found, it is necessary to change tempo. Here, instead of using the common time and alla breve signs, Praetorius suggests it might be better to employ the new practice of using Italian words, such as *adagio*, *presto*, etc.[4]

Praetorius clearly reflects[5] a level of rubato never mentioned in earlier treatises. For this practice he makes two general rules, first that a performance must not be hurried and second that all note values must be observed. Then he adds a comment that demonstrates how dramatic the revolution in the approach to tempo was. The conductor can now decide for himself changes in tempo which are entirely unnotated in the score.

> But to use, by turns, now a slower, now a faster beat, in accordance with the text, lends dignity and grace to a performance and makes it admirable … Some do not want such mixture of [tempi] in any one composition. But I cannot accept their opinion, especially since it makes motets and concerti particularly delightful, when after some slow and expressive measures at the beginning several quick phrases follow, succeeded in turn by slow and stately ones, which again change off with faster ones.

The purpose of this he says is to avoid monotony and he adds the same advice relative to dynamics.

> Besides, it adds much charm to harmony and melody, if the dynamic level in the vocal and instrumental parts is varied now and then.

When Praetorius returns to the subject of dynamics, he mentions that the Italians are beginning to use *forte*, *piano*, etc., to mark changes within a concerto. It is interesting that, once again, he suggests that the conductor is free to alter both dynamics and tempo.

---

[3] Ibid., 48ff.

[4] Ibid., 51.

[5] Ibid., 79ff.

> I rather like this practice. There are some who believe that this is not very appropriate, especially in churches. I feel, however, that such variety [in dynamics] and change [in tempo] are not only agreeable and proper, if applied with moderation and designed to express the feelings of the music, and affect the ear and the spirit of the listener much more and give the concerto a unique quality and grace. Often the composition itself, as well as the text and the meaning of the words, requires that one [change] at times—but not too frequently or excessively—beating now fast, now slowly, also that one lets the choir by turns sing quietly and softly, and loudly and briskly. To be sure, in churches there will be more need of restraint in such changes than at banquets.[6]

Finally, it is particularly interesting here, that Praetorius gives one Latin term, *lento gradu*, which he says was understood to mean that the voice was both softer and slower.

This apparent new freedom among the Italians is confirmed throughout the Baroque, following a fervent attempt to return emotions to music, after fifteen centuries of their being discouraged by the Church. And so the very nature of these recommendations reflect a prior regimentation in the concept of tempo, which the Baroque composers seemed eager to destroy. The very practice Praetorius discusses above, relative to the freedom of the performer to make his own decision on tempo, had been mentioned four years earlier, in 1615, by Frescobaldi:

> These pieces should not be played to a strict beat any more than modern madrigals which, though difficult, are made easier by taking the beat now slower, now faster, and by even pausing altogether in accordance with the expression and meaning of the text.[7]

We wish to emphasize that the reason for this new freedom in tempo was to aid in the expression of emotion. One feels this clearly in Monteverdi, as well as his concern about the old style of rigid tempi, when he pleads that his song must be 'sung to the time of the heart's feeling, and not to that of the hand.'[8] And we find exactly the same plea by Giovanni Bonachelli in 1642:

> In accordance with the feeling one must guide the beat, sensing it now fast, now slow, according to the occasion, now liveliness, and now languor, as indeed anyone will easily know immediately who possesses the fine manner of singing.[9]

By 1676, the great English critic, Thomas Mace, seems to suggest that this new freedom now also included decisions on the tempo of larger formal sections of the music. If, he says, the music falls into sections, these may be played,

> according as they best please your own fancy, some very briskly, and courageously, and some again gently, lovingly, tenderly and smoothly.

---

6   Ibid., 132 (112).

7   Girolamo Frescobaldi (1583–1643), *Toccatas and Partitas*, Book I.

8   *Madrigali guerrieri et amorosi* (Venice, 1638).

9   Giovanni Bonachelli, *Corona di sacri gigli a una, due, tre, Quattro, e cinque voci* (Venice, 1642).

He then continues with the same recommendation to the performer we have seen above.

> Beginners must learn strict time; but when we come to be masters, so that we can command all manner of time, at our own pleasures, we then take liberty … to break time; sometimes faster and sometimes slower, as we perceive the nature of the thing requires.[10]

This new Baroque style of leaving to the performer the decisions regarding tempi in performance is the explanation for what might otherwise seem to the modern reader a rather extraordinary incident involving Haydn in London. Haydn brought new symphonies with him for his second trip to London and when he went to the first rehearsal and sought to give the tempo for a manuscript work never before seen by the orchestra, he was immediately over-ruled by the 'Leader' (the Koncertmeister) who considered it *his* job to set the tempo. There must have developed some conflict for it carried over into a debate in the local newspapers. One who defended Haydn's right to set the tempo of his own music was the famous Charles Burney,

> There is a censure leveled at him … for marking the measure to his own new composition: but as even the old compositions had never been performed under his direction, in this country, till the last winter, it was surely allowable for him to indicate to the orchestra the exact time in which he intended the several movements to be played, without offending the leader or subalterns of the excellent band which he had to conduct.

During the nineteenth century we again find famous composers arguing for freedom in tempo, as we see, for example, in a letter by von Weber to the music director, Praeger, in Leipzig.

> The beat must not be like a tyrannical hammer, impeding or urging on, but must be to the music what the pulse-beat is to the life of man.
>
> There is no slow tempo in which passages do not occur that demand a quicker motion, so as to obviate the impression of dragging.
>
> Conversely there is no presto that does not need a quiet delivery by many places, so as not to throw away the chance of expressiveness by hurrying …
>
> Neither the quickening nor the slowing of the tempo should ever give the impression of the spasmodic or the violent. The changes, to have a musical-poetic significance, must come in an orderly way in periods and phrases, conditioned by the varying warmth of the expression.[11]

---

10 Thomas Mace, *Musick's Monument* [1676] (Paris: Editions du Centre National de la Recherche Scientifique, 1966), 429, 432.
11 Quoted in Felix Weingartner, *On Conducting* (New York: Kalmus), 41.

And Richard Wagner complained that the 'conductor-guild' of his time dictated that there should be no tempo modification in the music of Beethoven, a view he attributed to the 'incapacity and general unfitness of our conductors themselves.'[12] This attitude is still very strong in Europe, where it is presently heard in the advice that one should play only 'what the composer wrote.'[13]

Finally, after Brahms conducted his own *Fourth Symphony* with the famous Meiningen Orchestra he wrote Joseph Joachim complaining of things *not* notated in the score, 'In these concerts I couldn't make enough slowings and accelerations.'[14] And anyone who has heard the extant recording of Mahler playing at the piano a transcription of his own *Fifth Symphony* will have been astonished to hear tempi, and tempo alteration so radical as to be virtually unrecognizable in the score.

After reading all these similar comments by really great musicians, we hope the reader who is a musician will pause to contemplate on the degree which the twentieth century has taken something away from him and given it back to the composer. Or have we performers just lost sight of something?

The most serious consequence of the Church's decision to make music a branch of mathematics, as a part of its campaign to outlaw emotions from the life of the Christian, was the creation of the modern notational system by medieval church mathematicians. Adhering to the Church dogma, they created a notational system without a single symbol which has anything to do with emotion or feeling. Having to notate music with such an incomplete system forced composers to seek other, less effective, means of communicating with performers, such as the language at the beginning of the score. Couperin makes these same points in the preface to his *L'Art de Toucher*.

> Not having devised signs or characters for communicating our specific ideas, we try to remedy this by indicating at the beginning of our pieces, by some such word as Tenderly, Quickly, etc., as far as possible the idea we want to convey.

The most familiar form of this practice to musicians is, of course, what Praetorius calls in 1619, 'the new practice of using Italian words, such as *adagio, presto*, etc.' For musicians today these Italian words convey tempo, but originally they were intended to reflect character, not speed.[15] It will be quite surprising for the reader to see how Johann Mattheson (1681–1764) defined some of these familiar terms:

---

[12] *Wagner's Prose Works*, trans. William Ashton Ellis (New York: Broude), IV, 336.

[13] Isn't interesting that in our sister art, drama, which like music has both a written form and a performance form, in the past five hundred years not a single person has ever said to an actor, 'just say what the playwright wrote.'

[14] *Johannes Brahms im Briefwechsel mit Joseph Joachim* (Berlin, 1908), II, 205.

[15] Only a few, such as 'grave,' today carry a character association.

> An *Adagio* indicates distress; a *Lamento* lamentation; a *Lento* relief; an *Andante* hope; an *Affetuoso* love; an *Allegro* comfort; a *Presto* eagerness ...[16]

Whatever the original intent of these words were, their meaning had already become lost, according to Leopold Mozart, by 1756.[17] The importance of this truth can be seen clearly in his son's music. Wolfgang Mozart, in his beautiful and ethereal 'Ave verum corpus,' has written music in common time which is performed by virtually everyone today at a tempo of quarter-note = 144, yet Mozart calls this *Adagio*! Leaving aside his comment to his sister that in his life he had never written a really slow movement, this example clearly demonstrates that whatever 'adagio' meant to Mozart, it meant something beyond a reference to speed.

Things were made a bit more confusing during the Baroque by the French vocabulary used in place of the Italian terms. In particular, the word, 'Movement,' by which, according to Mattheson, the French meant 'what the Italians commonly indicate only with some adjectives such as: *affettuoso, con discrezione, con spirito*.'[18]

In other words, Movement meant the emotional quality and did not refer to speed or tempo. It is in this sense that when we speak of the 'First Movement,' or 'Second Movement,' in a Mozart symphony, for example, we are reflecting the original intent which was 'first emotion' and 'second emotion.' There may have been more correspondence of such terms with tempo than we might think today. We have known Europeans who say 'First tempo' and 'Second tempo' when referring to the two principal sections of the sonata form in Classical symphonies.

With this in mind we can understand the title of a book quoted by Mattheson, *Les mouvements differents sont le pur espirit de la Musique*.[19] Mattheson himself says movement is a 'spiritual thing,' not a physical thing, and depends not on 'precepts and prohibitions,' but 'feeling and emotion.' To find the correct movement, the performer must 'probe and feel his own soul' as well as 'feel the various impulses which the piece is supposed to express.'[20] The ability to correctly find the movement, Mattheson observes, is a knowledge which 'transcends all words' and 'is the highest perfection of music, and it can be attained only through considerable experience and great gifts.'

By refusing to use the Italian terms, the French apparently created some confusion among their own ranks. Couperin, for instance, explains,

---

[16] Johann Mattheson, *Der vollkommene Capellmeister* [1739], trans. Ernest Harriss (Ann Arbor: UMI Research Press, 1981), II, xii, 34ff.

[17] See his violin treatise.

[18] Johann Mattheson, *Der vollkommene Capellmeister*.

[19] Jean Rousseau, *Methode claire, certaine et facile pour apprendre à chanter la musique* (Paris, 1678).

[20] *Der vollkommene Capellmeister*, II, vii, 18ff.

> I find we confuse Measure or Time with what is called Cadence or Movement. Measure defines the number and quality of the beats; and Cadence is literally the intelligence and the soul which must be added to it.[21]

We find this same concern expressed in Jean Rousseau's viole treatise of 1687.

> There are people who imagine that imparting the movement is to follow and keep time; but these are very different matters, for it is possible to keep time without entering into the movement, since time depends on the music, but the movement depends on genius and fine taste.

Sebastien de Brossard, in an early dictionary of music (1703), considered time from a different perspective with regard to the recitative. Writing of *rubato* in Largo tempo, he observes,

> In Italian recitatives we often do not make the beats very equal, because this is a kind of declamation where the Actor ought to follow the movement of the passion which inspires him or which he wants to express, rather than that of an equal and regulated measure.[22]

With the hope to bring order to the general confusion regarding the designation of tempi there were a number of private inventors, caught up in the enthusiasm of the Industrial Revolution at the beginning of the nineteenth century, who worked toward creating a mechanical device for standardizing tempo. The winner of this race was the quack-inventor, acquaintance of Beethoven and emigrant to America, Johann Maelzel.[23] Maelzel's Metronome held promise for some, but for authentic musicians it only represented another rigid form of tyranny contradictory to musical feeling. Beethoven, for example, who made the instrument known, wrote on a score following the indication, '100 according to Maelzel,'

> but this must be held applicable to only the first measures, for feeling also has its tempo and this cannot entirely be expressed in this figure.[24]

Beethoven may have revised his thinking with more experience, for Franz Liszt claimed that when asked about the metronome, Beethoven replied, 'Better none.'[25] Here is a sampling of later views:

Berlioz,

> I do not mean to say that it is necessary to imitate the mathematical regularity of the metronome, which would give the music thus executed an icy frigidity; I even doubt whether it would be possible to maintain this rigid uniformity for more than a few bars.[26]

---

[21] François Couperin, *L'Art de toucher* (Paris, 1717, reprinted Wiesbaden: Breitkopf & Härtel, 1933), 24.
[22] Sebastien de Brossard, *Dictionaire de Musique* (Paris, 1703), 'Largo.'
[23] He more or less stole the idea from Dietrich Winkel of Amsterdam.
[24] Quoted in Erich Leinsdorf, *The Composer's Advocate* (New Haven: Yale University Press, 1981), 165.
[25] Letter to Breitkopf and Härtel, Nov. 16, 1863.
[26] His *Essay on Conducting*.

Brahms, regarding his *Requiem*,

> I think ... that the metronome is of no value ... The so-called 'elastic' tempo is moreover not a new invention.[27]

Verdi, a note in his *Te Deum*,

> This entire piece ought to be performed in one tempo as indicated by the metronome. This notwithstanding, it will be appropriate to broaden or accelerate in certain spots for reasons of expression and nuance.[28]

Wagner, regarding *Tannhauser*,

> As to the 'tempi' of the whole work in general, I can only say that if conductor and singers are to depend for their time on the metronomical marks alone, the spirit of the work must stand indeed in sorry case.[29]

Bruno Walter,

> The metronome marking is good only for the first few bars.[30]

Erich Leinsdorf,

> I do not consult the little clock.[31]

Well, the metronome is a horrible concept, a return to rigid formalism and the tyranny of rules. It is also unnecessary, for all the information on tempo is already provided by the composer—in the music itself. Thus, Franz Liszt wrote to a correspondent,

> A metronomical performance is certainly tiresome and nonsensical; time and rhythm must be adapted to and identified with the melody, the harmony, the accent and the poetry.[32]

And, when one considers the general limitation of our notational system, perhaps Mendelssohn said it best when he admits ignoring the notation completely:

> I think the movement might be taken too slow, which I found to be the case at the first rehearsal, until I no longer paid any attention to the notes or the heading, but adhered to the sense alone.[33]

---

[27] Ibid., 129.
[28] Ibid., 130.
[29] *Prose Works of Wagner*, III, 190.
[30] *On Music and Music-Making* (New York: Norton, 1957), 43.
[31] Leinsdorf, *The Composer's Advocate*, 130.
[32] Letter to Siegmund Lebert, Jan. 10, 1870.
[33] Letter to Nicolas Gade, March 3, 1843.

With the beginning of the twentieth century, when the Industrial Revolution reached down to the individual level with trains, washing machines, etc., there was, in the field of musical performance, a strong backlash against the artistic freedom of the nineteenth century. The unfortunate result was the production of generations of musicians who felt they were not allowed to apply their own feelings in their approach to scores. Nothing documents this so clearly as the typical adjudicator form given to judges of music contests. Here everything is judged against an anticipated performance which should reproduce precisely whatever is on paper. Nothing is more absurd, nothing is more unmusical and nothing is more unjust.

Early Reflections on Instruments and Ensembles

ONE SEES MUSICAL INSTRUMENTS pictured in the oldest of human art works, including the cave paintings of Spain and France, and finds them mentioned in the oldest extant literature. But it is much later before we begin to find insights into how the instruments were viewed aesthetically, which is the purpose of this essay.

Of course, we would know more but for the vast destruction, through wars and religious purposes, of books and even entire libraries. Consider as an example Aristoxenus (b. ca. 379 BC), a student of Aristotle, who wrote a great number of books, some of which were books on music. The titles of his lost books on music that we know of include *On Aulos Players*, *On The Aulos and Musical Instruments*, *On Aulos Boring*,[1] *On Music*, and *Brief Notes*. In fact, all that has come down to us from Aristoxenus is excerpts of two books, one chapter of his book, *Elements of Rhythm*, and three chapters of another, *Elements of Harmony*. The important early historian, Athenaeus (ca. 200 AD), knew some of these now lost books and quotes from them. We wish we had more information such as his quotation of Aristoxenus as saying he preferred string instruments to winds, as the winds were too easy—as, for example, people like shepherds can learn to play panpipes without even being taught![2]

There is another very interesting and mysterious comment about instruments by the Englishman, Roger Bacon (b. ca. 1214 AD), who studied at Oxford and at the University of Paris, where he received a doctorate in theology and then joined the Franciscan Order in about 1247. While the early Christian philosophers treated the numerous references to musical instruments in the Old Testament as being only metaphors, Bacon treats these passages as dealing with real instruments and takes at face value the descriptions of their use in the church services. For this reason, and especially for the reason that earlier ancient Greek philosophers often associated music with religion in general, we wish he had given us more information on his comment that the theologian must also know the 'numberless mystical meanings' of the various musical instruments.[3] Perhaps his silence reflects a general atmosphere he mentions in which the 'wise men' deliberately kept some truths for themselves.

> We see that such is the case among the professors of philosophy as well as in the truth of our faith. For the wise have always been divided from the multitude, and they have veiled the secrets of wisdom not only from the world at large but also from the rank and file of those devoting themselves to philosophy.[4]

---

[1] Athenaeus, *Deipnosophistae*, XIV, 634, quotes from this book that Aristoxenus knew five kinds of aulos, which he named: the virginal, child-pipes, harp-pipes, complete, and super-complete.

[2] Ibid., IV, 174. In Ibid., IV, 183, Athenaeus quotes from an unnamed book of Aristoxenus regarding string instruments.

[3] *Opus Majus*, 'Causes of Error,' XVI, in *The Opus Majus of Roger Bacon*, trans. Robert Burke (New York: Russell & Russell, 1962), I, 259ff.

[4] This discussion is found in Ibid., 'Causes of Error,' IV.

Another who took the Old Testament references literally was Hildegard of Bingen (1098–1179 AD), who wrote,

> They invented musical instruments of diverse kinds ... by which the songs could be expressed in multitudinous sounds, so that listeners, aroused and made adept outwardly, might be nurtured within by the forms and qualities of the instruments, as by the meaning of the words performed with them.[5]

In one of her famous 'visions,' Hildegard reveals an aesthetic preference for string instruments, which she says 'look up to God ... with the simplicity of a dove.' She means that the violin, for example, is held in such a way that the face of the instrument 'looks up toward God.' 'Players of wind instruments, on the other hand,' if one can imagine for example the modern clarinet and oboe player who sit with an instrument looking down, 'serve humbly upon the Earth.'

Because of the Church's attitude toward the musical instruments of the Old Testament, and their deliberate exclusion of any references to musical instruments in the services described in the New Testament, we read little of musical instruments during the long period when the Church controlled literature. When the 'dark ages' finally began to pass, writers frequently provide us with long lists of the instruments currently being used. Perhaps they had a sense of the need to write of things not permitted previously, but, in any case, they document that instrumental music had not disappeared during the long period when there is so little secular literature.

An early example of these new poetic descriptions is found in Robert Wace's (1100–1174 AD) *Roman de Brut*. Here, for a banquet of King Arthur, in addition to story-tellers, chess and dice games, the guests were treated to an extraordinary variety of musical entertainment.

> Now to the court had gathered many tumblers, harpers, and makers of music, for Arthur's feast. He who would hear songs sung to the music of the rote, or would solace himself with the newest refrain of the minstrel, might win to his wish. Here stood the viol player, chanting ballads and lays to their appointed tunes. Everywhere might be heard the voice of viols and harp and flutes. In every place rose the sound of lyre and drum and shepherd's pipe, bagpipe, psaltery, cymbals, monochord, and all manner of music. Here the tumbler tumbled on his carpet. There the mime and the dancing girl put forth their feats.[6]

During the early Renaissance one finds many such lists of instruments, particularly in French poetry. We will let one example represent them all, this by the famous poet and musician, Guillaume de Machaut (1300–1377).[7] In his 'Remede de Fortune,' Machaut describes a

---

5 'Vision Seven: 10,' in *The Book of Divine Works*, ed. Matthew Fox (Santa Fe: Bear & Company, 1987), 150.

6 Robert Wace, *Roman de Brut*, trans. Gwyn Jones (London: Dent, 1962), 69.

7 Machaut was probably educated at the cathedral school at Rheims and at the University of Paris. While still a young man be became associated with an important noble, John of Luxembourg, King of Bohemia. Machaut's reputation with other nobles can be seen in the fact that when Charles V visited Rheims a few years before the coronation, he advised the aldermen of the town to meet him 'chez maistre Guillyaume de Machault.' [Guillaume de Machaut, *Oeuvres*, ed. Ernest Hoepffner (Paris, 1908–21), I, xxv, xxxvff.]

dinner concert, carefully specifying not only that the musicians appear *after* the dinner, but that they arrive dressed for a concert, as it were. We should also admit here that just as it was an artistic challenge for painters to portray one of each possible instrument in some of their canvases, so the poets loved to list one of each instrument. We should not believe such an ensemble really played together, in spite of his suggestion that he heard them thus.

> And after the meal you should have seen the musicians arrive, all combed and comfortably attired. They played various harmonies, for there all in a circle I saw vielle, rebec, guitar, lute, Moorish guitar, small psaltery, cittern, and the psaltery, harp, tabor, trumpets, nakers, portative organs, more than ten pairs of horns, bagpipes, flutes, musettes, doucaines, cymbals, bells, timbrels, the Bohemian flute and the large German cornett, willow flutes, a fife, pipe, Alsatian reed pipe, small trumpet, busines, psaltery, a monochord (which has a single string), and a straw pipe all together. And it certainly seemed to me that such a melodious sound had never been perceived or heard; because I heard and perceived each one of them, according to the pitch of his instrument—vielle, guitar, cittern, harp, trumpet, horn, flute, pipe, bladder pipe, bagpipe, naker, tabor, and whatever could be played with finger, pick or bow—performing in perfect harmony there in the little park.[8]

The organizational system for ensembles of instruments, in the Middle Ages and early Renaissance, was one which distinguished between ensembles of 'loud' and 'soft' music, which probably had more to do with the size of room than for aesthetic reasons.[9] This organizational practice is mentioned in Eustache Deschamps' (1340–1410) 'Echecs amoureux.' A student of Machaut, Deschamps first mentions the 'loud' wind band, designated for a dance in the large hall ('a crowd' of dancers).

> Whenever that they were fain to dance
> And frolic, gathered in a crowd,
> The dancers called for music loud—
> It was this that always pleased them best,
> And ever added to their zest.
> One could hear each instrument
> That sounded forth its merriment.
> Trumpet, tabor, drum and bell
> Cymbals (which played so well)
> Cornemuse and shawm
> And horns that they did loudly blow.[10]

---

[8] Guillaume de Machaut, 'Remede de Fortune,' trans. James Wimsatt and William Kibler (Athens: The University of Georgia Press, 1988), 390ff.

[9] Eustache Deschamps, in his 'Ballade pour Machaut,' includes the shawms in the 'soft' ensemble, which is unusual for this time.

[10] Translation by Curt Sachs, *World History of the Dance* (New York, 1937), 287.

> Trompez, tabours, tymbrez, naquaires,
> Cymballes (dont il n'est mes guaires),
> Cornemusez et chalemelles
> Et cornes …

This same poem lists flutes, cromornes, rebec and rote as 'soft' instruments employed when 'less noise' is desired and which are pleasing for the appropriate entertainment.

There is one very early Renaissance book which attempts to provide us with the sound of many of these instruments. Perhaps we might even consider this an attempt at creating an aesthetic ranking. Juan Ruiz (1283–1350), in his *The Book of True Love*, describes an Easter procession in a fourteenth-century town, in which we see jongleurs and members of Religious Orders.

> And then the drums came forth with many other instruments.
>
> Then came out, with a strident sound, the two-stringed Moor's guitar,
> High-pitched as to its range, so to its tone both harsh and bold;
> Big-bellied lute which marks the time for merry, rustic dance,
> And Spanish guitar which with the rest was herded in the fold.
>
> The noisy, shrill rebec, with note so high it seems a squeak,
> Was joining in the tunes the Moor was twanging on his harp.
> And with them all, the *salterio* much higher than a peak;
> The picking *viyuela* among these others gaily skipped and hopped.
>
> The smaller zither [ca–o] and the harp and Moorish rebec played;
> Along with them the French recorder hummed a gay gavotte;
> The flute stood out above them higher than a lofty crag;
> Without the side drum's taps it is not worth an apricot.
>
> The bowing of the *vihuela de arco* produces sweet dance songs,
> At times quite soft and lulling, and at others very loud,
> Sweet sounds, delicious, bright and clear and always in good tune,
> Which make the people merry and delight the swarming crowd.
>
> The sweet *ca–o* came out with the little tambourine,
> Its jambles made of brass made sounds that are so sweet and clean;
> Portable organs there were playing country jigs and songs,
> And the poor comic minstrel girl played choruses between.
>
> The bagpipes and the Moorish flute, the *Sinfonia*,
> The *baldosa*, with their tight strings,
> And with all these the French *odrecillo* were playing well in tune,
> The silly bass bandora threw in its notes without delay.
>
> The horns and trumpets now came out with the timpani.
> It was a long time since there'd been such entertainment here,
> Such great rejoicing as the people mingled,
> The hillsides and the fields were full of jongleurs far and near.[11]

Leonardo da Vinci (1452–1519) was perhaps the most broadly talented man who has yet lived. Apart from his drawings in his notebooks, which include not only virtually every machine known to the fifteenth century (and some not known, such as the helicopter), but also anatomy, zoology, optics and architecture, there is that extraordinary resume he included

---

11   Juan Ruiz, *The Book of True Love*, trans. Saralyn Daly (University Park: Pennsylvania State University Press, 1978), 1225ff.

in a letter of job application which he wrote to Lodovico of Milan. After describing his abilities in designing instruments of war, from special cannons to armor plated vehicles and ships, he added,

> In time of peace I believe that I can give you as complete satisfaction as anyone else in architecture, in the construction of buildings both private and public, and in conducting water from one place to another.
>
> Also I can execute sculpture in marble, bronze, or clay, and also painting, in which my work will stand comparison with that of anyone else whoever he may be.

Were all those skills sufficient to convince Lodovico to hire Leonardo? Apparently not, for according to one sixteenth-century writer, Vasari, it was Leonardo's skill in music which won him the job![12] When he arrived he apparently won great applause by his performance on an instrument he had made, a silver lyre in the shape of a horse's skull.

Very few books today mention that Leonardo was a great performer in music. A contemporary, Paolo Giovio, reports that Leonardo's performances on the lyre were received by young and old with wonder and delight.[13] A sixteenth-century writer, Lomazzo, reports that his performance on the lyre 'surpassed all musicians of his time.'[14]

As with everything else the man was interested in, Leonardo's interest in music carried him into a study of the most remote corners of the subject, including sketches of numerous inventions and improvements of musical instruments and notes on acoustics. It is our great loss that Leonardo apparently wrote at least two books on music which are no longer extant. One of these, on the voice, he mentioned in one of his notes.

> My book 'On Voice' is in the hands of Messer Battista dell' Aquila, steward-in-waiting to the pope.[15]

And the main reason we mention him in this essay is a note which follows the above quotation:

> And I shall not enlarge on this as the subject is dealt with very fully in the book on musical instruments.[16]

If only we could find Leonardo's book on musical instruments, it would surely prove to be the most valuable book of its kind before the nineteenth century.

---

[12] Quoted in *The Literary Works of Leonardo da Vinci*, ed. Jean Paul Richter (London: Phaidon, 1970), I, 69.

[13] Paolo Giovio, *Leonardi Vencii Vita* [1528].

[14] Lomazzo, *Idea del Tempio della Pittura* [1590].

[15] *The Literary Works of Leonardo da Vinci*, I, 113. This source also gives the original library and shelf-marks where the autograph documents may be found.

[16] Ibid., I, 113.

In a treatise, 'Tractatus de Canticis,' by Jean de Gerson, Chancellor of the University of Paris, we begin to find more aesthetic characterizations of some instruments. He describes, for example, the psalterium and cithara as 'smooth and serene' and the viella as producing 'sweet and delightful music.' He even provides some interesting description for the prototype timpani, the naquaires, which he describes as consisting of one drum tuned to sound 'very dull' and the other 'very clear.'[17]

The first writer to deal more extensively with this topic was the great early theorist, Johannes Tinctoris (1435–1511). Music, to Tinctoris, still belonged to the old medieval definition of the liberal arts, where it resided as a branch of mathematics and in the Prologue to his own treatise *Concerning the Nature and Propriety of Tones*, Tinctoris identifies himself as one who professes 'the mathematical sciences.'[18] In this same work, in speaking of Church modes he says these were named,

> according to arithmetic, without which it is obvious no famous musicians escapes.[19]

In his treatise, *De Inventione et Usu Musicae*, Tinctoris writes at length of the principal instruments, as well as the best performers known to him. First, in Book III, he discusses the history of the early shawm, known first as *tibiae*, and in his time as *celimela*. Interestingly enough he mentions the continued existence of the double shawm [*duplici tibia*], which is surely the ancient aulos, but he calls this instrument the least perfect. The shawm he gives in three sizes, soprano, tenor [*bombarda*] and contratenor, the latter of which might be substituted by the trombone.[20] Together the ensemble is called *alta* [wind band]. The best player of the shawm he knew was Godefridus, a musician of Frederick III.[21]

Book IV and V Tinctoris devotes to a very detailed discussion of the wide variety of string instruments familiar to the Renaissance. The only string instrument he finds disagreeable is the Turkish *tambura*, which he calls a 'miserable and puny instrument which the Turks with their even more miserable and puny ingenuity, have evolved from the lyra.'[22] He later mentions that he heard this instrument in Naples played by Turks in captivity, to console themselves. To the ears of Tinctoris,

> The extravagance and rusticity of these pieces were such as only to emphasize the barbarity of those who played them.[23]

---

[17] Jean de Gerson, 'Tractatus de Canticis,' trans. Christopher Page, in 'Early fifteenth-century instruments in Jean de Gerson's 'Tractatus de Canticis,' *Early Music* 6, no. 3 (1978): 347, doi: 10.1093/earlyj/6.3.339

[18] *Concerning the Nature and Propriety of Tones*, trans. Albert Seay (Colorado Springs, 1976).

[19] Ibid., 3. He is speaking of the new church modes, not to be confused with the ancient Greek ones, which were named for tribes of people.

[20] Anthony Baines, 'Fifteenth-century Instruments in Tinctoris's De Inventine et Usu Musicae,' *The Galpin Society Journal* 3 (March 1950): 20ff, http://www.jstor.org/stable/841898

[21] Gustave Reese, *Music in the Renaissance* (New York: Norton, 1959), 147ff.

[22] Baines, 'Fifteenth-century Instruments in Tinctoris's De Inventine et Usu Musicae,' IV, 23.

[23] Ibid., IV, 25.

All of the strings he points out can play music in four parts and the lute, in particular, is used at feasts, dances and public and private entertainments. Among the most gifted players of the lute he points to Pietro Bono of Ferrara and Heinrich, a German in the service of Charles the Bold. The Germans, in particular, Tinctoris says 'improvise marvellously upon a treble part with such taste that the performance cannot be rivalled.'[24] This is particularly interesting as we do not usually think of this kind of artistic improvisation in Germany at so early a date.

He speaks of the *viola* [viol] as being used in Spain and Italy to accompany the recitation of epic poetry and mentions the musicianship of two Flemish brothers, Charles and Jean Orbus. In another references to the use of string instruments, he mentions the viol and rebec, which were also clearly his favorite instruments.

> I am similarly pleased by the rebec, my predilection for which I will not conceal, provided that it is played by a skillful artist, since its strains are very much like those of the viola. Accordingly, the viola and the rebec are my two instruments; I repeat, my chosen instruments, those that induce piety and stir my heart most ardently to the contemplation of heavenly joys. For these reasons I would rather reserve them solely for sacred music and the secret consolations of the soul, than have them sometimes used for profane occasions and public festivities.[25]

Another fifteenth-century German writer, Sebastian Brant, argued that wisdom should be attainable by all men. Those who fail in this common sense are to be found in the most widely read book of that century, after the bible, his *The Ship of Fools* (1494), where he gives his purpose as the instruction and pursuit of wisdom, reason and good manners.[26] In his allegorical ship he places one hundred and ten examples of 'fools' to illustrate the fate of those who fail to follow wisdom. He is quick to point out, however, that his boat is too small.

> One vessel would be far too small
> To carry all the fools I know.[27]

Our particular interest here is his references to the bagpipe, which had been an aristocratic favorite during the Middle Ages, because of its ability to play a non-stop dance melody—the nobles fearing getting out of step if even a single beat were missing! In *The Ship of Fools* we now find the bagpipe ridiculed in several places as the despised instrument of the lowest classes. As part of the title of his tale, 'Of Impatience of Punishment,' Brant warns,

> If bagpipes you enjoy and prize
> And harps and lutes you would despise,
> You ride a fool's sled, are unwise.[28]

---

[24] Ibid., 24.

[25] Ibid., 24ff.

[26] Sebastian Brant, *The Ship of Fools*, trans. Edwin Zeydel (New York: Columbia University Press, 1944), Prologue.

[27] Ibid.

[28] Ibid., 54. Bagpipes are again associated with fools in Tales Nr. 67 and 89.

In the main body of the story, he continues,

> A wise man lists to wise men's lore,
> Enriching thus his wisdom's store,
> Bagpipes are dunces' instrument,
> For harps they have no natural bent,
> And naught gives fools a greater joy
> Than wand and pipe, their favorite toy.

One of the most interesting commentators on music of the Italian Renaissance was Girolamo Cardano (1501–1576). After his marriage, Cardano moved to Milan, where his repeated requests for permission to practice medicine were turned down. He was able to gain appointment as a lecturer in mathematics for the Piatti foundation, which was the turning point in his career. He attracted large audiences for his lectures and published his first two books on mathematics in 1539. With this boost to his self-confidence, Cardano began to fight back against the doctors of Milan. He published a book called *On the Bad Practices of Medicine* which was immediately popular with the public.

> The things which give most reputation to a physician nowadays are his manners, servants, carriage, clothes, smartness, and caginess, all displayed in a sort of artificial and insipid way; learning and experience seem to count for nothing.[29]

Cardano eventually became one of the most famous physicians in Europe and went on to publish an incredible stream of books on nearly every subject, including mathematics, astronomy, physics, morals, dialectics, ethics, philosophy, the immortality of the soul, the mysteries of eternity, works of history, music, games of chance, chess, gems, dreams, and religious studies. His *De Subtilitate Rerum*, a work on science and natural philosophy became one of the best sellers during the second half of the sixteenth century. Another popular book, *Consolation*, was translated into English in 1573, read by Shakespeare and is considered to have influenced Hamlet's famous soliloquy. In all there were 131 published works, 111 in manuscript and another 170 which he burned, considering them worthless. It seems clear that this enormous output was driven by a passion to perpetuate his name, something he became obsessed with during his youth after noticing that a close family friend was never mentioned again after his death.

Cardano discusses the physical nature of musical instruments at length, including the materials used in their construction ('The best gut strings come from dogs'). Some of his observations make little sense, as when he distinguishes between a *fistula* in which the 'tone is formed in the throat' and the recorder or *syrinx*, 'which merely uses the breath but forms the tone within itself.'[30]

---

[29] Ibid., 12.

[30] Quoted in Clement Miller, *Hieronymus Cardanus, Writings on Music* (American Institute of Musicology, 1973), 51. In Ibid., 60, Cardano discusses the nature of breath used in a wind instrument, but he is generally misinformed.

His most interesting discussion provides several criteria for judging the excellence of musical instruments.[31]

1. The range should be ample, at least two octaves.
2. The sound should be pleasing, not harsh or clamorous.
3. The sound should be easy to produce. For these three reasons trumpets are imperfect and inferior: they are far more difficult to blow than recorders, their tone is raucous and clamorous, and they exceed an octave range by only one tone. Horns [*cornua*] are also more inferior because of the last two reasons.
4. They should sound well with the human voice and other instruments. On this account recorders are the least praiseworthy, for hardly any other instrument blends less well with the voice and other instruments.
5. Those with many strings are preferable to those with three or less.
6. They should be able to sustain a tone.
7. They should have a full tone.
8. They should be capable of producing very small and a great number of intervals. In this regard the lute is superior to the organ.

Cardano also ranks the aesthetic order of instruments according to their similarity to the human voice. Thus winds are superior to strings, although he hastens to say that the viol is preferable to the fife.[32] We learn the full extent of his meaning of 'similarity' in this remarkable description of the possibilities of the recorder.

> The things that are true for the recorder are true for all instruments, but they are even more appropriate for this instrument. A particular property is imitation of the human voice, not simple imitation (for this is common to all instruments) but rather exact imitation is proper to the instrument. This happens by using a relaxed tone in laments, a strong tone in excitement, a smooth, connected tone in serious moods, and so forth concerning the other emotions.[33]

Another interesting passage is one which reveals that bagpipe and string players sometimes simultaneously played and sang!

> It is common to all pipers and to string players who sing as they play that they should not move their heads about nor contort their lips nor do anything indecorous. Again, they should always adjust their voices and sound by listening, and should carefully watch others beating time. Thirdly, they should keep the beat, which is far easier to do in singing than in playing, since a constant pulse is less evident. Finally, in instruments which are played by blowing a pleasing quality must be kept in every respect, for although in singing one can pronounce words, in playing tonal sweetness and a suitable imitation of mood reach the highest summit of artistry.[34]

---

31 Ibid., 55.

32 Ibid.

33 Ibid., 69.

34 Ibid., 189.

Vincenzo Galilei (1520–1591), an important commentator on late Renaissance music in Italy, understands little inherent virtue of instrumental music in general. How, he asks, can these humble instruments be capable of anything more important than mere delight of the ear.

> If the object of the modern practical musicians is, as they say, to delight the sense of hearing with the variety of the consonances, and if this property of tickling (for it cannot with truth be called delight in any other sense) resides in a simple piece of hollow wood over which are stretched four, six, or more strings of the gut of a dumb beast or of some other material ... or in a given number of natural reeds or of artificial ones made of wood, metal, or some other material ... with a little air blowing inside them while they are touched or struck by the clumsy and untutored hand of some base idiot or other, then let this object of delighting with the variety of their harmonies be abandoned to these instruments, for being without sense, movement, intellect, speech, discourse, reason, or soul, they are capable of nothing else.[35]

The sixteenth century was a remarkable period for the manufacture of wind instruments, due to advances in the wood-working and metal-working trades. The most important developments, aside from the improvement of quality and the invention of a host of new instruments, was the new ability to make a true bass instrument and the development of the tradition of consorts.

With so many instruments now available, by the end of the century performers were beginning to be more selective. Some shawms, they found, sounded better than others; the smallest trombones were difficult to play. These choices were what resulted in the 'broken' consorts.

We can see that the shawm was beginning to lose its great popularity by the end of the century, which contributed to the impetus to develop its successor, the modern oboe. We can see an example of the shawm's falling out of favor in Thoinot Arbeau's (1519–1595) famous French treatise on dancing, *l'Orchesographie* (1588). In his description of the instruments used to accompany dance, Arbeau describes the shawm as being 'harsh and wailing and blown with force.'[36] While they tend to drown out any accompanying flutes, they sound good with percussion and especially if the treble and tenor are used together. It is clear he now thinks of this as a peasant instrument.

> There is no workman so humble that he does not wish to have shawms and sackbuts at his wedding.[37]

The most musical development, of course, was the consort principle, which replaced the old medieval loud-soft organizational plan. Now one heard homogenous ensembles rather than the old 'one instrument of a kind' ensembles. Soon civic, church and court wind bands were ordering 'cases' of shawms and of flutes, etc., meaning families of five or more instru-

---

35 Vincenzo Galilei, 'Dialogo della musica antica e della moderna,' in Oliver Strunk, *Source Readings in Music History* (New York: Norton, 1950), 313. His famous son, Galileo Galilei, was the first to point out the mathematical and physical impossibility of the account of Pythagoras' discovery of the overtone series by listening to a blacksmith—a story which had been unchallenged for two thousand years!

36 Thoinot Arbeau, *Orchesography*, trans. Mary Evans (New York: Kamin Dance Publishers, 1948), 50.

37 Ibid., 51.

ments of the same kind, but of different sizes, made by the same maker and contained in a single case. One can appreciate how important this was in a time where there was no standardized pitch and in which pitch differed from maker to maker. We can see a typical order, although here for a 'broken' consort, from Ghent, in 1540–1541:

> Item, paid to Pieter de Coninc, Goldsmith ... for two silver sackbuts, two descant and two tenor shawms ... to be delivered to the six shawm players of the city.[38]

These consorts must have sounded much more musical than the old medieval ensembles and so it is no surprise that the consort concept spread rapidly. Just how seriously did the aristocrats take this new principle? There is some suggestion that they actually began to organize their kennels of hunting dogs into consorts as well! Indeed one English treatise on organizing the estate recommends this as necessary for the best equipped household!

> If you would have your kennels for sweetness of cry then you must compound it of some large dogs that have deep, solemn mouths...which must as it were bear the bass in consort, then a double number of roaring and loud-ringing mouths which must bear the counter tenor, then some hollow, plain, sweet mouths which must bear the mean or middle part and so with these three parts of music you shall make your cry perfect.[39]

Nor is this an anomaly. Surely this can be the only explanation for the line in Lyly's play, *The Maydes Metamorphosis*, where a character says 'I can tune her with my hounds.'[40]

We even find a reference of this kind by Shakespeare. In his *A Midsummer Night's Dream*, the character, Theseus, says,

> Slow in pursuit, but matched in mouth like bells,
> Each under each. A cry more tunable
> Was never holla'd to, nor cheered with horn.[41]

---

[38] Ghent, Stads Rekeningen, 1540–1541, vol. 246v. Similar documents ordering 'cases' (consorts) of instruments exist in great numbers for many of these towns. In general, string instruments are not mentioned until after the middle of the sixteenth century.

[39] Quoted in Elizabeth Burton, *The Pageant of Elisabethan England* (New York: Scribner's), 190.

[40] John Lyly, *The Maydes Metamorphosis*, I, i.

[41] *A Midsummer Night's Dream*, IV, i, 123.

Early Views of Percussion

THERE IS AN EXTANT TEXT from the Seventeenth Dynasty of ancient Egypt which preserves a remarkable story about a drummer participating in a competition. Judging by the description of this contest in around 1,600 BC, it may have been something like the Olympic music competitions of ancient Greece, more athletic than musical in nature. The reader will in any case agree that no career in music today offers so delightful recompense.

> A certain Emhab had been practicing his drum secretly, keeping his fingers strong and supple to extract a variety of sounds from his instrument. Then one day he was invited to an audition to try his skills against those of another contestant. Emhab beat his rival by performing no fewer than seven thousand 'lengths.' The nature of such a 'length' is not explained, but this must be a technical term, perhaps describing a 'figure' or rhythmical phrase. Having gained the position as army drummer, Emhab spent a whole year drumming every single day, following his king on his campaigns and bravely executing every command until, finally, he was rewarded with a female slave, purchased for him by the king himself.[1]

Our greatest source of information about the use of percussion instruments in the ancient world is the Old Testament, a book assembled in about 700 BC from a number of earlier sources. Even given this patch-work background of the book, one is surprised by one passage, which includes percussion, in Psalm 81. This description seems much more appropriate to a truly pagan festival than a Jewish religious celebration. It is a ceremony uniquely out of place in the Old Testament.

> Raise a song, sound the timbrel,
> the sweet lyre with the harp.
> Blow the trumpet at the new moon,
> at the full moon, on our feast day.

Psalm 150 is perhaps the most familiar reference to musical instruments to be found in ancient literature.

> Praise him with the [shofar] sound;
> Praise him with lute and harp!
> Praise him with strings and pipe!
> Praise him with sounding cymbals;
> Praise him with loud clashing cymbals!

---

[1] Quoted in Lise Manniche, *Music and Musicians in Ancient Egypt* (London: British Museum Press, 1991), 75. Manniche says sticks were never used on drums in ancient Egypt, but this is incorrect as such sticks from that period actually survive in Berlin and are pictured by Carl Engel in *The Music of The Most Ancient Nations* (London: Reeves), 219.

One might be surprised by this recommendation for loud clashing cymbals in the religious service, but the Old Testament also gives us the actual names of some of these cymbal players.[2] In another place we are told that 'those who offer praises to the Lord with instruments' numbered four thousand![3] Another passage[4] speaks of cymbals, harps, lyres, trumpets, and singing altogether in the service. Perhaps such large forces are also intended by several references to 'Make a joyful *noise*.'[5] But what are we to make of the following?

> And David and all the house of Israel were making merry before the Lord with all their might, with songs and lyres and harps and tambourines and castanets and cymbals.[6]

Not so surprising are descriptions of the employment of percussion in religious processions, for example 'to the sound of the horn, trumpets, and cymbals, and made loud music on harps and lyres.'[7] Psalm 68 even gives us the order of the procession: singers in front, then 'maidens playing timbrels,' and finally the instrumentalists. The maidens playing timbrels in procession is again very reminiscent of the ancient pagan Greek festivals. Percussion instruments also appear in a description of a bridal procession:

> The bridegroom came forth, and his friends and brethren, to meet them with drums, and instruments of music.

In another interesting reference to percussion in the Old Testament we are told that it is the sons of Asaph, Heman and Jeduthun, 'who should prophesy with lyres, with harps, and with cymbals.'[8] It may seem odd to read of cymbals associated with prophesy, but then Miriam, the sister of Aaron is identified as 'the prophetess,' as well as a percussionist.[9]

Percussion instruments also appear with music to accompany public punishment. Even though this reference is symbolic, it would not serve as a symbol if the practice were unknown. The use of civic musicians to accompany punishment in the Middle Ages, for example, is well documented.

> And every stroke of the staff of punishment which the Lord lays upon them will be to the sound of timbrels and lyres.[10]

---

2   1 Chronicles 15:16ff; 16:5ff, 42; Nehemiah 12:34ff.

3   1 Chronicles 23:5.

4   2 Chronicles 29:25ff.

5   Psalm 95 and Psalm 100.

6   2 Samuel 6:5. An almost identical passage is found in 1 Chronicles 13:8, which adds the trumpet.

7   1 Chronicles 15:28.

8   1 Chronicles 25.

9   Exodus 15:20.

10 Isaiah 30:32.

Psalm 149 also has an unmistakable reference to the couches which guests reclined on during banquets of the ancient world. Again, percussion instruments are present.

> Sing to the Lord a new song ...
> Let them praise his name with dancing,
>   making melody to him with timbrel and lyre! ...
> Let them sing for joy on their couches.[11]

One interesting reference to banquet music describes a scene similar to a Greek *symposium*.[12]

> The mirth of the timbrels is stilled, the noise of the jubilant has ceased, the mirth of the lyre is stilled. No more do they drink wine with singing.[13]

Aside from banquets, there are several percussion references as a part of general merry-making with entertainment music. Typical is the command,

> Again you shall adorn yourself with timbrels and shall go forth in the dance of the merrymakers.[14]

We have a tragic epigram by a Greek poet of the second century which refers to the suicide of a percussion player, who is also named, with interesting detail of the several musical instruments he played during his career.

> Clytosthenes, his feet that raced in fury now enfeebled by age, dedicates to thee, Rhea of the lion-car, his tambourines beaten by the hand, his shrill hollow-rimmed cymbals, his double-flute that calls through its horn, on which he once made shrieking music, twisting his neck about, and the two-edged knife with which he opened his veins.[15]

A sixth-century poem by Agathias Scholasticus speaks of a cymbal-playing statue, with a strange emotion we cannot interpret.

> The sculptor set up a statue of a Bacchant, yet ignorant of how to beat the swift cymbals with her hands and ashamed. For so does she bend forward, and looks as if she were crying, 'Go ye out, and I will strike them with none standing by.'[16]

---

[11] A similar scene of music and dancing is found in the New Testament in Luke 15:25.
[12] In Greek this word meant 'drinking-party.'
[13] Isaiah 24:8ff.
[14] Jeremiah 31:4. Additional similar references can be found in Exodus 32:18, and Genesis 31:27.
[15] Philippus of Thessalonica, in *Greek Anthology*, VI, 94. The reference to the aulos 'with horn' describes a bell of animal horn which had begun to be used in Rome after the first century AD.
[16] *The Greek Anthology*, trans. W. R. Paton (Cambridge: Harvard University Press, 1939), V, 59.

There are also three specialized treatises on music which date from the sixth century, by Boethius (475–524 AD), Cassiodorus (480–573 AD) and Isidore of Seville (560–636 AD). The existence of their works in manuscript copies made possible the education of musicians for centuries, not to mention helping to preserve the liberal arts through the Dark Ages.

Cassiodorus makes a passing reference to a percussion instrument, the *acetabula*,[17] which 'yields such pleasure that, of all the senses, men think their hearing is the highest gift conferred on them.' We wish he had told us more.

Isidore, bishop of Seville, is the only writer known today representing Gothic Spain. His twenty-volume *Etymologiarum*, which is really the first encyclopedia, has the goal of presenting all the information a Christian needs to know. He divides music into voice, instrumental and percussion.[18] His comments of this third category, which he actually calls, *rhythmica*, include a rare verbal characterization of the sound of a percussion instrument. They consist of, he says, 'sounds produced by the beat of the fingers.' These, he finds, 'yield an agreeable clanging.'[19]

There are two references to percussion from the end of the Middle Ages which should be noted. The first is from a small body of work reflecting the lower side of society and a group of people we call, collectively, the Goliards.[20] While the poetry of the troubadours and Minnesingers were sung in the new indigenous languages of French and German, the Goliard repertoire is in Latin, the language of both cleric and student. One of these, a *Carmina Burana* song, '*Quocumque More Motu Volvuntur Tempora*,' begins,

> Whichever way the seasons turn in their movement,
> Accordingly I beat my trusty, well-tempered drums.

The second is by Johannes de Grocheo, in his treatise, *De Musica* of ca. 1300. In one of the earliest discussions of form, he mentions the instrumental *ductia,* accompanied by percussion instruments, which 'measure' it and the movement of the performer,

> and excite the soul of man to moving ornately according to that art they call dancing, and they measure its movement in ductiae and in choral dance.[21]

The famous late medieval Crusades were also the source of new musical instruments introduced to the West during these battles. Almost all the modern percussion instruments made their way west because of the crusades and subsequently the literature of Western Europe

---

[17] Letter to the Patrician Symmachus, in *Variae*, trans. Thomas Hodgkin (London: Frowde, 1886), IV, li. Presumed to be an instrument like the glockenspiel, but with metal cups instead of bars.

[18] *Etymologiarum*, III, xv, trans. W.M. Linsay, quoted in Oliver Strunk, *Source Readings in Music History* (New York: Norton, 1950). This important work, published a dozen times in the fifteenth century, has never been translated into English.

[19] Ibid., III, xxii.

[20] From Golias, a variant of Goliath, or perhaps gula (gullet). By the thirteenth century the term had become one of reproach.

[21] In Johannes de Garlandia, *De Mensurabili Musica*, trans. Stanley Birnbaum (Colorado Springs: Colorado College Music Press, 1978), 19.

often mentions the first sightings of these strange new percussion instruments. An example is a chronicle of 1457 describing the visit to the court of Charles VII by ambassadors from King Ludislaus of Hungary.

> One had never before seen drums like big kettles, carried on horseback.[22]

During the Renaissance, music rapidly became more artistic and as it did the accounts of percussion instruments began to change in character. In *Don Quijote*, Cervantes presents a survey of the instruments necessary to pastoral music which is followed by a description of cymbals.

> What soft flute sounds will come to our ears—what Zamoran bagpipes—what drums and tambourines—what timbrels—what lutes and violins! And just suppose, among all these other instruments, we hear the sound of cymbals [*albogues*]! Ah, then we'll have virtually everything that produces pastoral music.

Sancho asks,

> What are these cymbals? I've never heard of them, in all my life, and I've never seen them, either.

Don Quijote replies,

> Cymbals are flat sheets of metal, and they're used like brass candlestick holders, banging one against the other, on the hollow parts, to produce a sound which, though it may not be terribly pleasing or harmonious, is nevertheless not displeasing, and goes well with the rustic quality of the bagpipes and tambourines. The name *albogues* comes from Arabic, like all the words in Spanish that start with *al*.[23]

Finally, in one place Cervantes refers to a man as 'a great joker, as most drummers are.'[24]

The most interesting writer in seventeenth-century Italy on the nature of music was Athanasius Kircher (1601–1680), a German born scholar who spent most of his adult life in Rome. His greatest work was the *Musurgia Universalis* (Rome, 1650), a virtual encyclopedia of music, divided into ten books. Book Six, 'Organic music,' a medieval term for instrumental music, discusses as well geometry and acoustics. Here Kircher deals with the physical characteristics of the family of instruments, but, unfortunately, includes little information on performance practice or of aesthetic considerations. He makes the inaccurate assumption that string instru-

---

[22] Curt Sachs, *The History of Musical Instruments* (New York, 1940), 329.

[23] Miguel de Cervantes, *Don Quijote*, trans. Burton Raffel (New York: Norton, 1995), II, lxvii. In his *The Dialogue of the Dogs*, Cervantes writes that shepherds 'spend their days singing and playing bagpipes, flutes, rebecs, tabors, and other rare instruments.'

[24] Miguel de Cervantes, *The Dialogue of the Dogs*, trans. Harriet de On's, in *Six Exemplary Novels* (Great Neck: Barron's Educational Series, 1961), 32.

ments must be the most ancient,[25] partly because of their prominence in the Old Testament, but also because he assumes man always had available cords (potential musical strings) to tie things with.[26]

In discussing the skins used for percussion instruments, Kircher relates a charming contemporary example of folklore about sheep.

> Just one little sheep feeds us, clothes us, and entertains us with four types of musical instruments, with intestines for strings, with shinbones and horns for pipes, and finally the skin turning into a drum, so that consequently the Hebrews have declared of it not inelegantly that the live animal has one voice; dead, seven.[27]

We find several references to percussion in the plays of the great Spanish playwright, Pedro Calderon (1600–1681). Military drums appear relatively frequently in the stage directions of Spanish plays and in Calderon's *The Mayor of Zalamea* a soldier-drummer appears several times. At the beginning of the play, another soldier who does not appreciate this instrument is thankful the instrument is not playing:

> … by keeping quiet for a while
> Showed mercy and stopped splitting our poor heads.

For a prison scene at the end of the play (III, xvii) a stage direction requests that the sound of 'rolling drums' off-stage accompany the dialog.

Moorish drums are called for in Calderon's *Love after Death* (II, ii). After a stage direction indicates off-stage drums playing, we read,

> MALEC. No Moorish tabors give that sound,
>   A sound that with such terror comes;
>   No! it's the sound of Spanish drums
>   That thunders through the mountains round.
> TUZANI. This is a sound foreboding woe.

Marin Mersenne (1588–1648) studied mathematics, physics, the classics and metaphysics at the Jesuit College of Le Mans and later at the college at La Fleche, where one of his classmates, and life-long friend, was René Descartes. Mersenne's studies and experimentation in music resulted in his *Harmonie universelle* (1636), a work of encyclopedia proportion organized in five treatises. The fifth of these, *Traite des instruments,* included under percussion instruments which were to be considered musical, only those which produced a pitch—pitch, but not 'noise,' being describable by mathematics.

---

[25] Logic would suggest instruments made of natural objects, such as flutes from bones, percussion instruments from turtle shells and trumpets from sea shells, must be older than string instruments which require a relatively advanced technology to construct.

[26] Athanasius Kircher, *Musurgia universalis* [1650], trans. Frederick Crane (unpublished dissertation, State University of Iowa, 1956),

[27] Ibid., 161.

> All the bodies which make noise and which produce a sensible sound when they are struck can be placed in the rank of percussion instruments.[28]

The most interesting discussion which Mersenne engages in on this subject is relative to popular myths associated with church bells. He relates a number of superstitions believed by the public regarding the disturbances in the air caused by the ringing of the great cathedral bells. Among these, some believed it could cause the death of the fetus in the womb. Mersenne adds,

> Since it is experienced that the drum, the thunder, and the trumpet make more effect on the mind or the senses than the sound of other instruments, it is easy to conclude that the great effects of music or other sounds can happen only through great movements, which are made of a lot of air, or that the violence must make up for the size of the air when there is little air which serves the noise.[29]

The most famous Puritan of the English Baroque, John Bunyan (1628–1688), wrote some passages about percussion that were not too complimentary. First there is an unusual reference to signal music in his 'The Holy War,' where he describes a drummer who served under Lord Lucifer and the Diabolonians.

> This, to speak truth, was amazingly hideous to hear; it frightened all men seven miles round, if they were but awake and heard it.[30]

Later the drummer gives various signals and again the observation is made, 'no noise was ever heard upon earth more terrible.'

Curiously, in his autobiography, there is a passage which hints that Bunyan had a familiarity with dance music such as we might not have expected. He quotes 1 Corinthians 13:1, 'If I speak in the tongues of men and of angels, but have not love, I am a noisy gong or a clanging cymbal,' as a metaphor for the men of the church. But then, his explanation of this verse includes the following:

> A clanging cymbal is an instrument of music, with which a skillful player can make such melodious and heart-inflaming music, that all who hear him play can scarcely hold from dancing.[31]

---

[28] V, vii, 1.

[29] V, vii, 28.

[30] 'The Holy War,' in *The Works of John Bunyan*, ed. George Offor (London: Blackie and Son, 1853), III, 342, 347.

[31] Ibid., I, 44ff. Having a more primitive translation, Bunyan gives 'tinkling' for 'clanging' and 'charity' for 'love.'

The appearance of drums in both the Elizabethan and Jacobean plays was fairly common.[32] Rather unusual, however, is a stage direction in Beaumont and Fletcher's *The Loyal Subject* (I, iii) which calls for 'Drums in cases.'

The one form which seems to have been associated with the drums was the 'dead march.'[33] A typical example is found at the beginning of Act V of Beaumont and Fletcher's *Bonduca*:

> *A soft dead march within.*

Sometimes the stage directions call for soft drums, as in Beaumont and Fletcher's *Bonduca* (II, i), 'Drum softly within,' and perhaps in another work by these authors, *The Maid in the Mill* (II, v),

> *Drums afar off. A low March.*

An interesting example of soft drum playing is found in Heywood's *The foure Prentises of London*,[34] where after a stage direction reads simply 'soft march,' Godfrey commands,

> But soft, that Drumme should speak the Pagans tongue.

The character of drum players is sometimes questioned in early literature. An example is found in Beaumont and Fletcher's *The Burning Pestle* (V, i) a cannon is not in working order and the reason given for the missing flint is 'The Drummer took it out to light Tobacco.'

Nothing is more familiar in Europe still today than to find street entertainers employing a drum to draw a crowd. Thus, it is no surprise to find in the *Spectator*, a famous early English newspaper, for 8 November 1714,

> The celebration of this night's solemnity was opened by the obstreperous joy of drummers, who, with their parchment thunder, gave a signal for the appearance of the mob under their several classes and denominations.

---

32 Also see: Beaumont and Fletcher's *The Mad Lover* (I, i), [Drums within], and *The Pilgrim* (III, iv); Thomas Dekker: the beginning of *The Whore of Babylon* (V, iii); the end of *The Shoemakers' Holiday* (I, i); *Lust's Dominion* (IV, i and iii); *If This be not a Good Play* (IV, iii); in George Chapman's *The Blind Beggar* (Scene vii); Thomas Heywood's *The Rape of Lucrece*; *The Golden Age*; *The Iron Age*, Part II; *The foure Prentises of London*; *If you know not me, you know no body*; and a rare speaking part for a drummer in Beaumont and Fletcher's *The Two Noble Kinsmen* (III, v). The ancient pipe and tabor is mentioned in Thomas Dekker's *The Shoemakers' Holiday* (III, iii). In *Sir Thomas Browne's Works*, ed. Simon Wilkin (London: Pickering, 1836), IV, 191, one will find a treatise called 'Of Cymbals, etc.,' which reviews references to this instrument in early literature.

33 See also Thomas Dekker's *Sir Thomas Wyatt* (I, ii); in Cyril Tourneur's, *The Atheist's Tragedy* (III, i), for the funeral of Charlemont; Thomas Heywood's *The foure Prentises of London* [*The Dramatic Works of Thomas Heywood* (New York: Russell & Russell, 1964), II, 178. This edition is a reprint of an 1874 one which, in a misguided attempt to ease the reading, omitted all references to scenes and most Acts. Therefore we cite page numbers.] and *If you know not me, you know no body* [Ibid., I, 238].

34 Heywood, Ibid., II, 223.

Early Views on Memorization

You must have the score in your head, not your head in the score.
Hans von Bulow (1830–1894), letter to Richard Strauss

THE ABOVE ADVICE BY VON BULOW is Commandment Nr. 1 learned by all conductors in most of the world today. Bulow went on to say that if, in the circumstances of some global catastrophe, all scores of the Beethoven symphonies were destroyed, there would be no concern because he could write them all out. That is clearly hyperbole, but not the fact that any number of nameless young Italian conductors routinely conduct entire operas by memory, string quartets in Europe commonly play from memory and one piano, violin and cello ensemble in London performed the *entire* known trio repertoire from memory. While those examples may appear exceptional, the fact that no singer, violinist or pianist, even the most humble, would ever think of appearing in public looking at the music should remind us that memorization is a common expectation of the profession.

Robert Schumann wrote the following in his private diary in 1833:

> Whether it be done out of charlatanism or daring, [playing from memory in public] is always a proof of uncommon musical powers.

Schumann's wife, Clara, was one of the first modern pianists to perform entirely from memory. She was criticized by some who considered this somehow demeaning to the composer. It was during this brief period when this attitude prevailed that Mendelssohn, on the famous occasion when he revived the Bach *St. Matthew Passion*, walked to the podium only to discover that a stage-hand had mistakenly placed the score of the *Marriage of Figaro* on his music stand. Rather than have criticism of not using a score detract from the Bach, Mendelssohn gravely turned the pages of *Figaro* for three hours while he conducted the *St. Matthew Passion* from memory.

The literature of Europe begins with the ancient Greek accounts of the rhapsodists, the first of whom known to us was the blind poet and singer, Homer. Performing *before* the advent of modern written Greek, he and his followers sang[1] works like the *Iliad* and *The Odyssey* from memory in public. It was these performances which kept these works alive until such time as the invention of the written form of the Greek language would allow them to be written out.

And, of course, musical notation did not yet exist, so whatever regular musicians were doing, they were also doing it from memory. These early demonstrations of memory by rhapsodists and musicians did not go unnoticed by the ancient philosophers. How did they do

---

[1] The few accounts which are extant suggest something between speech and singing, but we call it singing to emphasize the distinction with oratory.

it, they wondered? Plato wrote that he regarded the powers of memorization to be Hippias' most brilliant achievement.[2] We wish we had more detailed information by the early writer, Ammianus Marcellinus, who testified that Hippias obtained these great powers of memory 'by drinking certain potions.'[3]

St. Augustine (354–386 AD), who was also a musician and wrote a treatise on music, gave some thought to the nature of memory. He believed that in the case of memory derived from the senses, it is not the object but the image of the object that is stored in the memory. On the other hand, with regard to conceptual knowledge he held the reverse is true: it is the things themselves which are retained. He is incorrect, of course, for they too are images, symbolic descriptions, not the real things, which are stored in our left hemispheres.

> Here [in the memory] also is all learnt of the liberal sciences and as yet unforgotten; removed as it were to some inner place, which is yet no place: nor are they the images thereof, but the things themselves.[4]

It is worthy of note here, when he says the information is stored in 'no place,' that he could not account for the actual location of memory. He offers only the suggestion that all knowledge is genetic, 'they were already in the memory, but thrown back and buried as it were in deeper recesses,' which some suggestion draws to the surface.[5]

Aurelian of Reome, in his treatise, *Musica Disciplina* (ca. 843 AD), gave the credit for memory to the ancient Greek gods, remarking that music was associated with one of the daughters of Jupiter, who was also goddesses of memory, 'because this art, unless it is imprinted in the memory, is not retained.'

The philosopher, Giordano Bruno (1548–1600) was famous in his lifetime for his memory and Henry III of France demanded of him the secret of his mnemonic method. Bruno's answer probably did not satisfy the king, but it must have discouraged further questions.

> Unless you make yourself equal to God, you cannot understand God: for the like is not intelligible save to the like. Make yourself grow to a greatness beyond measure ... free yourself from the body; raise yourself above all time, become Eternity.[6]

Like Augustine, St. Thomas Aquinas (1225–1274 AD) seemed to associate memory with the senses. In his opinion, sight gives the most pleasure with regard to knowledge, but for sensory pleasure touch is the most appreciated due to our desire for 'food, sex, and the like.'[7] Aquinas includes the senses as one of the 'sensitive powers,' among which are also imagination and

---

[2] 'Hippias Minor,' 368b.

[3] Rosamond Kent Sprague, *The Older Sophists* (Columbia: University of South Carolina Press, 1972)., 100

[4] *The Confessions*, Book X.

[5] Ibid.

[6] Quoted in Stuart Isacoff, *Temperament* (New York: Vintage, 2001), 148.

[7] *Summa Theologiae*, XX, 2. It is odd that he associates the sense of touch, rather than taste, with food!

memory.⁸ It seemed obvious to him that imagination was tied to the senses, for how could a blind man imagine color?⁹ Memory he includes as he felt it was evident that it was based on images.¹⁰

Juan Ruiz, in his *The Book of Love*, 1330, wrote that the soul stores 'true understanding and good will' in memory and compels the body to do good works by which man is saved. Poor memory, therefore, is partly responsible for sin! He also makes the interesting contention that painting, writing and sculpture were invented for the purpose of keeping things in the memory.¹¹

Well, there were some early thinkers who were on the right track. Alcuin (735–804 AD), the famous English scholar who was a member of the court of Charlemagne, pointed to an observation by Tullius (578–535 BC), one of the legendary kings of ancient Rome, that, 'Memory is the storehouse of all our experiences.'¹² That is correct and it is a good starting place. But we would go further: Memory is the storehouse of *everything* we know. If we don't remember something, then for us, personally, it does not exist. In this Aurelian was right with regard to music, 'unless it is imprinted in the memory, is not retained.' If we do not remember Mahler's Third Symphony, then we have no first-person evidence that it exists. If nothing else, that should tell us how important memory is.

There are two other thoughts that some earlier writers had which seem valid. The first has to do with some association between memory and the emotions. Thomas Aquinas guessed this correctly:

> No impression is made on the body as a result of an apprehension, unless united to the apprehension there be some emotion, such as joy, fear, desire, or some other passion.¹³

The great German philosopher and mathematician Gottfried Wilhelm Leibniz (1646–1716) also associated emotion with effective memory. His mention of music in this regard reminds us that music was often used in church schools as a means of helping the boys learn Latin.

> Those signs are most mnemonic which are most perceptible, so to speak, such as words which are not merely heard but are heard with joy—for example, songs.¹⁴

The use of music as an aid to memorize text, which Leibniz mentions above, had been observed for a long time. A similar comment can be found in John Donne (1573–1631). Much of the instructions in the bible were given in the form of music, he maintains, for God then

---

8 *Summa Contra Gentiles*, LXXIII. Intuition, however, is information secretly provided us by angels. [Ibid., XCII]
9 *Summa Theologiae*, XV, 29.
10 Ibid., XXXVI, 63.
11 Juan Ruiz, *The Book of True Love*, trans. Saralyn Daly (University Park: Pennsylvania State University Press, 1978), 10ff.
12 Alcuin, *Rhetoric*, trans. Wilbur Howell (New York: Russell & Russell, 1965), 137.
13 *Summa Contra Gentiles*, CIII.
14 Ibid., I, xxiii.

'was sure they would remember.'[15] This same thought is found in an earlier anonymous treatise on music, *De Musica Mensurata* (ca. 1279). Written at a time when most poetry was still sung, this author observes,

> And also things composed in verse are received more easily in the store-house of memory than things composed in prose, and since they are impressed easily on the memory they are more quickly recalled. Also verses arouse the minds of the listeners more favorably than prose.[16]

Some modern clinical research has also confirmed this. In 1982, researchers from the University of North Texas found that background music seemed to enhance the memorizing of vocabulary words.[17] This seems obvious enough and one scholar believes the very reason why early poetry was sung was for the purpose of aiding the memory.

> Melody can be an important feature in the mnemonics of oral tradition in song, as we know from the studies of folklorists who scrutinize the transmission and diffusion of song: melody helps recall the words.[18]

With regard to the memorization of music this association of music and emotion seems especially critical, particularly so since the communication of emotions is what music is all about. In this regard we suspect that Augustine was on the right tract when he wrote, 'that it is not the object but the image of the object that is stored in the memory.' In other words, it may be that an emotional 'image' is what enables us to remember music. If you ask any (classical) musician, 'Do you know Beethoven's Fifth Symphony?,' he will answer, 'Yes.' And it is a truthful answer. But he does not mean he could write out the viola part. One is music (right hemisphere of the brain), the other is data, notation (left hemisphere). We call the left hemisphere elements of music, 'music,' but they are not music, they are grammar.

One question remains and that is, Why? Why do musicians all over the world feel compelled to make the effort to memorize their music before they perform in public? The answer to this question begins with an observation by the great seventeenth-century composer and keyboard artist, Francois Couperin:

> The fact is we write a thing differently from the way in which we execute it.[19]

He means that the musician does not play what is on paper.

---

[15] John Donne, 'A Lent Sermon Preached at White-hall, February 12, 1619,' in *Selected Prose*, ed. Helen Gardner (Oxford: Clarendon Press, 1967) 183.

[16] The Anonymous of St. Emmeram, *De Musica Mensurata*, trans. Jeremy Judkin (Bloomington: Indiana University Press, 1990), 75.

[17] http://www.soundtherapy.co.uk/research/musicresearch.php

[18] Gregory Nagy, *Pindar's Homer* (Baltimore: Johns Hopkins University Press, 1982), 50

[19] Couperin, *L'Art de toucher*, 23.

The reason for this lies in the history of our music notation. To make a very long story short, the Church, during a period when they sought to expel emotions from the life of the Christian, turned music into a branch of mathematics. The Church was responsible for the creation of our notational system and it was created by mathematicians, not by musicians. Subsequently, no composer can possibly notate what they really *feel*, because we have a notational system in which there is not a single symbol for feeling! The reason we speak of the 'interpretation' of music is because the musician is consequently forced to try to discern what the composer *felt* and not what he wrote.[20] The dullest of all performances are those by musicians who play what is on paper. Indeed, such performances are often called, 'unmusical.'

Memorization is an important means of discovering what a composer *really* had in mind, because it allows the musician to free himself from the visual data-form. Music, after all, is for the ear, not the eye. Once the eye is eliminated, the ear comes into play. And that is the key, to *hear* what a composer felt and would have written if he had a sophisticated notational system which answered to his every need. But memory not only allows us to understand what a composer really felt, but it also allows us to understand why he wrote what he did. This is to say, memory allows one to arrive at an understanding of even rational, or left hemisphere, knowledge. Nothing illustrates this more vividly than the old Sufi parable:

> A student was walking through the village, whereupon he came to the house of his teacher. There he saw his teacher, on his hands and knees, apparently looking for something in the grass.
> 'Master, what are you looking for?'
> 'I am looking for my house key,' his teacher replied, 'Come and help me look for it!'
> The student joined his teacher in the grass, but after a time he concluded that there was probably no key in the grass at all and that he was participating in some sort of lesson.
> 'OK, Master, where did you actually lose your house key?'
> His teacher answered, 'Well, actually, I lost it somewhere inside my house.'
> 'Why, then,' said the student, 'are we looking out here in the grass?'
> 'Because there is more light here,' explained the teacher!

I should like to close this discussion by offering some observations of my own, as a conductor who conducted both rehearsals and concerts from memory for forty years. The most important step forward in my experience came from the conducting classes at the Akademie für Musik in Vienna, where I studied in 1968–1969. I learned there a system of memorizing scores which I believe all major European conductors used at that time. It was not a method of memorizing music, it was a method of organizing the mind to facilitate the memorization of music. Using this system I found during my career that there was no score I could not memorize, even in the case of many complex, non-tonal scores for which I was doing the premiere performance. I often set challenges for myself, in this regard, such as not only conducting the Stravinsky *Rites of Spring*, but rehearsing it without scores from the very first rehearsal.

---

[20] It is interesting that the French (Couperin [Ibid., 13]), German (Orff Schulwerk) and Japanese (Suzuki) all begin 'music' long before introducing the student to notation.

It was always my experience that after learning a score in this way I came to understand things which I would have never 'seen' if I had only looked at a score. This is a remarkable experience, to be walking somewhere, or doing dishes, thinking about the music and suddenly realizing something about the music which had not been apparent to the eye. I believe this single experience is what pays every artist back for whatever effort he has put into memorization.

But there is something more at work here than the capacity of the eye, because we are always really talking about the brain. It is very clear to me that the brain, or some part of it, has the ability to work on a problem all by itself without our (us, or the Id) being aware of it. One obvious demonstration of this which I believe a great many conductors have discovered is that if one studies a score just before going to sleep one always wakes up in the morning knowing more of the music than he thought he knew when he fell asleep. The brain, retaining the image of the score pages, clearly continued to memorize while you slept soundly.

But this level of 'brain-work,' it seems to me, is only a functional process. It has also been my experience that the brain has the ability to 'think' about some musical problem all on its own, without one previously having thought to himself, 'I will think about this.' Indeed I have had the experience that the brain appeared to have been 'thinking' about some musical detail that I was completely unaware of in the first place. I can think of one instance where I suddenly 'understood' something Mozart had in mind whereas I had been looking at this very same score for fifty years without ever realizing the now evident problem existed.

I don't regard the above example as evidence that my particular brain just works very slowly. Rather, one must remember that musical experiences and understanding lie in the right hemisphere of the brain which is incapable of communicating rational thoughts, expressed in writing or in speech, even silent speech—'thinking.' Therefore it may be, instead, a case where the right hemisphere had to simply wait until the rest of me, the left hemisphere, developed through life experience to a level that I could understand what was there all along, waiting patiently for fifty years for me to catch up. I might add that in recent years I have had some extraordinary instances where very important insights regarding scores I have known for decades has been presented to me during dreams. Was this a case of the right hemisphere waiting until life's distractions during the awake state were eliminated rendering me more susceptible for non-rational communication?

For me, the above is proof that our brain has capabilities far beyond those man has yet found a need to call upon.

Bibliography

CHAPTER 1 MUSIC IN ANCIENT GREECE

Aristotle. *Categories*.
Aristotle. *De Anima*.
Aristotle. *Ethica Nicomachea*.
Aristotle. *Magna Moralia*.
Aristotle. *On Interpretation*.
Aristotle. *Problemata*.
Aristoxenus. *Elementa Rhythmica*. Oxford: Clarendon Press, 1990.
Aristoxenus. *The Elements of Harmony*. Translated by Henry S. Macran. Hildesheim: Georg Olms Verlag, 1974.
Athenaeus, *Deipnosophistae*.
Bacon, Roger. *The Opus Majus of Roger Bacon*. Translated by Robert Burke. New York: Russell & Russell, 1962.
Barker, Andrew. *Greek Musical Writings*. Cambridge: Cambridge University Press, 1989.
Conway, Geoffrey S. *The Odes of Pindar*. London: Dent, 1972.
Homer. *The Homeric Hymns*. Translated by Apostolos N. Athanassakis. Baltimore: Johns Hopkins University Press.
Ovid, *Metamorphoses*.
Plato. *Apology*.
Plato. *Gorgias*.
Plato. *Ion*.
Plato. *Laws*.
Plato. *Republic*.
Plato. *Symposium*.
Plutarch, *Lives*.
Plutarch. *Concerning Music*.
Plutarch. *Customs of the Lacedaemonians*.
Strabo. *Geography of Strabo*. Transl;ated by Horace L. Jones. Cambridge: Harvard University Press, 1960.
Tibullus. *Poems*.
Voltaire. *The Works of Voltaire*. New York: St. Hubert Guild, 1901.

CHAPTER 2 ON THE ANCIENT GREEK MODES

Aristophanes. *Ecclesiazusae*.
Aristotle. *Politica*.

Aristotle. *Probemata*.
Athenaeus. *Deipnosophistae*.
Bianconi, Lorenzo. *Music in the Seventeenth Century*. Translated by David Bryant. Cambridge: Cambridge University Press, 1989.
Chamberlin, Henry H. *Last Flowers*. Cambridge: Harvard University Press, 1937.
Doni, Giovanni Battista. *Compendio del trattato de' generi e de' modi*. Rome, 1635.
Erasmus, Desiderius. *The Collected Works of Erasmus*. Toronto: University of Toronto Press, 1992.
Glarean, Heinrich. *Dodecachordon*. Translated by Clement Miller. American Institute of Musicology, 1965.
Hucbald, Guido, and John on Music. Translated by Warren Babb. New Haven: Yale University Press, 1978.
Mattheson, Johann. *Neu-Eroffnete Orchestre*. Hamburg, 1713.
Mattheson, Johann. *Der vollkommene Capellmeister* [1739]. Translated by Ernest Harriss. Ann Arbor: UMI Research Press, 1981.
Mersenne, Marin. *Harmonie universelle*.
Murray, Gilbert. *The Complete Plays of Aeschylus*. London: George Allen, 1952.
Ornithoparchus, *Musicae active mirologus* and Dowland, *Introduction: Containing the Art of Singing*. New York: Dover, 1973.
Pickard-Cambridge, Arthur. *The Dramatic Festivals of Athens*. Oxford: Clarendon Press, 1953.
Plato. *Laches*
Plato. *Protagoras*.
Plato. *Republic*.
Plutarch. *Concerning Music*.
Plutarch. *Lives*.
Tyson, Donald. *Three Books of Occult Philosophy*. St. Paul: Llewellyn Publications, 1993.

Chapter 3 The View of the Performance of Music in Ancient Societies

Aristotle. *Politics*.
Aristotle. *Probemata*.
Aristoxenus. *The Elements of Harmony*. Translated by Henry S. Macran. Hildesheim: Georg Olms Verlag, 1974.
Athenaeus. *The Deipnosophist*.
Cicero. *De Senectute*
Cicero. *Pro Sexto Roscio Amerino*.
Cicero. *De Officiis*.
Cicero. *De Oratore*.
Cicero. *On Behalf of Milo*.

Epictetus. *The Discourses of Epictetus*. Translated by P. E. Matheson. New York: Random House, 1957

Epicurus. *Epicurus*. Translated by Cyril Bailey. Oxford: Clarendon Press, 1926.

Farmer, Henry G, 'The Music of Ancient Mesopotamia,' in *The New Oxford History of Music*. London: Oxford University Press, 1966.

Guthrie, Kenneth. *The Pythagorean Sourcebook*. Grand Rapids: Phanes Press, 1987.

Herodotus. *The Histories*.

Horace. *Carmina*.

Horace. *Epistles*.

Jebb, Richard C. *Bacchylides*. Hildesheim, Georg Olms Verlagsbuchhandlung, 1967.

Homer. *The Odyssey*. Translated by A. T. Murray. London: Heinemann, 1960.

Nagy, Gregory. *Pindar's Homer*. Baltimore: Johns Hopkins University Press, 1982.

Ovid. *Letters in Exile*.

Plato *Laws*.

Plato. *Phdaerus*.

Pliny the Elder. *Natural History*.

Plutarch. *Lives*. 'Alcibiades.'

Plutarch. *Lives*. 'Pericles.'

Plutarch. *Concerning Music*.

Plutarch. *Conjugal Precepts*.

Plutarch. *Customs of the Lacedaemonians*.

Plutarch. *Laconic Apophthegms*.

Polybius. The Rise of the Roman Empire.

Polybius. *The Rise of the Roman Empire*.

Propertius. *Poems*.

Reale, Giovanni. *A History of Ancient Philosophy*. Albany: State University of New York Press, 1987.

Sallust. *The Conspiracy of Catiline*.

Sendrey, Alfred. *Music in the Social and Religious Life of Antiquity*. Rutherford: Fairleigh Dickinson University Press, 1974.

Seneca. *Epistolae*.

Strabo. *The Geography of Strabo*. Translated by Horace L. Jones. Cambridge: Harvard University Press, 1960.

Suetonius. *Lives of the Caesars*.

Tacitus. *The Annals*.

Thucydides. *The Peloponnesian War*.

Varro, Marcus. *On the Latin Language*.

Virgil. *Georgics*.

Wilkinson, L. P. *Letters of Cicero*. New York: Norton, 1966.

Xenophon. *A History of My Times*.

CHAPTER 4 MUSIC AS VIEWED BY MEDIEVAL CHURCH PHILOSOPHERS

Anderson, Warren D. *Ethos and Education in Greek Music*. Cambridge: Harvard University Press, 1966.
Bacon, Roger. *The Opus Majus of Roger Bacon*. Translated by Robert Burke. New York: Russell & Russell, 1962.
Carpenter, Nan Cooke. *Music in the Medieval and Renaissance Universities*. Norman: University of Oklahoma Press, 1954.
The Greek Anthology. Translated by W. R. Paton. Cambridge: Harvard University Press, 1939.
Julian. *The Works of the Emperor Julian*. Translated by Wilmer Wright. London: Heinemann, 1913.
McEvoy, James. *The Philosophy of Robert Grosseteste*. Oxford: Clarendon, 1982.
Psellus, Michael. *Chronographia*. Translated by E. R. A. Sewter. Baltimore: Penguin Books, 1966.
Sextus Empiricus, *Against the Musicians*, in *Against the Professors*. Translated by R. G. Bury. Cambridge: Harvard University Press, 1949.
Wilkinson, L. P., 'Philodemus in Ethos in Music,' *Classical Quarterly* 32, no. 3–4 (July 1938): 174–181, doi: 10.1017/S0009838800025878

CHAPTER 5 BOETHIUS ON MUSIC

Boethius. *Fundamentals of Music*. Translated by Calvin Bower. New Haven: Yale University Press.
Boethius. *Consolatione Philosophiae*. Translated by Samuel Fox. London: George Bell, 1895.
Cassiodorus. *The Letters of Cassiodorus*. London: Frowde, 1886.

CHAPTER 6 ON CASSIODORUS

Capella, Martianus. *Martianus Capella and the Seven Liberal Arts*. Translated by William Harris Stahl. New York: Columbia University Press.
Cassiodorus. *Divine Letters*. Translated by Leslie W. Jones. New York: Octagon Books, 1966.
Cassiodorus. *Variae*. Translated by Thomas Hodgkin. London: Frowde, 1886.
Cassiodorus. 'On Dialectic,' in *An Introduction to Divine and Human Readings*. Translated by Leslie Jones. New York, Octagon Books, 1966.
Durant, Will. *The Age of Faith*. New York: Simon and Schuster, 1950.
Strunk, Oliver. *Source Readings in Music History*. New York: Norton, 1950.

CHAPTER 7 LATE MEDIEVAL MUSIC TREATISES

Aurelian of Reome. *The Discipline of Music*. Translated by Joseph Ponte. Colorado Springs: Colorado College Music Press, 1968.
Farmer, Henry George. *Al-Farabi's Writings on Music*. New York: Hinrichsen, 1934.

Hucbald, Guido, and John on Music. Translated by Warren Babb (New Haven: Yale University Press, 1978), 104

Strunk, Oliver. *Source Readings in Music History*. New York: Norton, 1950.

Chapter 8 Early Reflections on Repertoire

Apel, Willi. *Harvard Dictionary of Music*. Cambridge: Harvard University Press, 1947.

Aristophanes. *Peace*.

Aristotle. *Ethica Nicomachea*.

Aristotle. *Magna Moralia*.

Aristotle. *Problemata*.

Athenaeus. *The Deipnosophists*. Translated by Charles Burton Guilick. Cambridge: Harvard University Press, 1951.

Ausonius. *Ausonius*. Translated by Hugh G. Evelyn White. London: Heinemann, 1921.

Beowulf. Translated by Francis Gummere, in *Epic and Saga*, Vol. 49, *The Harvard Classics*. New York: Collier.

Bianconi, Lorenzo. *Music in the Seventeenth Century*. Translated by David Bryand. Cambridge: Cambridge University Press, 1989.

Brant, Sebastian. *The Ship of Fools*. Translated by Edwin Zeydel. New York: Columbia University Press, 1944.

Erasmus, Desiderius. *The Collected Works of Erasmus*. Toronto: University of Toronto Press, 1992.

Euripides. *Medea*.

Euripides. *The Bacchae*.

Homer. *The Homeric Hymns*. Translated by Apostolos N. Athanassakis. Baltimore: Johns Hopkins University Press, 1976.

Juvenal. *Satire*.

Marcus Aurelius. *Meditations*.

Plato. *Gorgias*.

Plato. *Laws*.

Plato. *Republic*.

Plato. *Symposium*.

Plutarch. *Lives*.

Psellus, Michael. *Chronographia*. Translated by E. R. A. Sewter. Baltimore: Penguin Books, 1966.

Saint Ambrose. 'Death as a Good,' in *Seven Exegetical Works*. Translated by Michael P. McHugh. Washington, D.C.: The Catholic University of America Press.

Strunk, Oliver. *Source Readings in Music History*. New York: Norton, 1950.

Voltaire. *The Works of Voltaire*. New York: St. Hubert Guild, 1901.

Xenophon. *Cyropaedia*. Translated by Walter Miller. Cambridge: Harvard University Press, 1960.

Chapter 9 Early Reflections on Acoustics and the Perception of Music

Bacon, Francis. *Natural History* in *The Works of Francis Bacon*. Cambridge: Cambridge University Press, 1869.
Barker, Andrew. *Greek Musical Writings*. Cambridge: Cambridge University Press, 1989.
Berkeley, George. *The Works of George Berkeley, Bishop of Cloyne*. Edited by A. Luce. London: Nelson, 1964.
Chaucer. *The House of Fame*.
Cicero. *De Natura Deorum*.
Cicero. *De Oratore*.
Durant, Will. *The Age of Reason Begins*. New York: Simon and Schuster, 1961.
Erasmus, Desiderius. *The Collected Works of Erasmus*. Toronto: University of Toronto Press, 1992.
The Greek Anthology. Translated by W. R. Paton. Cambridge: Harvard University Press, 1939.
Guthrie, Kenneth. *The Pythagorean Sourcebook*. Grand Rapids: Phanes Press, 1987.
Hall, Joseph. *The Works of Joseph Hall, D. D.* Edited by Philip Wynter. New York: AMS Press, 1969.
Locke, John. *The Works of John Locke*. London, 1823; reprinted in Aalen: Scientia Verlag, 1963.
Magnus, Albertus. *De Animalibus*. Translated by James Scanlan. Binghamton, NY: Medieval & Renaissance Texts, 1987.
Mersenne. *Harmonie universelle*.
Newton, Isaac. *The Correspondence of Isaac Newton*. Cambridge: University Press, 1959—.
Newton, Isaac. *Opticks*.
Pliny the Elder. *Natural History*.
Plotinus. *The Enneads*. Translated by Stephen MacKenna. London: Faber and Faber, 1962.
Wilson, John. *Roger North on Music*. London: Novello, 1959.

Chapter 10 Early Experience with the 'Pyramid Principle'

Bunyan, John. *The Works of John Bunyan*. Edited by George Offor. London: Blackie and Son, 1853.
Erasmus, Desiderius. *The Collected Works of Erasmus*. Toronto: University of Toronto Press, 1992.
Glarean. *Dodecachordon*. Translated by Clement Miller. American Institute of Musicology, 1965.
Hawkins, John. *A General History of the Science and Practice of Music* [1776]. New York: Dover Reprint, 1963.

Mace, Thomas. *Compendium of Music*. Translated by Walter Robert. American Institute of Musicology, 1961.
Marchetto of Padua. *Lucidarium*. Translated by Jan W. Herlinger. Chicago: University of Chicago Press, 1985.
Praetorius. *Syntagma Musicum*. Kassel: Bärenreiter, 1958.
Stokes, Francis, trans. *On the Eve of the Reformation*. New York: Harper & Row, 1909.
Strunk, Oliver. *Source Readings in Music History*. New York: Norton, 1950.

CHAPTER 11 EARLY THOUGHTS ON TEMPI

Berlioz. *Essay on Conducting*.
Bonachelli, Giovanni. *Corona di sacri gigli a una, due, tre, Quattro, e cinque voci*. Venice, 1642.
Brossard, Sebastien. *Dictionaire de Musique*. Paris, 1703.
Couperin, François. *L'Art de toucher* [Paris, 1717]. Wiesbaden: Breitkopf & Härtel, 1933.
Ellis, William Ashton. *Wagner's Prose Works*. New York: Broude.
Frescobaldi, Girolamo. *Toccatas and Partitas*.
Johannes Brahms im Briefwechsel mit Joseph Joachim. Berlin, 1908.
Leinsdorf, Erich. *The Composer's Advocate*. New Haven: Yale University Press, 1981.
Mace, Thomas. *Compendium of Music*. Translated by Walter Robert. American Institute of Musicology, 1961.
Mattheson, Johann. *Der vollkommene Capellmeister* [1739]. Translated by Ernest Harriss. Ann Arbor: UMI Research Press, 1981.
Praetorius. *Syntagma Musicum*. Kassel: Bärenreiter, 1958.
Rousseau, Jean. *Methode claire, certaine et facile pour apprendre à chanter la musique*. Paris, 1678.
Walter, Bruno. *On Music and Music-Making*. New York: Norton, 1957.
Weingartner, Felix. *On Conducting*. New York: Kalmus.

CHAPTER 12 EARLY REFLECTIONS ON INSTRUMENTS AND ENSEMBLES

Arbeau, Thoinot. *Orchesography*. Translated by Mary Evans. New York: Kamin Dance Publishers, 1948.
Athenaeus. *Deipnosophistae*.
Bacon, Roger. *The Opus Majus of Roger Bacon*. Translated by Robert Burke. New York: Russell & Russell, 1962.
Baines, Anthony. 'Fifteenth-century Instruments in Tinctoris's *De Inventine et Usu Musicae*.' *The Galpin Society Journal* 3 (1950.): 19–26, http://www.jstor.org/stable/841898
Brant, Sebastian. *The Ship of Fools*. Translated by Edwin Zeydel. New York: Columbia University Press, 1944.
Burton, Elizabeth. *The Pageant of Elisabethan England*. New York: Scribner's.
da Vinci, Leonardo. *The Literary Works of Leonardo da Vinci*. Edited by Jean Paul Richter. London: Phaidon, 1970.

Gerson, Jean de. *Tractatus de Canticis*. Translated by Christopher Page, in 'Early 15th-century instruments in Jean de Gerson's 'Tractatus de Canticis,' *Early Music* 6, no. 3 (1978): 339–349, doi: 10.1093/earlyj/6.3.339

Giovio, Paolo. *Leonardi Vencii Vita* [1528].

Hildegard of Bingen. *The Book of Divine Works*. Edited by Matthew Fox. Santa Fe: Bear & Company, 1987.

Lomazzo. *Idea del Tempio della Pittura* [1590].

Machaut, Guillaume de. *Oeuvres*. Edited by Ernest Hoepffner. Paris, 1908–21).

Machaut, Guillaume de. *Remede de Fortune*. Translated by James Wimsatt and William Kibler. Athens: The University of Georgia Press, 1988.

Miller, Clement. *Hieronymus Cardanus, Writings on Music*. American Institute of Musicology, 1973.

Reese, Gustave. *Music in the Renaissance*. New York: Norton, 1959.

Ruiz, Juan. *The Book of True Love*. Translated by Saralyn Daly. University Park: Pennsylvania State University Press, 1978.

Sachs, Curt. *World History of the Dance*. New York, 1937.

Strunk, Oliver. *Source Readings in Music History*. New York: Norton, 1950.

Tinctorius. *Concerning the Nature and Propriety of Tones*. Translated by Albert Seay. Colorado Springs, 1976.

Wace, Robert. *Roman de Brut*. Translated by Gwyn Jones. London: Dent, 1962.

Chapter 13 Early Views on Percussion

Browne, Thomas. *Sir Thomas Browne's Works*. Edited by Simon Wilkin. London: Pickering, 1836.

Bunyan, John. *The Works of John Bunyan*. Edited by George Offor. London: Blackie and Son, 1853.

Cervantes, Miguel de. *Don Quijote*. Translated by Burton Raffel. New York: Norton, 1995.

Engel, Carl. *The Music of The Most Ancient Nations*. London: Reeves.

The Greek Anthology. Translated by W. R. Paton. Cambridge: Harvard University Press, 1939.

Heywood, Thomas. *The Dramatic Works of Thomas Heywood*. New York: Russell & Russell, 1964.

Johannes de Garlandia. *De Mensurabili Musica*. Translated by Stanley Birnbaum. Colorado Springs: Colorado College Music Press, 1978.

Kircher, Athanasius. *Musurgia universalis* [1650]. Translated by Frederick Crane. Unpublished dissertation, State University of Iowa, 1956.

Manniche, Lise. *Music and Musicians in Ancient Egypt*. London: British Museum Press, 1991.

On's, Harriet de. *Six Exemplary Novels*. Great Neck: Barron's Educational Series, 1961.

Sachs, Curt. *The History of Musical Instruments*. New York, 1940.

Strunk, Oliver. *Source Readings in Music History*. New York: Norton, 1950.

Chapter 14 Early Views on Memorization

Alcuin, *Rhetoric*. Translated by Wilbur Howell. New York: Russell & Russell, 1965.

Anonymous of St. Emmeram, *De Musica Mensurata*. Translated by Jeremy Judkin. Bloomington: Indiana University Press, 1990. Couperin, François. *L'Art de toucher*.

Donne, John. 'A Lent Sermon Preached at White-hall, February 12, 1619,' in *Selected Prose*. Edited by Helen Gardner. Oxford: Clarendon Press, 1967.

Isacoff, Stuart. *Temperament* (New York: Vintage, 2001.

Nagy, Gregory. *Pindar's Homer*. Baltimore: Johns Hopkins University Press, 1982.

Ruiz, Juan. *The Book of True Love*. Translated by Saralyn Daly. University Park: Pennsylvania State University Press, 1978.

Sprague, Rosamond Kent. *The Older Sophists*. Columbia: University of South Carolina Press, 1972.

St. Augustine. *The Confessions*.

St. Thomas Aquinas. *Summa Contra Gentiles*.

St. Thomas Aquinas. *Summa Theologiae*.

About the Author

Dr. David Whitwell is a graduate ('with distinction') of the University of Michigan and the Catholic University of America, Washington DC (PhD, Musicology, Distinguished Alumni Award, 2000) and has studied conducting with Eugene Ormandy and at the Akademie für Musik, Vienna. Prior to coming to Northridge, Dr. Whitwell participated in concerts throughout the United States and Asia as Associate First Horn in the USAF Band and Orchestra in Washington DC, and in recitals throughout South America in cooperation with the United States State Department.

At the California State University, Northridge, which is in Los Angeles, Dr. Whitwell developed the CSUN Wind Ensemble into an ensemble of international reputation, with international tours to Europe in 1981 and 1989 and to Japan in 1984. The CSUN Wind Ensemble has made professional studio recordings for BBC (London), the Köln Westdeutscher Rundfunk (Germany), NOS National Radio (The Netherlands), Zürich Radio (Switzerland), the Television Broadcasting System (Japan) as well as for the United States State Department for broadcast on its 'Voice of America' program. The CSUN Wind Ensemble's recording with the Mirecourt Trio in 1982 was named the 'Record of the Year' by The Village Voice. Composers who have guest conducted Whitwell's ensembles include Aaron Copland, Ernest Krenek, Alan Hovhaness, Morton Gould, Karel Husa, Frank Erickson and Vaclav Nelhybel.

Dr. Whitwell has been a guest professor in 100 different universities and conservatories throughout the United States and in 23 foreign countries (most recently in China, in an elite school housed in the Forbidden City). Guest conducting experiences have included the Philadelphia Orchestra, Seattle Symphony Orchestra, the Czech Radio Orchestras of Brno and Bratislava, The National Youth Orchestra of Israel, as well as resident wind ensembles in Russia, Israel, Austria, Switzerland, Germany, England, Wales, The Netherlands, Portugal, Peru, Korea, Japan, Taiwan, Canada and the United States.

He is a past president of the College Band Directors National Association, a member of the Prasidium of the International Society for the Promotion of Band Music, and was a member of the founding board of directors of the World Association for Symphonic Bands and Ensembles (WASBE). In 1964 he was made an honorary life member of Kappa Kappa Psi, a national professional music fraternity. In September, 2001, he was a delegate to the UNESCO Conference on Global Music in Tokyo. He has been knighted by sovereign organizations in France, Portugal and Scotland and has been awarded the gold medal of Kerkrade, The Netherlands, and the silver medal of Wangen, Germany, the highest honor given wind conductors in the United States, the medal of the Academy of Wind and Percussion Arts (National Band Association) and the highest honor given wind conductors in Austria, the gold medal of the Austrian Band Association. He is a member of the Hall of Fame of the California Music Educators Association.

Dr. Whitwell's publications include more than 127 articles on wind literature including publications in Music and Letters (London), the London Musical Times, the Mozart-Jahrbuch (Salzburg), and 52 books, among which is his 13-volume *History and Literature of the Wind Band and Wind Ensemble* and an 8-volume series on *Aesthetics in Music*. In addition to numerous modern editions of early wind band music his original compositions include 5 symphonies.

David Whitwell was named as one of six men who have determined the course of American bands during the second half of the 20th century, in the definitive history, *The Twentieth Century American Wind Band* (Meredith Music).

A doctoral dissertation by German Gonzales (2007, Arizona State University) is dedicated to the life and conducting career of David Whitwell through the year 1977. David Whitwell is one of nine men described by Paula A. Crider in *The Conductor's Legacy* (Chicago: GIA, 2010) as 'the legendary conductors' of the 20th century.

> 'I can't imagine the 2nd half of the 20th century—without David Whitwell and what he has given to all of the rest of us.' Frederick Fennell (1993)

About the Editor

CRAIG DABELSTEIN began studying the piano at age seven and took up the saxophone at age twelve. Mr Dabelstein has Bachelor of Arts (Music) and Bachelor of Music degrees from the Queensland Conservatorium of Music, where he majored in the performance of classical saxophone repertoire. He also has a Graduate Diploma of Learning and Teaching and a Graduate Certificate in Editing and Publishing from the University of Southern Queensland.

He has held the principal alto and tenor saxophone chairs in the Australian Wind Orchestra and has been an augmenting member of the Queensland Philharmonic Orchestra, the Queensland Symphony Orchestra, and the Queensland Pops Orchestra. For many years he was also a member of the Queensland Saxophone Quartet.

He has been a casual conductor of the Young Conservatorium Symphonic Winds, and has previously been a saxophone teacher at the Queensland Conservatorium of Music. He is a regular conductor of the Queensland Wind Orchestra, having served as their artistic director and chief conductor from 2004 to 2009.

Craig Dabelstein is a research associate for the *Teaching Music Through Performance in Band* series of books, contributing analyses to volumes 7, 8, 1 (rev. edn), and the *Solos with Wind Band Accompaniment* volume. He served as the copyeditor and layout designer of the *Australian Clarinet and Saxophone Magazine* from 2007 to 2009 and he has written many CD and book reviews for *Music Forum* magazine. He is the editor of the second editions of the books by Dr. David Whitwell including *A Concise History of the Wind Band*, *Foundations of Music Education*, *Music Education of the Future*, *The Sousa Oral History Project*, *Wagner on Bands*, *Berlioz on Bands*, *The Art of Musical Conducting*, and the *Aesthetics of Music* series (8 volumes) and *The History and Literature of the Wind Band and Wind Ensemble* series (13 volumes). From 1994 to 2012 he was a staff member at Brisbane Girls Grammar School. He now teaches woodwinds and conducts bands at St. Joseph's College, Gregory Terrace, Brisbane.

www.ingramcontent.com/pod-product-compliance
Lightning Source LLC
Chambersburg PA
CBHW081352230426
43667CB00017B/2814